THE NORTHERN IRELAND SOCIAL DEMOCRATIC AND LABOUR PARTY

The Northern Ireland Social Democratic and Labour Party

Political Opposition in a Divided Society

IAN McALLISTER

Foreword by
RICHARD ROSE

HOLMES & MEIER PUBLISHERS, INC.
IMPORT DIVISION
IUB Building
30 Irving Place, New York, N.Y. 10003

First published 1977 by
THE MACMILLAN PRESS LTD
London and Basingstoke
Associated companies in Delhi
Dublin Hong Kong Johannesburg Lagos
Melbourne New York Singapore Tokyo

British Library Cataloguing in Publication Data

McAllister, Ian
    The Northern Ireland Social Democratic and
    Labour Party.
    1. Social Democratic and Labour Party – History
    1. Title
    329.9′416   JN1572.A98

    ISBN 0–333–22347–0

Printed in Great Britain by
UNWIN BROTHERS LTD
Woking and London

For my mother and father

Contents

List of Tables and Figures

List of Abbreviations

CRC	Community Relations Commission
CSJ	Campaign for Social Justice in Northern Ireland
EEC	European Economic Community
GAA	Gaelic Athletic Association
IRA	Irish Republican Army
NDP	National Democratic Party
NICRA	Northern Ireland Civil Rights Association
NILP	Northern Ireland Labour Party
NIO	Northern Ireland Office
PR	Proportional Representation
RLP	Republican Labour Party
RTE	Radio Telefis Eireann
RUC	Royal Ulster Constabulary
SDLP	Social Democratic and Labour Party
STV	Single Transferable Vote
TD	Teachta Dala
UDA	Ulster Defence Association
UPNI	Unionist Party of Northern Ireland
UUUC	United Ulster Unionist Council
UWC	Ulster Workers' Council

Foreword

Politics is not an easy profession, and often it is scorned by the ordinary citizen, who takes for granted the advantages of representative government and free elections, and the public order that government provides. The citizens of one part of the United Kingdom, Northern Ireland, cannot take for granted the ordinary virtues of government. Since 1968 political life in the province has been in turmoil, and since 1971 men with guns have been more important than elected officeholders in its politics.

The lasting dangers that confront an Ulster politician are as real as those that confront a British soldier temporarily stationed in the province. During the time of the troubles, two members of the Senate of the old Stormont Parliament have been murdered, and more have been shot with intent to kill. Every man elected to the 1975 constitutional Convention was given the right to carry a gun, and some politicians have needed multiple bodyguards. The knock at the door of a politician's house may be a constituent asking for help – or it may come from the hand of a political assassin.

When politics invites such risks, it takes courage to speak out, whether on the majority or the minority side. Politicians in the majority can at least take solace from the fact that they have enjoyed the fruits of office in the past. As and when the government of Northern Ireland is returned to Ulster hands, representatives of the electoral majority can hardly be excluded. In Northern Ireland, minority politicians face a fate far worse than years of desultory speechmaking on opposition benches. They face the risk of seeing their party disrupted and destroyed by gunmen, whether from their own community or from the other side.

The existence of the Social Democratic and Labour Party is thus a triumph against the odds, for it is a party with a minority, not a majority vocation. The party was created after a half-century of Catholic isolation from the government of Northern Ireland. In part, the isolation was self-imposed, for traditional Catholic politicians looked to Dublin, not Stormont hill in Belfast, as the capitol of what they considered their country, a 32-county Irish Republic independent of Britain. They were prepared to spend a lifetime paying tribute to this ideal, while the Ulster Unionists, pledged to maintain the province as part of the United Kingdom, took all the power at Stormont. Sporadically the Irish Republican Army launched campaigns to unite Northern and Southern Ireland. But the sharp and effective response of Stormont demonstrated that Unionists were well able to defend what they held, by force of arms as well as by superior electoral numbers.

As its compound name suggests, the SDLP is an amalgamation of disparate groups within the Catholic community of Northern Ireland. Some of its members would emphasise its 'social' or 'labour' concerns and others its 'democratic' character. Many now identify with it simply as 'the party', being prepared to sink differences of left and right in order to maintain it as a single spokesman for the Catholic community. In consequence, an undivided party founded in 1970 is now the third oldest of the eight parties in Ulster. Moreover, it is far stronger electorally than the two groups senior to it.

The successes of the party are several. First of all, it has become the sole electoral voice of the Catholic community, in competition with traditional republicans and candidates seeking Catholic votes while putting the British before the Irish dimension. Secondly, it has participated in, rather than abstained from, representative bodies. This contrasts with the republican tradition of nominating candidates who refuse to recognise the separate institutions of Northern Ireland government – except in so far as they are incarcerated in its gaols. Thirdly, the SDLP became the first party representing pro-Irish and Catholic voters to hold office in a Northern Ireland government, participating in the short-lived 'power-sharing' Executive formed under British government sponsorship in 1974, with Brian Faulkner of the Unionists as head, and Gerry Fitt, leader of the SDLP, as its deputy head. Fourthly, the SDLP has secured the endorsement of successive Conservative and Labour governments in Britain for its recommendation for governing Northern Ireland by an Executive sharing power between Protestants and Catholics, and recognising an Irish dimension.

The achievements of the SDLP have not been easily won. From its origin, its leaders have had to compete for the political support of Catholics against the republican movement, in its political (Sinn Féin) and military (IRA) wings. The violence of the province, where British, Protestant loyalist and republican armed forces are all active, makes it difficult to argue the case for resolving differences through peaceful electoral means. Equally important, the party's minority status – the SDLP has never won more than 24 per cent of the vote at an Ulster election – means that it faces opposition from politicians who can legitimately claim to represent the majority of the electorate.

The SDLP has been unsuccessful in realising one of its major goals – the creation of a political party drawing large numbers of votes across the sectarian divide. Unlike the old Ulster Nationalists, who welcomed clerical support, the SDLP is a secular party. It does not claim to be a spokesman for the Catholic hierarchy, or for Catholics *qua* Catholics. But its avowed long-term aspiration for the unification of Ireland inevitably confines its appeal to Catholics, in a society in which national identity and religion are closely related. In this respect, it resembles the far weaker Northern Ireland Labour Party, with support confined to Protestants, because it is committed to British as well as labour and trade union interests. Neither of these parties has been as successful as the Alliance Party in drawing support across the Protestant – Catholic boundary. But the size of Alliance's steady vote – about one-tenth of the electorate – emphasises how limited is the short-run scope for a party that puts a bi-confessional appeal before the issue of national identity.

The potential conflict between the SDLP's immediate dependence upon British patronage at Westminster and its long-term aspiration to belong to a united Ireland has been muffled within the party, because of the advantages of maintaining a united party. But the SDLP's orientation to 'the two Souths' has constituted a great barrier to the achievement of power-sharing. When listing their objections to sharing office with the SDLP, loyalist politicians do not refer to its Catholic base of support, but rather to its rejection of British for Irish allegiance. For example, the fact that SDLP party leaders travel on Irish passports and raise party funds in Dublin is cited as proof of disloyalty to Ulster institutions, and as a disqualification from holding office in Ulster in institutions established by the Crown in Parliament at Westminster.

Ultimately, the limitations of the SDLP, like those of any political party, are determined by the actions of other parties with which it must compete. In the system of inter-party relations in Northern Ireland, the SDLP controls only part of the action. As long as individuals tend to vote along religious and national identity lines, the pro-British loyalist parties supported by Protestants will command a majority of votes and seats. The single transferable vote system of proportional representation used in Northern Ireland, by allocating seats much more strictly in accord to votes than in Britain, can only register defeat for any party representing a minority.

The SDLP is not a normal political party, any more than Northern Ireland is typical of the United Kingdom as a whole. The SDLP is not only a vote-getting party, but also part of a protest movement. It gives electoral voice to the views of the Catholic third of Northern Ireland. The power-sharing policy that the SDLP puts forward is not based upon electoral strength, but upon a moral claim to reparation. The party has pointed to the exclusion of Catholics from office in the half-century of Stormont, and asks that they now be guaranteed a share of posts in power as a condition of establishing any future institutions of government in Ulster. In reply, loyalists argue that Catholics excluded themselves from office by refusing to recognise Northern Ireland as a British territory; until they show British loyalty, they have no right to lose elections yet still expect to be given office.

The debate about power-sharing between the SDLP and loyalists leads off on the long march backward in time. There is no point in pursuing that controversy here. Moreover, the message that one finds at the end of the search in the seventeenth century is the same as today: conflict between the two communities.

The value of Ian McAllister's study of the Social Democratic and Labour Party is that it is concerned with the present tense of Ulster politics. As the chief electoral spokesman of one of the two communities in the province, the SDLP must necessarily be involved – as a winner or a loser – in any resolution of the current conflict. An Ulsterman himself, McAllister displays the province's characteristic concern with the complexities of Northern Ireland politics, and with the roots as well as the visible evidence of the party's activities. The story of the SDLP is told clearly, carefully and objectively. The reader can judge from this account how much the SDLP has achieved, and what is left undone.

At the end of the day the great political divide in Northern Ireland separates those who wish to settle their differences peacefully by elections, from those who are ready to settle them by force of arms. In this respect, the SDLP and loyalist politicians have a common preference for the ballot, not the bullet, as the ultimate arbiter of political differences. Those who commit themselves to party politics in Northern Ireland do not do so casually, they actively reject the stark and brutal efforts to settle the province's political future by force.

University of Strathclyde   RICHARD ROSE

Introduction

In Western democracies most well-organised and supported groups can exercise some political influence on the decision-making process. The ability to formulate demands, present them to the political system and ultimately to influence policies, is a process that almost all take for granted. But in a deeply polarised society a numerical minority will encounter great difficulty in exerting influence at any stage of decision-making process, and this exclusion from power raises severe problems for any office-seeking group broadly representative of a minority. How can it reconcile the desire for political office with that of permanent minority status?

One group that has faced this problem is the Northern Ireland Social Democratic and Labour Party (SDLP), a political party that has endeavoured since 1970 to articulate the political demands of the province's Catholic minority.[1] The dilemma for the Catholic minority has been to find an effective channel to express its demands while consisting of only one-third of the population of the state. The SDLP, using constitutional methods and relying on elections, has provided one means. In the context of this study the focus of attention is thus the political party, but this is not an exclusive, nor necessarily the most effective, channel. Before briefly examining the possible alternatives, it is useful to define the concepts that will recur throughout this work.

The concept of *community* provides the foundation for the various forms of political activity. The community is defined as a collection of people who share a common political and/or social attribute (or attributes) and among whom a high degree of shared political activity takes place. It follows that the community's solidarity will militate against any political activity that transgresses its boundaries and, correspondingly, any variation in the nature of political activity will result from endogenous forces. The term *Catholic community* is used to specify a collectivity that has the common elements of community and draws its social cohesion from the common identification with Catholicism. The *minority* is a surrogate for the Catholic community in Ulster that recognises, but does not emphasise, its common religious attribute. Within the community, political activity may be defined in various forms. A *tradition* is a broad concept denoting a set of political attitudes that are passed from generation to generation and more or less accepted by each. A *movement* is the organised political expression of a point of view and can involve more than one kind of group. A *political party* is an organisation concerned with political aims to be furthered by winning public office through electoral competition. An *organisation* is an institution incorporating regular procedures and rules through which a group of individuals come together to act in the attainment of a defined aim or aims.

The method by which a community sets out to articulate its political demands is contingent, among other things, on *size*. For a majority community within a democratic system, the simplest way to express its demands is through elective institutions, provided that voting is free from intimidation, the electoral system fairly run, a choice of candidates offered and that the representative institution takes politically important decisions.[2] On the other hand, for a minority community the choices are wider and harder. The options are determined by whether the community forms only one of a number of minorities, none of which can attain a majority, or whether it is faced by a united and cohesive majority. If the society is composed of a number of minorities, then the need for a coalition to constitute a governing majority will encourage compromise. The situation where, as in Northern Ireland, a majority faces a minority and the political party representing the majority has been electorally dominant for a long period, is by far the most intractable and rare. Some comparisons emphasise this uniqueness.

If language is used as a criterion of community identification, out of 132 countries throughout the world only eight possess a majority faced by a minority made up of more than one quarter and less than one half of the country's population. Moreover, only two of the eight, Canada and Belgium, are Western democracies.[3] If elections are examined, of 23 industrial countries operating national competitive elections in the twentieth century, only three possess instances where one party gained an absolute majority of seats in the legislature on five or more successive elections. The longest period of unbroken rule is found in Canada, between 1935 and 1953. By comparison, the Ulster Unionist Party obtained an absolute majority of the seats in the Northern Ireland parliament from 1921 to prorogation in 1972, a period of 51 years' unbroken rule covering 12 elections.[4]

The permanent exclusion from political power has made size a central consideration for the Ulster Catholic community and a major influence on the means they have chosen to express their political demands. It is possible to identify four separate channels of which two are constitutional (in so far as they follow accepted procedures dictated by law and convention) and two extra-constitutional (in that they infringe these procedures). They are defined and applied to Irish politics below.

The first constitutional form is the organised electoral group, expressed most frequently in the *political party*. Recognising the institutions of the state, the political party mobilises support through the electoral system and directs the consequent demands through representative institutions. Success for the party depends upon numerical strength, which in turn determines its ability to influence or participate in government. To derive the optimum advantage from this support, the political party must organise and co-ordinate its activities cross-locally and enforce strict discipline among its elected representatives.

In the nationalist tradition of Irish politics, the most effective expression of the political party was the Irish Party, formed into a cohesive parliamentary force under Parnell's leadership. The party exercised a decisive influence on Irish politics and, though a small minority in the Westminster House of Commons, by holding the balance of power between the two British parties also influenced the course of United Kingdom politics. The party was notable for the primacy of the parliamentary principle, for the unscrupulous use of parliamentary obstruction to further home rule demands, and for the fact that it won the support of a majority within the Irish electorate. Within the unionist tradition, the political party has been utilised since partition as the main means of ensuring the preservation of the Northern Ireland state, since this was conditional upon the return of a pro-union electoral majority. The Unionist Party achieved this aim by introducing a complex framework that linked a mass party in the country, organised on a province-wide basis, with a disciplined body within the Stormont parliament.

A second organised group that shares the constitutional orientation of the political party but which is essentially non-electoral, is the *pressure group*. In seeking to influence government rather than replace it, the pressure group generally represents one interest only and thus its function is primarily articulative. The success of this form of organisation depends on the structure of the regime and the political system it seeks to influence, and on the nature and extent of its support.

Constitutional pressure groups have never played more than a secondary role in Irish politics due to the ascendancy of the broader political movements. The role of the Catholic and Protestant churches in the education controversy of the 1920s is one example of pressure group politics in Ulster. The various housing action groups that emerged in the 1960s and the Campaign for Social Justice in Northern Ireland also acted as pressure groups in urging the government to take remedial action on specific social issues. As the groups rarely encompassed more than a small circle of members, the best method of attaining their aims was to collate evidence, using this as a basis to lobby individuals holding influential positions within the regime.

A third method of expressing political demands is that of the *protest group*. As the means of direct action employed are illegal, it is extra-constitutional in form. Although non-violent in intent, the protest group uses the *implicit* threat of violence emanating either from fringe supporters or from hostile counter-demonstrators and police.[5] A major condition for success is the mobilisation of large numbers of demonstrators, and as the threat of violence is central to the group's approach, disruptive counter-demonstrators may also serve this end by adding to the erosion of the regime's stability.

The Irish National Land League was an important nineteenth-century Catholic manifestation of the protest group. The League organised the peasantry for peaceful picketing and social ostracism in order to publicise evictions and depress rents. While never strong in Ulster, the League's ability to mobilise mass support in aid of political reform made it a precursor of the Northern Ireland Civil Rights Association (NICRA). In pursuit of the equal rights of British citizenship, the NICRA organised street demonstrations and picketing and like the League attracted mass support as well as counter-violence, which tangibly strengthened and legitimised its cause.

The fourth and final method of political expression, *armed force*, is overtly extra-constitutional. It deploys the *explicit* threat of violence as a political means and seeks to replace the regime by posing a direct military challenge to it.[6] The distinction between a defensive and offensive armed force has little relevance in the extent of the challenge it makes, for both equally aim to usurp the regime of its fundamental power, the monopoly of the legitimate means of force. In contrast to the protest group, for example, the size of support for the armed force is not paramount; the dedication and loyalty of its membership and the effectiveness of their tactics are likely to be of more concern. However, at a minimum, the passive acquiescence of the community from which the armed force operates makes it more difficult for the regime to extirpate.

Instances of the organised expression of armed force abound throughout Irish history. Regional defensive organisations mushroomed in response to the rampant agrarian discontent of the eighteenth century: Protestant secret societies such as the Oakboys, the Peep O'Day Boys and the most famous, the Orange Boys, were opposed by clandestine Catholic groups such as the Whiteboys and the Defenders. The use of offensive physical force in the attainment of a political goal was inaugurated in 1798 by the United Irishmen, whose separatist ideals created an armed republican tradition that has continued to this day in the Irish Republican Army (IRA), via Young Ireland, the Fenians, the Irish Republican Brotherhood, and the pre-Treaty IRA. The explicit threat of force against the state was first used by the Protestant community in modern times in 1912 with the activation and extensive arming of the Ulster Volunteer Force, then a corporate part of the unionist movement, in opposition to the third Home Rule Bill.

Although the four channels for the expression of political demands defined above are analytically separate, groups and individuals initially in one category can invoke the means of another channel in order to advance a political aim. For example, Parnell recruited a wide and politically heterogeneous following by blurring the issues and refusing to define how far he would deviate from constitutional politics to attain his demands.[7] In a similar vein, William O'Brien concluded that 'the methods vary with the circumstances . . . mere methods are accidents, not principles.'[8] The method to be used in pursuit of a political goal is thus decided not only by constitutional or moral considerations, but also by practicality and expediency.

The position of a minority creates two initial alternatives: withdrawal or political action. The negative alternative of withdrawal reduces the regime's legitimacy and is a route frequently taken by minorities consigned to political impotence, since it makes 'politics a more remote and therefore less painful experience'.[9] Often non-political substitutes such as religion replace politics, so that a minority can look forward to the prospect of change in the next world, if not in the present. The positive alternative of political action, which is normally an act of allegiance towards the regime, contains four possible choices.

Firstly, the minority may seek to redress their grievances through the judicial system, where ideally the weight of argument and not the weight of numbers is the guiding principle. The Catholic community never seriously attempted to exploit this channel due to their intense suspicion of a Unionist-dominated judiciary that, in any event, enforced a form of law that could not adjudicate on the content of legislative decisions.[10] The second choice, armed rebellion to overthrow the state, has been frequently endorsed by Catholics, but in Northern Ireland never brought their aim of Irish unity any closer, for Protestants had the dual advantages of numerical strength and political legitimacy. The third choice, street protest to attain limited reform, did in the late 1960s make some progress in winning reform within the established system, but its influence was unsustained, due largely to the tendency for protest to be accompanied by violence.

The fourth choice for political action, electoral competition, is potentially the most far-reaching in giving a minority political influence. The conditions under which a minority may exercise influence on government by electoral means are if the majority were to actively recruit minority support or if the majority were to fragment and leave the minority in the advantageous position of being able to help reconstruct the governmental majority. Neither of these conditions apply to Ulster because of the dominance of the constitutional question in political debate. Since the Catholic community seeks Irish reunification, they are 'disloyal' in Protestant eyes as their aim is nothing less than the destruction of the state. This basic consideration precludes the majority seeking Catholic support under any circumstances, either voluntarily or in coalition.

If, then, the Catholic community cannot exercise any influence on the majority, what can it do within the framework of electoral competition in Ulster? There are four possibilities. Firstly, the simple demand for an end to partition can be sustained, a goal that would end Catholic minority status by widening the boundaries of the state. But this aim promises little hope of attainment and only serves to exacerbate Protestant distrust of the 'disloyal' Catholic minority and to increase unionist cohesion. Secondly, the basis of the franchise and the electoral system might be changed, which, although not negating the ascendancy of the majority, could shift the balance of power in localised areas. The introduction of proportional representation (PR), a system that gives a fairer representation to competing groups and especially minorities, has favoured Catholic political groups. PR in local elections, coupled with the universal franchise, has given Catholics increased representation on local authorities, and in a few cases, the power of a majority. The use of PR in provincial elections has encouraged Catholic electoral activity and made it more difficult for the majority to maintain discipline among its members.

A third choice involves changing the dimension of the conflict from the constitutional question to one of class or societal benefit. The efforts of various labour groups to promote the salience of class over religion have met with little success. Almost all have been forced to declare their position on the constitution, hence limiting their support to one or other community. Other attempts to encourage the growth of inter-communal politics have been similarly unforthcoming, with the most notable, the Alliance Party, receiving only modest support for the aim of communal reconciliation. The fourth choice for a minority engaged in electoral competition is to seek a change in the rules determining the formation of the government. If the rules confer power on a legislative majority, then to reformulate them, so that power must be shared equally (or proportionately) between the communities, is an obvious and direct means of ending the minority's exclusion from authority and responsibility.[11] Since 1973 this demand for institutionalised power-sharing within the Northern Ireland state has become the central SDLP demand and largely replaced orthodox anti-partitionist claims.

This, then, is the context in which the study of the SDLP is set. To reiterate, the problem for the Catholic community has been how to articulate its political demands effectively in a democratic system while holding the status of a permanent minority. The party political approach, expressed through the SDLP, has provided one method. Within the framework of electoral competition, the party has sought to redraw the political 'rules of the game' in order to secure representation in government as of right and hence end the Catholic minority's permanent exclusion from power.

The object of this book is to examine how the SDLP has sought to achieve this aim, and more generally, to assess the party's impact on the Northern Ireland political system. Part One deals with the post-war social and political changes within the Catholic community and the immediate events leading up to the formation of the SDLP. Part Two analyses the party's organisational structure, policies and personnel, using a quantitative approach where possible, and Part Three recounts the SDLP's experience within the political system, with emphasis on its relationship to the regime, between the party's inception in 1970 and the collapse of the constitutional Convention in 1976.

During the preparation of the book, which is based on a PhD thesis accepted by the University of Strathclyde, Glasgow, many individuals gave generously of their time. Professor Richard Rose oversaw the research and provided encouragement and advice at every stage. Dr John Oliver, Dr John Whyte and John Duffy commented on the manuscript as a whole, and individual chapters were commented on by Ben Caraher, Denis Haughey and Hugh Logue. The final stage of the work was completed while the author was a Research Fellow at the Institute of Irish Studies, the Queen's University of Belfast, where the Institute's Director, Professor E. R. R. Green, made many valuable comments in the course of numerous conversations. Needless to say, any errors of fact or interpretation which remain are entirely my own responsibility. Dr Patrick McGill compiled the information on post-war Nationalist MPs used in Chapter 6, and Dan McAreavy and Martin Lacey, both of the SDLP headquarters staff, supplied me swiftly with the party's published documentation. Most of the research was carried out in the Library of the New University of Ulster, Coleraine, where the Librarian, F. J. E. Hurst, and the Assistant Librarian, Joan Scally, graciously made every facility available to me.

Institute of Irish Studies   IAN MCALLISTER
The Queens University of Belfast
June 1977

Part One

CONTINGENT CIRCUMSTANCES

1 Social Mobilisation

The transition to organised politics presupposes the existence of many social changes conducive to its initial growth. The individual influence of these social changes may not be large, but collectively they may well have a considerable effect on political activity. Thus the population begins to be socially mobilised through changes in various areas of social life which 'singly, and even more in their cumulative impact . . . tend to influence and sometimes to transform political behaviour.'[1] The immediate result is a higher level of political awareness, which is increased by improved transportation and communications. This in turn serves to emphasise political and social inequalities. The sense of injustice aroused by inequality translates itself into pressures for political reform which the existing system is likely to find impossible to meet. The eventual outcome is an extension of political participation by all sections of the population and a need for organised groups to structure and exploit this growing mass involvement.

In Northern Ireland the replacement of the Nationalist Party by the SDLP as the political representatives of the Catholic community has highlighted the importance of many social changes occurring in the province in the 1950s and 1960s. While the problem of general inequality remained the same for Catholics, attempts to adequately articulate their grievances were contingent on a number of changes in the social sphere. This chapter examines some of these changes and assesses their significance in the growth of organised politics.

RELATIVE DEPRIVATION AND RELIGIOUS DISCRIMINATION

Runciman has defined relative deprivation as the sense of deprivation involved in a comparison of one's own situation with that of the real or imagined situation of some other person or group.[2] Thus, if one person or group is relatively better off than another, then the second is *relatively* deprived of the advantage enjoyed by the first. In Northern Ireland, despite the socio-economic deprivation of the region as a whole in comparison with the rest of the United Kingdom, the Catholic minority is relatively deprived when compared to the Protestant majority. The instrument by which the minority is deprived of advantage is religious discrimination. An important qualification has to be made in that it is the Catholic community's *perception* of relative deprivation rather than the *objective truth* that is the salient factor.

Substantial evidence of religious discrimination against Catholics has been compiled and documented at length, particularly in the last ten years.[3] It is therefore necessary only to trace the broad outline of the allegations. Runciman has isolated three main areas in which inequality may take place: the political, the economic and the social.[4] Catholic grievances will be outlined in each of these areas in turn.

Until comparatively recently the main political grievance was the restricted franchise, the gerrymandering of electoral boundaries and the exclusion of Catholics from government-appointed statutory bodies. Up until 1968 plural voting and residential and property qualifications were part of the local government franchise. This resulted in a striking difference between the numbers of electors registered for local and Stormont elections, where no similar restrictions operated: in 1967, for example, the local government electorate was 694,483, compared to 933,724 for the Stormont parliament.[5] This became an emotive issue for Catholics since they were by far the more heavily penalised by the restrictions. Gerrymandering of local government boundaries was potentially more serious since even if Catholics were enfranchised and formed a numerical majority in the area, boundary manipulation ensured that this majority could never be realised in the council chamber. Statistical evidence of the unfair distribution of boundaries has been well documented, notably in the Cameron Commission's investigation of the causes of the 1968 disturbances.[6] Catholic representation on government-appointed statutory boards has also been low. In 1969 the Campaign for Social Justice published the results of a survey of the religious composition of 22 public boards, which showed the avearage level of Catholic membership to be only 15 per cent.[7]

While political inequality tends to be symbolic, economic deprivation has a direct impact on those subject to it. Religious discrimination exists in many areas of employment, both public and private, although accurate statistical information is lacking. The 1970 report of the Northern Ireland Commissioner for Complaints had particular difficulty in investigating and categorising alleged cases of discrimination in the public sector.[8] There is thus a paucity of Catholics in public employment, and especially in the higher echelons of the Northern Ireland Civil Service. In 1962 Barritt and Carter discovered that the percentage of Catholics in the post of Staff Officer and above had remained unchanged at 6 per cent between 1927 and 1959, and in some ministries, such as Home Affairs, no Catholics at all were employed in these grades.[9] By contrast, Catholic applications to the Imperial Civil Service – administratively separate from Stormont and hence not subject to Unionist control or patronage – has frequently exceeded the proportion of Catholics in the population.

Prior to the reorganisation of local government in 1973, inequalities in jobs at the disposal of the local authorities were also marked. Catholics were rarely to be found in senior posts, and in some areas virtually no

Catholics were employed at any level. One of the best documented cases concerned the working of Fermanagh County Council. Notwithstanding the Catholic majority in the county, the Unionist-controlled Council rarely employed Catholics in anything other than temporary manual work. For example, of the Council's 75 school bus drivers, all but seven were Protestants.[10] The consequence of job discrimination has been a high level of Catholic unemployment. Rose's survey found that two-thirds of the unemployed were Catholics or 'almost double what would be expected from the proportion in the population.'[11] There is also a strong regional imbalance, with the area of Ulster lying to the west of the River Bann, which contains a high proportion of Catholics, having an unemployment rate approaching 20 per cent, whereas the more prosperous (and Protestant-dominated) east has a figure appreciably lower.

The third field of deprivation affecting the Catholic community is social inequality, where the main area of contention has been the allocation of council housing. Since the lack of adequate housing results in cramped and unpleasant living conditions, it inevitably strengthens feelings of inequality. While Rose's survey found no evidence of any systematic pattern of discrimination at the aggregate level,[12] the Cameron Commission found ample evidence of unfair methods of allocation.[13] A later housing study concluded that areas with over 50 per cent of Catholics were almost exclusively represented in the group of local authority areas with the worst housing conditions.[14]

This, then, is the broad outline of the foundation for the Catholic sense of grievance. It is largely irrelevant that Prostestant socio-economic conditions have been only marginally better than those of their Catholic fellow-neighbours: what is important is the Catholic feeling of relative inequality. Similarly, the objectivity of the grievances is also not of great importance – although a strong factual basis obviously exists for them – it is the Catholic belief that they are held to reflect the existing state of affairs. The political response is thus 'not proportionate to the incidence of complaints. It is disproportionately greater. Catholics are not concerned with the quantity of complaints or the cash value of their deprivations, but rather, with *any* evidence of discrimination.'[15] The question remains, however, why it was not until the 1960s that steps were taken to try and ameliorate these long-standing grievances. In other words, why did no Catholic political party or group emerge to adequately articulate them before 1960? In this context three social changes were of significance.

THE CONDITIONS FOR THE SUCCESSFUL ARTICULATION OF
GRIEVANCES

(i) A Large Catholic Middle Class
The Cameron Commission identified the emergence of a larger Catholic

middle class as 'an important and new element in the political and social climate of Northern Ireland'. This new middle class, the Commission noted, was 'less ready to acquiesce in the acceptance of a situation of assumed (or established) inferiority and discrimination than was the case in the past.'[16] The significance of this middle class for Northern Ireland politics was therefore clear, but from what social base in the society did it originate? The answer lies in change in two main areas, the economy and the educational system.

The increasing economic prosperity of the 1950s and the early 1960s produced a growing demand, not only for skilled workers and raw material, but for professionally trained administrative and middle-management employees. The decline of the province's large manufacturing industries was matched by an inflow of newer, smaller and highly specialised industries. Whereas the old manufacturing concerns required relatively little specialised or professional expertise, these new industries demanded highly skilled workers and competent management, design and research staff. This diversification had the further effect of stimulating the growth of service industries, which again necessitated both specialised administrative and technical skills.

These changes in the economy were paralleled by an increasing governmental priority on education. The insistence of the Catholic Church on separate education had meant that 'the deficiencies of the educational system affected them preponderantly.'[17] The 1947 Education Act sought to remedy these deficiencies and give financial provision to Catholic voluntary schools while at the same time allowing them to retain their independent status. The new educational opportunities allowed many children of Catholic working class families to have post-primary education which they would in all probability not otherwise have had. In the 17 years following the 1947 Act the number of pupils in grant-aided schools increased by 39 per cent, while the total number of pupils in secondary education as a whole doubled between 1946 and 1952 alone.[18]

Many of the beneficiaries of this education continued on to university. Entry to The Queen's University, Belfast, is guided by the principles of equal opportunity and non-discrimination; and as a large proportion of its intake has always come from Ulster, many availed themselves of this opportunity to receive higher education. Queen's itself began to expand in response to the growing demands for more graduates: between 1930 and 1965 the student population quadrupled and the Economics and Science faculties alone expanded by eight and nine-fold, respectively.[19] But the raw statistics concerning the expansion of Queen's student population hardly takes into account the effect of its particular atmosphere. At the pinnacle of an educational system that is segregated from early primary school, the University is unique in being religiously heterogeneous and its tolerant atmosphere helps to dampen the natural acerbity between the communities. In a survey of Queen's students conducted by Barritt and

Carter, 78 per cent of the respondents claimed friendship with those of the opposite faith,[20] a remarkable figure considering the rigid pre-university educational segregation.

Post-war educational changes thus propelled more Catholics with a better education and a liberal outlook into an Ulster society that was hardly able to absorb them. With many holding degrees and comparable qualifications, they demanded employment commensurate with their ability. The smaller and less well educated Catholic middle class had previously been content with employing its members in jobs which served their own community rather than jobs serving the society as a whole. Many owned small shops or public houses and occasionally doubled up as undertakers, insurance brokers or similar part-time occupations. These occupations were hardly attractive to graduates who were seeking upward mobility in the growing Northern Ireland economy. But public employment was effectively closed to them by religious discrimination as were many commercial enterprises and the result was the frustration of 'blocked opportunities'. Many went into the more secure teaching, medical or legal professions, which demanded professional expertise yet were free from possible discrimination. In the 1960s the political groups that emerged to challenge the orthodox political leadership of the Catholic community were largely drawn from this residue of graduates. One main factor preventing them immediately assuming political leadership was the influence of the Roman Catholic Church.

(ii) Laicisation
The second condition for the successful articulation of grievances was the *laicisation* or secularisation of politics. Historically the Roman Catholic Church has claimed jurisdiction over all aspects of the secular and spiritual life of its members, including their political life. Prior to the twentieth century this doctrine went unchallenged in Ireland, although the role of the clergy in the fall of Parnell in 1890 did provoke heated controversy. Before the 1829 Catholic Emancipation Act there was virtually no lay leadership and thus the clergy became the undisputed leaders of the Catholic community. This situation persisted into the twentieth century in many parts of Ireland, such as the rural west, where a sufficiently progressive or able laity never emerged. In Northern Ireland the priesthood retained this position partly because the Catholic majoritarian position in Ireland as a whole had given way after 1921 to that of a separated minority and partly because the laity was unwilling or unable to take the initiative. The main instrument in perpetuating clerical power within the Catholic community has been the policy of exclusivism. The two areas it has been most rigorously applied are in the social relations of the community and in education.

The notion of exclusivism dates from the period of religious persecution when it was introduced as a device to preserve the numbers of the faithful

and the intensity of their commitment. Throughout Europe this relic of
religious defensiveness was gradually relaxed in the twentieth century. In
Northern Ireland, however, since the Church faced a Protestant majority
the leaders of whom barely tolerated, let alone welcomed, the minority in
their midst, exclusivism in social life became a matter of practical
expediency.

The view of the Church on mixed marriage, and in particular the *Ne
Temere* decree, is one aspect of the policy. The aim of the decree, now
relaxed, was to ensure that in a mixed marriage the faith of the Catholic
partner and of any children would be preserved. In general social
relationships the Church has, whenever possible, organised parallel social
bodies for its people and has discouraged groups or meetings that included
non-Catholics. The Gaelic Athletic Association, for example, was set up in
1884 with the help of a Catholic bishop to further Gaelic sports in Ireland.
In order to reinvigorate and protect the game, exclusivism was implemented and expressed in the famous Rule 27 which forbade members 'to play,
or to watch or to help promote, soccer, rugby, cricket or hockey.'[21] Again
this rule has been recently relaxed. Overall, the policy of segregation
coupled with the hostile political and social environment militated against
outside contacts on any appreciable scale and maintained the 'peculiar
authority, and often affection'[22] enjoyed by the priest.

This 'peculiar authority' is enhanced by the role of the priest manager in
the Catholic educational system. Throughout Europe the dispute over
secular education was, with few exceptions, resolved by 1900, but its
divisiveness has been sustained in Northern Ireland. The reinforcement of
the religious cleavage by the constitutional question has placed the
educational issue at the forefront of the political conflict. Originally a
committee under Robert Lynn had recommended the setting up of a
completely secular, integrated system of education, but both Protestant
and Catholic groups were opposed on the grounds that they had a moral
duty to teach religion. An amendment was passed to the 1925 Education
Act permitting religious instruction to be given and subsequently a further
Act was passed in 1930 which made it compulsory. The bitterest conflict
arose over the post-war reconstruction of the educational system and
centred on the level of grant to be made towards the running costs of
Catholic voluntary schools. Latterly the debate has returned to the
question of non-denominational education, with the Catholic Church
preserving its influence throughout, with all the significance this has in the
process of political socialisation.

Since 1921 the Church has therefore been able to maintain its important
position within the Catholic community and impose its standards and
values on them in numerous areas of everyday life. But there has been a
tendency to regard it as more monolithic and powerful than either its
image deserves or its critics claim. Like other institutions and organisations, the Church has been exposed to a multiplicity of forces making for

change. Dissension within the Church has developed between both the clergy and the laity, and within the clergy itself between the hierarchy and the priests. Post-1945 changes in the political, social and economic spheres have kept up a continuous attrition and many aspects of the policy of exclusivism have either been relaxed or removed.

In Ulster the political outlook of the Church has been ambiguous. One of the cornerstones of the faith has been the notion of respect for law, yet the Church has disapproved of partition and while simultaneously opposing the state has urged respect for authority and a denial of physical force as a political means. In the secular state in which Ulster Catholics found themselves in 1921 this ambiguity fostered passivity and the abstentionist strategy of the Nationalist Party was underlaid by a submissive and uncooperative attitude in social life.

Among the multitude of reasons contributing to the erosion of these attitudes in the late 1950 and 1960s, probably of most direct relevance were the growth of ecumenism and the emergence of a competent lay leadership. The growth of the ecumenical movement is not itself a motive for change but rather reflective of an increasing secularisation in society, coupled with a growing tolerance for other religious views. Within the Catholic Church this external image was improved by the liberalising influence of Pope John XXIII, who set a precedent by explicitly approving of state intervention in economic life.[23] From the perspective of the Catholic community, it showed that qualitative change could take place and transferred the onus for maintaining the dynamic of this change to the middle-class Catholic laity.

The accession of a lay group willing to take the leadership created the conditions for the formation of constructive political groups. The foundations for the policy of exclusivism and passivity in political life disappeared and as these traditional constraints on involvement in conventional political activity were removed, so too by a combination of their sensitivity to the change and in deference to public opinion, the clergy largely relinquished their leadership role. In a survey of priests carried out in Co. Tyrone in 1968 this trend was confirmed. It was found that while priests were 'acutely aware of the problems cited as political issues there was a general reluctance . . . to take on a leadership role and initiate and carry on the burden of agitation.'[24] Regionally the process was an uneven one: in Belfast and some smaller urban centres secularisation had been accomplished by the 1940s or even earlier, but in the more remote rural areas it persisted well into the 1960s.

The focus of many of these changes came in a desire for greater involvement in the running of the Northern Ireland state. A Social Studies conference held at Garron Tower, Co. Antrim, in 1958 crystallised the feeling that Catholics should be allowed to participate in public life without prejudicing their ultimate aspiration to Irish unity. The strongest protagonist of this approach was Dr G. B. Newe, who emphasised the part

Catholics could play in public life. In a paper read to the conference, he asserted that they had a duty 'to co-operate with the *de facto* authority that controls . . . life and welfare.' He dismissed the Republic's argument that they were the *de jure* government of Northern Ireland as fallacious and 'a salve to the conscience' and concluded that Catholics would have to 'show a readiness to serve' and to act in many committees from which they had previously been excluded, and excluded themselves, from participation.[25]

While many at the conference did not go as far as Newe – one speaker called it 'co-operation at almost any price'[26] – there was a generally held belief that Catholics would have to actively participate in the state. Thus the redefinition of the functions of the clergy, the liberalising influences at work in the world-wide Catholic Church and the strong desire of middle class Catholics to participate, made the 1958 Garron Tower conference a turning-point in the Ulster Catholic's view of political activity. A more general change conducive to this shift in attitude was the modernisation of life in the province.

(iii) Modernisation

In his study of modernisation in Turkey, Daniel Lerner isolated two main factors responsible for the shift from a non-participant, kinship-based traditional society to a participatory, individual, urban-based society. The first catalyst in the move to modernity is *physical mobility* or the ability to move with relative ease from one place to another. The second is *psychic mobility* or 'the capacity to see oneself in the other fellow's situation'. This in turn depends on the development of the media, which promotes social integration and diffuses modern political values.[27] The two concepts have considerable relevance in explaining the social change occurring within the Catholic community in the 1960s. Physical mobility has been of direct concern in helping to determine the population balance between the two communities and the development of the media, especially television, has helped to erode traditional attitudes. More specifically, the media created unprecedented opportunities for publicising Catholic political demands in the 1960s.

The population balance between the two communities has always been important, since if the Protestant community ceased to have numerical superiority, they would forfeit political power. Despite the Protestant fear of being outnumbered by the higher rate of Catholic fertility, Catholic emigration has consistently nullified their higher birth rate. The greater degree of relative deprivation to which Catholics have been subject has forced large numbers of them to seek work abroad, and this emigration is thus politically significant not only as a device for maintaining the inter-communal balance, but also in the particular groups of Catholics it affects most. A study by Boal and Compton indicated that it reaches its peak among Catholic males in the 20 to 24 age category, where the percentage emigrating is almost twice that of any other single group.[28] For the young and mobile, emigration is an obvious alternative to the prospect of prolonged unemployment. Once initiated, the continuance of such a population movement is semi-automatic, for 'so long as there are people to emigrate the principal cause of emigration is prior emigration.'[29] It may also be argued that these groups, in age, religion and political inclination, often tend to be the most disaffected and rebellious, while those left behind may be more politically satisfied or passive.

There is evidence of a shift in this trend since the war. Although the overall pattern of a slow decline in the Catholic population continues, there are significant regional variations, particularly in Belfast and Londonderry. Here a decline in the Catholic population of 10 per cent between 1861 and 1937 became a 3 per cent increase between 1938 and 1961: in Londonderry there was a 4 per cent increase between 1951 and 1961 alone. Catholics who might otherwise have emigrated have tended to move into the two large urban centres, no doubt attracted by the better job prospects and higher wages. This is reflected in the population statistics. Between 1911 and 1926 Northern Ireland ceased to be a predominantly rural country and by 1961 a majority – 54 per cent – lived in urban areas. Another indication is given by the numbers employed in agriculture, which in 1949 stood at just under 7 per cent of the insured population, but had been more than halved by 1964. In short, emigration has declined among those to whom it is traditionally most attractive, while there has been a move to urban living and the expanding pool of young Catholics who might otherwise have emigrated has created a potential reservoir of criticism to the regime.

Urbanisation has been facilitated by improved transportation and travel opportunities. The large numbers travelling in and out of Ulster have helped to widen horizons and undermine parochial outlooks. Between 1951 and 1962 the number of passengers carried by air transport in the province more than quadrupled while the number of cars doubled. Whereas that other mode of transport which had an important social impact, the railway, tended to exacerbate the religious cleavage by bringing Catholics into Belfast, the growing use of the motor car has had a more liberalising influence by increasing contacts between the rural and urban areas and giving individuals the relative freedom to choose where to live and work.

Thus physical mobility has been an initial catalyst in the modernising process. The advent of the media and the stimulation of psychic mobility has helped to consolidate this change and integrate the new urban areas. When television broadcasting commenced in Northern Ireland in 1954, just under 10,000 licences had been issued, a figure that increased nineteen-fold in the next eight years. Television had a slow if discernible effect on political and social outlooks, due largely to the fact that the BBC only gradually incorporated matters of specific concern to Catholics. Although the broadcasting authorities are obliged by law to give a fair balance to differing points of view, Catholic representatives, both lay and clerical, were only gradually given exposure on the new medium. The eventual inclusion of Catholic spokesmen on various topical programmes helped to give their point of view a respectability that it had not previously enjoyed. The result was the emergence of Catholic self-confidence and a stimulation of the already revived interest in politics among middle-class Catholics. Many became aware of the media's potential in publicising grievances and in this the United States example of agitation for negro civil rights proved seminal.

CONCLUSION

The problem of inequality for the Catholic community in Ulster remained almost completely static from 1921 on: what began to change was the context in which the problem was set. Religious discrimination and the resulting relative deprivation became increasingly anachronistic in an urban, secular society and Catholic mobilisation made its removal a more pressing necessity. The emergence of an able middle class, coupled with *laicisation*, modernisation and a general rise in the level of expectations, created the social preconditions for an attempt to resolve the problem.

Tangible expressions of this change at the social level are seen in the Catholic community's desire to *participate* in public life, to be *flexible* in outlook and to bring a measure of *cohesion* to political activity. These nascent themes were first given shape at the Garron Tower conference in 1958, but at the time they had not yet been formulated into any firm demands for reform. One social organisation symbolising much of the new atmosphere was the growth of the credit union movement, a form of community self-help that combined pre-industrial obligations of mutual aid with modern techniques of financial management.

At the political level, social mobilisation and modernisation induced a heightened political consciousness and a feeling of common political identity at all levels of the Catholic community. This in turn became translated into a demand for political participation on a cross-local basis. The main institutional means of formalising and preserving this expanding participation is the mass political party, organised cross-locally and structured around centralised control. As Huntington has noted, the power vacuum in a modernising society can be permanently filled only by political organisation: 'in the modernising world he controls the future who organises his politics.'[30] The eventual emergence of the SDLP was substantially a reflection of this new level of political participation and awareness.

2 Political Conditions

For many years the Northern Ireland Nationalist Party voiced the only demand with which the Catholic community showed any lasting concern: Irish reunification. In the 1950s and 1960s the social attitudes supportive of this outlook began to change, and notably the belief that greater material benefits could be obtained by constructive participation in the institutions of the state began to challenge traditional anti-partitionist principles. Gradually the Nationalists ceased to be the single socially approved vehicle for political action. In parallel with these social changes, the range of political alternatives grew beyond the simple options of constitutional action or physical force. The new alternative that emerged was mass, non-violent protest that combined neutrality on the border issue with a demand for the rights of British citizenship. Since the Nationalist Party had never been wholly dominant in the Catholic community, the introduction of a new channel that promised more tangible gains signalled the demise of the Nationalists. This chapter focuses on the political conditions that were necessary to provide a suitable environment for the formation of the SDLP, and deals particularly with the dilemma of the Nationalist Party and the political options open to the Catholic community in the 1960s.

THE DILEMMA OF THE NATIONALIST PARTY

After 1921 the continuing identification of the Catholic community in Ulster with the aim of Irish unity, coupled with their permanent minority status, meant that any political influence they wielded before partition was lost. While the Unionists consolidated control of the new state's institutions, disaffected Catholic politicians were equally united by a resolve not to accord it any formal or practical recognition. Constitutional nationalists were thus in a dilemma: they had no incentive to participate in the normal political activity of the state because they could never hope to influence, let alone become, the government, yet they were committed to parliamentary politics. To disavow parliament would mean abandoning the only legal channel capable of highlighting their constituents' grievances. More seriously, it would leave the way open for the non-parliamentary adherents of republicanism to assume Catholic political leadership and seek to achieve their national aspirations by force.

In the event, the Nationalists overcame the dilemma by a half-hearted commitment to constitutional politics. They failed to organise and restricted their activities to enclaves where they possessed a numerical majority. Moreover, they frequently abstained from parliament and continued to emphasise partition to the exclusion of other social issues affecting the welfare of their supporters. In many ways this solution to the problem was the worst they could have adopted, for it left them open to attack from all sides. Unionists accused them of being quasi-revolutionaries, moderate Catholics of not adequately seeking to redress their grievances, and militant republicans vilified them for not having the courage of their convictions to oppose partition by force. To understand why constitutional nationalism manoeuvred itself into such an exposed position, it is necessary to look at the origins of the Nationalist Party.

During the three decades before 1914, the Irish Parliamentary Party dominated political activity throughout Ireland. In the eight elections between 1885 and December 1910 the party consistently secured all but a handful of the seats outside the historic nine counties of Ulster and roughly half the seats within Ulster. However the advent of the First World War brought the abeyance of the long-promised Home Rule Bill and was followed two years later by the 'blood sacrifice' of the Easter Rising. According to one historian, 'the blow to the Irish Party received in 1916 was not far short of mortal.'[1] Thus, from 1916 until 1922 physical force displaced parliamentary politics as a political means. In the 1918 election the Irish Party was crushed and retained only six of the 76 seats it had held in 1910, as against 73 seats for the hitherto electorally untested Sinn Féin. The only area in which the party survived was Ulster, where it held five seats; and in one, the Falls division of Belfast, the incumbent Joe Devlin roundly defeated a popular instigator of the 1916 Rising, Eamon de Valera.

Since both the political parties that emerged in the Free State after the bitter civil war – Cumann na nGaedheal (later Fine Gael) and Fianna Fáil – were derivatives of Sinn Féin, they were without any natural links with the Ulster remnant of the Irish Party. As neither harboured any desire to extend their activities to the North, the Nationalists became an isolated and an alienated political group: isolated from the all-Ireland movement of which they had been part before the First World War, and alienated from the state in which they found themselves in 1921. In sum, the nature of the Nationalists, their origins and the position in which they found themselves gave rise to three major characteristics: firstly, the absence of organisation; secondly, the tendency to abstain from parliament; and thirdly, the single-claim nature of their appeal.

Among the Nationalist elected representatives, the absence of organisation meant the loss of cohesion and co-ordination. At Stormont they existed only as a loose collection of individuals acting, on the admission of one Nationalist MP, 'in harmony but not in harness.'[2] The disregard for organisation was linked to the nature of their appeal, for since 'nationalism appeals for votes in terms of an ascriptive characteristic, there is less need for organisation than in a party competing against others with attributes that all can share.'[3] Most Nationalists recognised this fact: as one MP noted, they had 'to have regard to the spirit of nationalism rather than the precise shape in which they visualised it.'[4]

At the constituency level local energies went untapped and MPs relied on personal followings rather than on an organised party membership for support. Without a formal membership, candidate selection was carried out through the 'convention' system, a method whereby prominent Catholics in the constituency, often invited by the local priest, would come together to make a collective choice. A contemporary critic observed that 'charges of "fixing" and selective invitations by the sponsors to such conventions have been the rule rather than the exception.'[5] The absence of organisation obviously left the way open for gross abuses and it aided clerical participation and influence since they were looked to as the 'natural' leaders of the community. This helped to cement the popular identification of Catholicism and nationalism, and it encouraged 'a narrow sectarian approach on the part of some Nationalist members.'[6]

A further consequence of the lack of organisation was the virtual abandonment of constituencies where a Catholic majority was not assured, resulting in a high percentage of unopposed returns at elections. Table 2.1 illustrates how the proportion of uncontested seats in Ulster was almost identical between 1918 and 1970 with the period 1832 to 1880. This is in direct contrast to both the rest of Ireland and Britain where the high figures for the early period were reduced in the twentieth century by the growth of party organisation.

The tendency to abstain from parliament was a second characteristic symptomatic of the general political malaise. The Nationalists boycotted Stormont until 1927, and after an unproductive period of participation again withdrew in 1932 after a dispute between Joe Devlin and the House of Commons Speaker. In practice they periodically abstained from parliament, having reserved for themselves the right, in Cahir Healey's words, 'to come in or stay outside as and when our people may decide.'[7] One aspect of this non-cooperation was the refusal to fulfil basic constitutional obligations. For example, despite being by far the largest opposition group in the House of Commons, the party did not allow itself to become the official opposition until 1965, as this would have implied a recognition of the state. For many years there was no formal opposition at all in Stormont and during the seven years preceding the reversal of Nationalist policy, an anomalous situation persisted in which the Speaker recognised the four Northern Ireland Labour MPs as the official opposition while the government recognised the Nationalists.

Another side to this unwillingness to participate was the collusion with the extra-parliamentary republican tradition. In order to avoid losing seats to Unionists in Catholic constituencies by splitting the vote, a pact

TABLE 2.1 Uncontested Seats in the British Isles, 1832–1970

Electoral periods	Ulster[a]		Rest of Ireland[b]		Britain	
	Number of uncontested seats	As percentage of total	Number of uncontested seats	As percentage of total	Number of uncontested seats	As percentage of total
1832–80	133	38.2	209	25.2	1,707	46.4
1885–1910 (Dec)	112	42.4	344	61.4	638	14.7
1918–70	234	37.5	84	3.3	369	3.9

NOTES [a]For the election years 1832 to 1910 (Dec) nine counties; thereafter six counties.
[b]For the election years 1832 to 1910 (Dec) twenty-three counties; thereafter twenty-six counties.

SOURCES J. Vincent (ed.), McCalmont's Parliamentary Poll Book, 1832–1918 (Brighton: Harvester Press, 1971); Thomas T. Mackie and Richard Rose, The International Almanac of Electoral History (London: Macmillan, 1974); Sydney Elliott, Northern Ireland Parliamentary Election Results, 1921–72 (Chichester: Political Reference Publications, 1973).

was made in the early 1950s by which the Nationalists agreed to contest only Stormont elections and thus left Westminster elections open to Sinn Féin candidates. In the public mind the distinction between physical force republicanism and constitutional nationalism was blurred and in the 1955 and 1959 elections, the same workers often aided both groups, notably in Fermanagh and Tyrone.[8]

Thirdly, there was the obsession with partition which excluded all other issues from political debate, regardless of how seriously they affected the Catholic community. Thus such pressing issues as religious discrimination, the housing shortage and educational policy were rarely raised by Nationalist MPs. Before the withdrawal from Stormont, Joe Devlin had initiated some moves on these questions by cultivating a rapport with the Unionist Prime Minister, James Craig. But no attempt was made to inculcate this approach among the other Nationalist MPs or set it on a secure parliamentary footing; and thus when Devlin walked out of Stormont in 1932 and died soon after, the rest of the party reverted to the established policy of abstention and concentration on partition. In fact, until November 1964, the party never issued any clear statement of policy.

The Nationalist Party thus changed little, either in structure or outlook, from 1921 to 1960. But meanwhile social change had begun to erode the attitudes that formed the foundation for their appeal. The social mobilisation of the Catholic community and the general modernisation of the society challenged the traditional policies of isolation and non-cooperation while at the same time improved educational opportunities produced a potential leadership in an able and articulate middle class and the traditional leadership, the clergy, steadily relinquished active participation in politics. All these changes were beginning to have a profound effect on political attitudes and, in particular, the legacy of *laicisation* produced a greater readiness to criticise hitherto unquestioned authority in non-religious fields.

From the late 1950s onwards, pressure increased on the Nationalists to refashion their appeal in conformity with the shifting priorities of the times. This, again, necessarily reopened their dilemma and after forty years of ossification the problem was still the same: to participate more fully in politics, as their critics demanded, would imply a recognition of the state that they had bound themselves never to do. 'Our task', one representative asserted, 'is to safeguard our mandate for a united Ireland.'[9] To remain as they were left them in an increasingly exposed position and vulnerable to political competition from within the Catholic community. The 1960s inaugurated almost a decade of ferment and debate concerning the role and possible ends of Catholic political activity that has never completely ceased. The next section will analyse the direction and scope of that discussion.

THE OPTIONS FOR CATHOLIC POLITICS IN THE 1960s

Two specific events helped to pave the way for the discussion that began in the early 1960s about the nature and ends of Catholic political activity in Ulster. The first was Sinn Féin's decisive electoral defeat in the 1959 Westminster general election, when they received 11.0 per cent of the valid vote, compared to 23.7 per cent in 1955. This was interpreted as a rejection of force as a political means. The second event was a speech made by the then Taoiseach, Sean Lemass, to the Oxford Union in October 1959 in the course of which he accepted that partition existed with the consent of a majority in Northern Ireland and hence accorded the state *de facto* recognition.[10] Both events cemented the belief that a successful solution to the Northern Ireland problem could only emanate from within Ulster society itself.

The emerging political debate concerned the direction that any solution might take. Five main options entered into the general discussion: firstly, Catholics could decide to continue to press reform on the Nationalist Party; secondly, to reassert physical force as a political means; thirdly, to abandon nationalism altogether and transfer allegiance to the class-based parties, such as the Northern Ireland Labour Party (NILP), or to moderate Unionism; fourthly, to create new anti-partitionist political parties; or, fifthly, to exploit new political channels outside the party system.

Reform of the Nationalist Party was untenable as the efforts of the various pressure groups urging change on the party illustrated. Under the moderate leadership of Eddie McAteer the impression was conveyed of gradual reform, yet in practice very little was done, save for the introduction of annual conferences in 1965. The inability to change meant that by the time civil rights was a dominant theme, Nationalist representatives were rarely invited to participate, although a few did so on an individual basis.[11] If reform of the Nationalist Party was impractical, so also was the second option, the use of force. This was demonstrated by the dismal failure of the 1956 to 1962 Irish Republican Army border campaign. Incidents were limited to remote rural areas where they attracted little support and the only effect of the campaign was to discredit the Catholic community by making them appear extremist. To republicans, Catholic passivity was the most disastrous factor. The mordant statement that called off the hostilities noted the apathy of the Catholic population, 'whose minds have been deliberately distracted from the supreme issue facing the Irish people – the unity and freedom of Ireland.'[12]

The third alternative was to eschew nationalism and transfer support to the class-based parties, such as the NILP or the O'Neillite wing of the Unionist Party. The NILP was, however, strongly loyalist and such was its connection with fundamental Protestantism that it gained some notoriety when two Labour members on Belfast City Council voted in 1964 against the opening of children's playgrounds on Sundays. The NILP's inability to compete with the Unionist Party on the constitutional issue also meant that its electoral support has been transient and vulnerable to rapid erosion in periods of communal tension.[13] If Labour proved an unenticing option for Catholics, the Unionist Party under the mild progressivism of Terence O'Neill appeared a more feasible proposition. O'Neill did in fact attract some Catholic support, but his central problem was the inability to win sufficient Catholic backing to balance defections from the intransigent Unionists who were distrustful of his conciliatory approach. The paradox of O'Neillism was that its 'moderation lay in avoiding bigotry. It did not extend so far as to endorse change sufficient to dispel the Catholic sense of grievance.'[14] The ultimate collapse of O'Neill's policies flowed from his failure to 'convince the Unionist Party that in the long run his policies would strengthen Ulster and the union.'[15]

If these three alternatives appeared unprepossessing, the final two options, to create new anti-partitionist political parties and exploit new political channels outside the party system, were more promising. Two anti-partitionist political parties which were formed in the 1960s and tried to displace the Nationalists were the National Democratic Party (NDP) and the Republican Labour Party (RLP). The NDP originated in 1965 from National Unity, a pressure group formed in 1959 to urge reform on the Nationalist Party. After a meeting organised by National Unity at Maghery, Co. Armagh, in April 1964 a 'National Political Front', composed of Nationalist MPs and co-opted individuals, was set up to coordinate reform of the Nationalist Party. After some months it was clear that the Nationalists were impervious to change and the National Political Front came to form the nucleus for the NDP. For the next five years the NDP organised mainly in the Belfast area and did not encroach into the Nationalist's rural strongholds. As the areas left were *ipso facto* Protestant, the new party was electorally unsuccessful, but it did establish a number of cardinal principles – a card-carrying membership, political organisation and a belief in constructive political action – that were seminal influences on the SDLP in the first few years.[16]

The only other party political competitor to the Nationalist Party in the 1960s was the Republican Labour Party. The core of the RLP membership were anti-partitionist Labour supporters who had split from the NILP in 1949 when it had eventually decided 'to maintain unbroken the connection between Great Britain and Northern Ireland as part of the Commonwealth.'[17] As the RLP's leader, Harry Diamond, concluded, 'there is no room for pure Labour.'[18] In 1964 Diamond was joined by Gerry Fitt, then Irish Labour MP for the Stormont constituency of Belfast Dock, converting 'two one-man parties into one two-man party.'[19] Like the NDP, the RLP's support was localised and it would not challenge the Nationalists and risk splitting the Catholic vote. Consequently, both parties were relatively unsuccessful but they did display a desire to participate in the system and forcefully pursue their constituents' grievances. Harry Diamond was noted for his regular attendance at Stormont while Fitt's election to Westminster in 1966 provided a focal point for the dissemination of the civil rights case and the NDP, too, were often acclaimed for their constructive approach.

The fifth and final option, the creation of political channels outside the party system, was the most important alternative and when utilised had far-reaching consequences. In this context two bodies emerged, differentiated by the means they used to articulate their demands. One employed established, institutional channels, the second the methods of mass protest. As with all protest groups, both sought to attain their aims by influencing a third party, which, while neutral in the conflict, could nevertheless be mobilised on the protesters' behalf.[20] In Northern Ireland this third party was the British government and British public opinion.

The institutional pressure groups, such as the Campaign for Social Justice in Northern Ireland (CSJ), endeavoured to voice discontent by collating factual evidence of discrimination and using this as a basis for lobbying individual Westminster MPs. This strategy drew on the strong anti-Unionist sentiments of a sizeable minority of British Labour MPs, who later formed themselves into the Campaign for Democracy in Ulster, a pressure group that publicised Catholic demands on the British mainland. Individual CSJ members provided the stimulus for the formation of the Northern Ireland Civil Rights Association in January 1967. While housing allocation had mainly concerned the institutional pressure groups, the NICRA saw the 'maintenance of civil liberties'[21] as its sphere of interest, and on this basis a number of Unionists initially involved themselves in the body. The impetus to adopt mass protest came with the illegal occupation of a council house at Caledon, Co. Tyrone, sparking off the first civil rights march from Coalisland to Dungannon in August 1968.

These groups demonstrated a measure of flexibility and initiative hitherto absent in Catholic political thinking. Moreover, all the groups, both pressure group and party political, showed a relative unconcern with the perennial border issue. The pressure groups were avowedly non-party and hence, by default, took no stand for and against the union. The two political parties, the NDP and the RLP, both advocated reunification but with the qualification that it could take place only with the consent of a majority in the province, a condition that effectively removed the question from their day-to-day politics. The greatest innovation was that, without exception, all the groups wished to work *within* the existing political system using constructive (if in some cases unconventional) political action to improve the conditions of the Catholic community.

THE FEBRUARY 1969 GENERAL ELECTION

While the NICRA exhibited the image of a united, cohesive body, in practice its leadership was fragmented and its organisation merely a loose collection of local *ad hoc* committees. Whatever the practical shortcomings, NICRA's image served to undermine the Nationalists, whose antipathy towards mass protest had been well-known, and further presented an unprecedented tactical unity in the face of the common Unionist adversary. The reactions of both the Nationalist and Unionist establishments to NICRA are important in interpreting the outcome of the February 1969 election.

The Nationalist response was determined by the development of the party after 1965 when they agreed to become the official opposition at Stormont in response to O'Neill's initiatives. As the party strove to gain a measure of political respectability, they became sensitive to accusations that they were compromising the inviolable principle of Irish unity. Before the NICRA was formed the Nationalist reaction had already been mooted in July 1965 when McAteer expressed the hope that it would 'never be thought necessary to organise freedom marches here to abolish second-class citizenship.'[22] Even after the movement's obvious political potential was being realised, this conservative attitude still predominated. At the party's third annual conference in June 1968 the issue of civil disobedience was brought up. Coming shortly after the successful and widely publicised occupation of the Caledon council house, the response was cautious. Replying to a motion put by Austin Currie advocating 'a policy of civil disobedience' to act as 'a safety valve against the possibility of violence . . . ,'[23] delegates approved Currie's action but were reticent about the use of such a tactic in 'a constitutional party'. McAteer urged his followers not to think 'about going home and taking up the pikes . . . we must not allow ourselves to be goaded into precipitate action . . .'[24]

While the perennial quandary of the Nationalist Party – to reject or embrace parliamentary politics – had been exacerbated by these political changes, the Unionist government was in a similar predicament. Threats to the Unionist regime had invariably been violent, ephemeral and ineffective. Faced with a threat of physical force, the government could easily retaliate with force. But non-violent street protest presented a novel threat since it could not be ignored, nor broken by undue force. Confronted with this threat, the Unionist answer was to concede some of what the NICRA orginally demanded. Success in gaining any concessions was unrivalled and, in sum, 'greater than Catholics had won in 47 years of parliamentary opposition.'[25] The popular response amongst Catholics was a strong endorsement of street protest as a legitimate political tactic. A survey conducted in February 1969 found that 47 per cent of Catholic respondents approved of demonstrations and 70 per cent saw them as politically helpful.[26]

Thus the civil rights movement created a new unity of purpose, a cohesion and a refreshingly pragmatic strategy that brought an invigorated interest in political activity. Austin Currie, for one, perceived the extent to which the civil rights success emphasised

The increasing irrelevance to the Northern Ireland political scene of all the existing opposition parties as presently constituted. The united civil rights campaign has highlighted the absurdity of opposition political disunity . . . and it has shown the necessity for a new alignment of political forces in the North.[27]

In time these embryonic themes would have no doubt grown and resulted in a formal fusion between the NICRA and the political parties, but in the event the catalyst was the February 1969 general election.

The concessions announced by O'Neill in November 1968 alienated the Unionist right-wing as well as the NICRA who were still seeking a universal local government franchise. Similarly, O'Neill's 'crossroads' broadcast only brought a short respite and the resulting NICRA moratorium on demonstrations was broken by the People's Democracy march from Belfast to Londonderry. Intermittent counter-violence accompanied it, culminating in the ambush at Burntollet Bridge, Co. Londonderry, on 4 January. Clashes between police and rioters ensued in Londonderry and the moratorium ended. Burntollet further polarised attitudes; and when O'Neill announced that a commission of inquiry would be set up to investigate the causes of the violence, a number of ministers resigned. Twelve dissident Unionist MPs met at Portadown to call for O'Neill's replacement. With his parliamentary support ebbing and many Unionist constituency associations in open revolt, O'Neill transcended the overt opposition to him in the Unionist Party and appealed directly to the province by calling a general election.

The election for the 52 seats in the Northern Ireland House of Commons amounted to virtual plebiscite on the leadership of the Unionist Party and the issue overshadowed the disorganisation of Catholic politicians. The NICRA refused to participate in the election, in keeping with its non-electoral structure, although some of its more ambitious leaders stood on an individual basis, using civil rights demands as the substance for their political platform. Initially another non-electoral group, the People's Democracy, also decided not to participate, but reversed the decision in response to the demand for new candidates.[28]

The pattern of nominations showed the fervour the election aroused and the level of uncontested seats, at 14 per cent, was by far the lowest since 1921. On the Catholic side, in eight constituencies the incumbents were challenged by another anti-partitionist competitor, and in five of these contests the sitting members were defeated: three Nationalists and one each, Republican Labour and National Democratic. The three Nationalists were defeated by Independents, John Hume, Ivan Cooper and Paddy

O'Hanlon, all of whom had been active in the NICRA. The veteran Republican Labour MP, Harry Diamond, was defeated by Paddy Devlin, chairman of the NILP and another civil rights activist.

In many senses the Foyle division of Londonderry entertained the most significant contest. The Nationalist leader, Eddie McAteer, was defending his seat against John Hume and Eamonn McCann, the latter a prominent figure in the Derry Labour Party. McAteer's campaign was restrained and defensive and he approached the contest with 'more avuncular sorrow than anger'.[29] McAteer had in fact decided to retire from politics almost a year before and the Nationalist nomination had been offered to Hume, who refused. To forestall the disintegration of his party, McAteer was persuaded to remain. Hume's advent into politics was not as opportunistic as some critics claimed, for he had always asserted that civil rights demands would ultimately have to proceed through parliamentary channels. In his manifesto, he saw the election as a 'mandate' for a new movement, a non-sectarian 'political movement based on social democratic principles with open membership and elected executives . . . ' acting as a 'strong, energetic opposition to conservatism . . .'[30] In the event, he received his mandate by a respectable majority, decisively symbolising the demise of the Nationalist Party.

For O'Neill the outcome of the election was indecisive and pro-O'Neill candidates were returned in only 27 constituencies. Within the Catholic community the election marked a renewed interest in politics and electoral activity made possible by the civil rights campaign. The successes of candidates associated with the NICRA were not limited to the three Independents. The People's Democracy, ill-organised and with a mainly student membership, won 4.2 per cent of the valid vote and failed to capture a seat only because they chose to fight in traditionally uncontested Unionist and Nationalist constituencies. The common denominator of the victors was that they possessed a 'greater social consciousness, activism and ecumenical image than their predecessors.'[31] As the election acted as a catalyst for political change, so the existence of three articulate and unaligned MPs produced a focal point for discussion concerning the possible coalescence of a new parliamentary grouping among the non-Nationalist Catholic representatives. But it was not until August 1970, nearly 18 months after the election, that the new alignment was formally cemented.

CONCLUSION

The continuity of allegiance accorded to the Nationalist Party was finally ended by the social changes in the Catholic community and by a shift in the salient political issues. Attempts to reform the Nationalists by encouraging them to assimilate the new demands were universally unsuccessful and left parliamentary anti-partitionist politics in deadlock. The problem was resolved by the introduction of a new alternative, mass protest, which won such a level of popular endorsement that it undercut traditional patterns of allegiance. This change in the direction of support was formally registered at the 1969 Stormont general election.

The three emergent themes of the 1960s, participation, cohesion and flexibility, were gradually absorbed into Catholic politics. The two political parties, the NDP and the RLP, demonstrated the will to *participate* constructively in parliamentary politics, underpinning this with a total commitment to electoral activity. To this the civil rights movement added cohesion and flexibility. *Cohesion* emerged in the sense that the community became united behind a number of political demands, contrasting sharply with the previously fragmented nature of anti-partitionist politics. *Flexibility* was seen in the ease with which the unproductive electoral politics of the past were by-passed. The result was the adoption of new methods and goals taking as their point of reference the framework of the Northern Ireland state.

The short period during which the NICRA received unequivocal endorsement from Catholics for street protest – from late 1968 until mid-1969 – had a profound influence on Northern Ireland politics. As the demonstrations provoked increasing counter-violence and polarisation in the society at large, support waned, especially from those leaders of the movement who had been elected in February 1969. From then on, they asserted, the appropriate place to present the political demands of the Catholic community was on the floor of the Stormont House of Commons.

3 Opposition Unity and Disunity

Many factors may converge to stimulate the formation and development of a political party and their weight in specific situations helps to determine the subsequent form that the party eventually takes. In Ulster a number of influences were at work in the late 1960s with the ability to shape new political alignments. Of all these potential influences, perhaps the most significant was negative: the constitutional arrangements. The adoption of the Westminster model of government in a divided society had resulted in a permanent government and opposition. The effect of this on Catholic politics was to militate against the establishment and consolidation of any tradition of parliamentary activity. In 1968 and 1969 those Catholics who primarily sought reform of the system rather than Irish unity therefore by-passed parliamentary politics by utilising street protest. Those that later stood for election on civil rights platforms did so as Independents, *outside* the already existing anti-partitionist political parties, and hence served as an impetus towards the reformation of the opposition groups.

The fragmentary nature of the Catholic opposition in Stormont reflected the low regard of Catholics for parliamentary politics. The successes of the NICRA, however, increased interest in politics, especially after the February 1969 election and the unanimity of political purpose won by the civil rights movement contrasted sharply with parliamentary fragmentation. The result was that the factions on the opposition benches were forced to create some working arrangement between themselves as a response to the changing priorities of the political environment. This chapter examines the attempts to forge such an arrangement and the events leading up to the formation of the SDLP in August 1970.

THE STORMONT PARLIAMENTARY OPPOSITION IN 1969

Of the thirteen members of the opposition returned at the 1969 election, it is possible to identify four groups. The Nationalist Party constituted the largest, with six members, and was therefore obligated to become the official opposition. They had, however, already withdrawn from this position on 15 October 1968 in protest at the actions of the police in Londonderry ten days previously. The second largest group was the three

Independents, all of whom were committed to the formation of a new political party. The two remaining groups, the Republican Labour Party and the Northern Ireland Labour Party, both had two MPs each, all representing Belfast constituencies.

The origins, nature and outlook of the Nationalist Party have been extensively discussed in the last chapter, but two facts emerged to have a bearing on their demeanour during 1969 and 1970. Firstly, they were now without their witty and able leader at Stormont, Eddie McAteer, who retained titular leadership as 'President' of the Nationalist Party, while the 'Chairmanship' of the parliamentary party (in reality the party itself since it existed only in parliament) went to Roderick O'Connor, an implacable opponent of internal reform. Secondly, among the six MPs dissension was rife and two members, Austin Currie and Tom Gormley, had become particularly severe critics.

Currie had been returned for the East Tyrone constituency in a by-election in 1964 at the age of 24. His youth made him aware that few younger people were coming forward to involve themselves in nationalist politics, exacerbating the party's elderly, conservative image. He strongly favoured political organisation and a greater emphasis on socio-economic policies, but his efforts to stimulate reform were generally ignored. Tom Gormley was less vocal in his criticism but no less penetrating. Elected in 1969 on a platform that included a commitment to opposition unity, Gormley resigned from the party during the November 1969 annual conference to focus attention on the lack of progress being made towards this aim. He became an Independent and withdrew from Stormont in July 1971 with the rest of the opposition, although he subsequently joined the Alliance Party in February 1972 to become one of its first MPs.

The accession of an inflexible leader, coupled with defections and criticism from within, made the Nationalist Party even more averse to change than hitherto. Some Nationalists believed that they had a duty to support O'Neill, despite what they saw as his lack of reciprocation to their own conciliatory gestures. The urge to back liberal Unionism and 'hold the centre' against both extremes was prompted by the heightening inter-communal tension and the assessment that if O'Neill fell, a loyalist would succeed him and the reform programme would be halted. In the event, O'Neill's resignation in April 1969 removed the Nationalist option of supporting the Unionist government, but it did illustrate their tenuous political position.

The three Independents were the moving forces behind the efforts to achieve opposition unity. All three had been elected on platforms that included NICRA demands as well as the formation of a new, non-sectarian political movement organised around a political party and based on social democratic principles. By contrast to this apparent unity of purpose, the two NILP MPs encompassed differing outlooks. Vivian Simpson was the more representative of the Protestant-oriented NILP in that he was uninterested in civil rights; as the NILP's first Catholic chairman, Paddy Devlin was the exception. At the NILP annual conference in May 1969 a large majority had voted in favour of members individually supporting the civil rights campaign, but reservations had been voiced about the decision by the two extremes, expressed by William Boyd and Eamonn McCann, respectively.

The two Republican Labour MPs concurred with the NILP in their lack of enthusiasm for any new political party or opposition unity. Gerry Fitt envisaged 'a radical alliance on the left, but not a terribly close one. We were not elected to form a new party.'[1] On the issue of support for civil rights, both Fitt and Paddy Kennedy were unequivocally in favour and Fitt had been instrumental in publicising the NICRA case among sympathetic Labour MPs at Westminster. At this stage an embryonic division existed between the two as to the efficacy of parliamentary action: Fitt's interpretation of Connolly socialism had been tempered by his experience at Westminster while Kennedy still emphasised the single, non-negotiable aim of Irish unity.

This, then, was the opposition in the Stormont parliament in 1969. All of the four groups were divided on policies to differing degrees, but added to this was a further dimension of cleavage in the form of personality differences. These two cleavages existed in abundance and could have well have delayed the emergence of any new political party even longer than actually occurred if it had not been for the practical experience of working together derived from the debates on the Public Order (Amendment) Bill.

After the violence that followed the civil rights march in Londonderry on 5 October 1968, marches, sit-downs and general street protest became the operative form of Catholic political activity, but they attracted violent fringe supporters and counter-demonstrations from extreme loyalists. To deal with the deteriorating situation, the government announced the amendment of the existing Public Order (NI) Act of 1951. The Public Order (Amendment) Bill, introduced at Stormont on 4 March 1969, made it an offence, among other things, to sit, kneel or lie in a public highway, or to organise a counter-demonstration, and doubled the period of notice for demonstrations from 48 to 96 hours. These measures were intended to cope with both Protestant and Catholic agitation, but the opposition immediately declared their dissatisfaction and called it retrogressive, unnecessary and repressive. Although they recognised the need to control counter-demonstrations – and indeed Roderick O'Connor had introduced a Private Member's Bill at Stormont in January 1969 to legislate 'against the menace of counter-demonstrations'[2] – the opposition saw the government's Bill as unnecessary and a threat to the last legitimate channel of protest. Hume concluded that the government were 'removing the last means that people have of putting forward their point of view . . . now the last peaceful, non-violent means left open to the people, that of sitting on the street, is being taken away from them.'[3]

The opposition's decision to fight the Bill clause by clause consigned it to a tortuous passage through the Commons and Senate. Throughout the summer more than 100 hours were spent on debate and the Bill's progress was successfully impeded on a number of occasions. On 20 March, after an all-night sitting, the government pushed through an amendment to try and break the filibustering tactics and the nine members of the opposition in the chamber staged a sit-down protest, singing 'We Shall Overcome'. After being removed by police they were suspended from the House by the Speaker for one week. It was not until 6 January 1970 that the Bill finally reached the Senate, where further heated exchanges ensued. On 5 February the measure eventually became law after opposition MPs and Senators had unsuccessfully petitioned the Governor, Lord Grey, to withhold the Royal Assent.

The debates on the Public Order (Amendment) Bill were important because they showed that, although Catholic MPs were in a permanent minority at Stormont and could not hope to halt legislation approved by the Unionist Party, they could impede the progress of legislation with which they disagreed. In addition, the opposition tactics demanded a high degree of co-operation between all the groups and individuals involved and this, coming only one week after the first Stormont sitting, set an important precedent for the future evolution of the opposition during the rest of the parliamentary session. Table 3.1 illustrates the amount of activity created by the Bill through an analysis of the opposition's voting record. It clearly shows the vigorous participation initiated by the Bill's passage, especially among the three Independents. Even the Nationalist

TABLE 3.1 Opposition Voting in the Stormont House of Commons
on the Public Order (Amendment) Bill,
12 March 1969 – 19 June 1969

Political Group	Number of MPs	Average percentage of divisions against the Bill in which group participated[a]
Nationalists	6	57.3
Independents	3	93.9
Republican Labour Party	2	54.5
Northern Ireland Labour Party	2	86.4
Total	13	69.4

NOTES [a]Based on a total of 55 divisions.

SOURCE HC Deb (NI) 72–3.

figure is notable given their propensity towards intermittent attendance. The practical experience gained from the debates provided a foundation for the discussions that began to try and achieve opposition unity through the summer and autumn of 1969.

THE ATTEMPTS TO FORM A NEW ALIGNMENT

At least four serious attempts were made between March 1969 and August 1970 to forge the disparate Stormont opposition into a united grouping, but all were frustrated by the personal and political animosities with which the various factions were infused. The first attempt was instigated by a number of British Labour MPs who tried to amalgamate the non-Nationalist Stormont MPs into a new body. Secondly, there was the ambiguously named 'Opposition Alliance' which appointed shadow spokesmen yet was neither a political party nor became the official opposition. Thirdly, in early 1970 the National Democrats organised a conference to explore areas of common ground between the component parts of the opposition. The fourth and final effort to secure a new alignment came in the form of an electoral pact between the two major political figures in Londonderry, Eddie McAteer and John Hume. All these abortive attempts are of importance because their very failure had a significant bearing on the evolution of the SDLP and help to explain its complex and often contradictory origins. Furthermore, one of the main reasons why the SDLP has subsequently laid so much public and private emphasis on preserving Catholic political unity was a recollection of the laborious efforts needed to achieve it.

The British Labour Party has traditionally contained a small core of MPs sympathetic to the Ulster Catholic community. After James Callaghan had made his second visit to the province in October 1969 as Home Secretary and delivered a speech to Labour's annual conference at Brighton calling on Catholic politicians to unite, some tentative discussions were initiated by these interested MPs to persuade the non-Nationalist MPs and the NILP to link up. Given their differing outlooks neither prospective partner greeted the plan with any enthusiasm and it was quickly dropped in favour of a merger between the NILP and the British Labour Party. The NILP convened a special conference in January 1970 at which the planned merger was overwhelmingly ratified, although Paddy Devlin and Eamonn McCann both argued that a thirty-two-county labour movement should have greater priority than the financial and organisational advantages that might flow from affiliation to the British Labour Party. In the event, the merger was never consummated because the NILP's absorption into the British party would have been conditional on the writing in of an acceptance of partition into the Labour constitution, and would have precipitated much internal conflict.

The possibility of a merger did not prevent discussions continuing between the Labour Party and the Catholic politicians at Stormont. At a meeting in London in early December 1969 Maurice Foley, the Labour chairman, Arthur Skeffington and other officials met Gerry Fitt, John Hume, Ivan Cooper, Austin Currie and Paddy Devlin to discuss the prospects for the formation of a social democratic party in Ulster. It was reported at the time that the British politicians raised the possibility of the NILP-affiliated trade unions being persuaded to switch their allegiance to such a new and electorally more promising party.

While the British Labour Party discussions produced no tangible results, and only involved the original six Stormont MPs who later formed the SDLP, the 'Opposition Alliance' incorporated, at least nominally, eleven of the thirteen opposition MPs. The impetus for the Alliance came from the successful co-operation occasioned by the Public Order (Amendment) Bill debates and it was designed to formalise already existing arrangements. But disagreements soon arose as to how comprehensive these formal structures should be in co-ordinating parliamentary work, especially among the Nationalists and Simpson, who were concerned about losing their own distinctive political identities.

Meetings were held throughout September 1969, theoretically involving all thirteen, but in practice Simpson and O'Connor rarely attended. Hume was the main advocate of shadow spokesmen and he further proposed that a whip should be elected monthly, the post rotating around the parties. Eight MPs favoured the plan while the remaining five – four Nationalists and Simpson – resisted it. It was not until 3 December 1969 that the Opposition Alliance was finally agreed upon, with the election of a whip who would hold the post until the following April and the appointment of shadow spokesmen.[4] The term 'shadow ministers' was avoided so as not to invite parallels with the Nationalist Party's formation of a shadow cabinet during their period as the official opposition. James O'Reilly became whip and a general spokesman to reply to the prime minister, but as the arrangement was not a political party, he was in no sense leader. Seven government ministries were shadowed, involving ten MPs. Simpson and O'Connor refused to participate while Gerry Fitt felt unable to accept a post because of his Westminster commitments.

The contradictory aspects of the Alliance ensured that it never evolved beyond a loose structure encompassing the disunited participants. The first contradiction was that although the arrangement implied at least a *de facto* recognition of the state, it refused to become the official opposition, presumably because the Nationalists had just withdrawn from the position. Secondly, all were agreed on the Alliance's practical functions, but put different interpretations on its significance. Those antagonistic to the concept of opposition unity saw it as merely an organisational expedient to co-ordinate the common parliamentary interests of the opposition groups. Those favourably disposed to unity viewed it as the first step towards a single political party, with the activities of the spokesmen helping to evolve a common policy and gradually assuage the sharp divisions between the members. The Alliance failed as a portent of the future because of its inherent contradictions, but also because of a lack of opportunity to demonstrate its potential usefulness. Despite their length and intensity, the debates on the Public Order (Amendment) Bill represented the peak of opposition influence on the content of government legislation and on the course of government action. From then on, the growing disturbances on the streets rapidly began to displace Stormont as the focal point for politics.

As the opposition's inability to construct a new political party became more evident, the National Democratic Party organised a conference in Belfast to give 'the radical elements in Northern politics . . . an opportunity to discuss any points of difference and possible areas of co-operation.'[5] The conference met on 1 March 1970 and concentrated on economic issues and attitudes towards the Government of Ireland Act. Despite a strong plea from Hume and others for unity, no progress was made at the conference, which clearly illustrated the impasse faced by any group in Ulster politics without either parliamentary representation or the means to exploit extra-parliamentary channels. The NDP had obviously hoped to gain access, via the conference, to the Stormont discussions on opposition unity, but the nature of these moves was such that they precluded the participation of any group that did not first possess electoral representation.

A final event before August 1970 demonstrated the potential of unity. Since the 1950s the fragmentation of Catholic politics guaranteed the return of Unionists in three of the twelve Westminster constituencies that contained a Catholic majority. In 1966 Fitt's election for West Belfast broke the Unionist monopoly and this was followed at a by-election in 1969 by the success of Bernadette Devlin as a 'Unity' candidate. The demand for single Catholic candidates paved the way for Unity candidates in the 1970 Westminster general election. In Londonderry John Hume announced the support of himself and his Independent Constituency Association for the Unity candidature of Eddie McAteer. Both leaders described the pact as 'purely practical', but hoped that it could lead to permanent co-operation. Hume declared at a press conference that unity was now more essential than ever, for

> It is abundantly clear that we face critical times ahead, and we must enter them as a united political force if we are to serve the best interests of the people we represent. It is our conviction that our agreement can lead to a strong political movement throughout Northern Ireland and to a lessening of political fragmentation.[6]

McAteer's election manifesto was in fact almost identical to Hume's manifesto for the 1969 Stormont general election. It enunciated the three basic points that would be central to any new political movement, namely, left-of-centre socio-economic policies, a democratic organisation with open membership and reunification only by the consent of a majority in Northern Ireland. The example of co-operation between these two major political figures did not, however, prove to be the catalyst in the formation of the new movement both had declared themselves intent on forming. The main stumbling-block was the mainstream Nationalist Party, who possessed neither the will nor the incentive to participate in a new party for which most did not see the need.

THE FORMATION OF THE SDLP

After the failure of the four major attempts to form a new alignment the six MPs who were the main protagonists continued to hold informal talks throughout March and April 1970 with the aim of launching a political party on their own, without the initial participation of the other MPs. Agreement existed on the form the new party would take, but Fitt was reticent about wholeheartedly committing himself without having first convinced his own Republican Labour Party to agree to the amalgamation. A policy document was drawn up based on the three principles of left-of-centre socio-economic policies, democratic organisation and reunification by consent. A name was also agreed – the Social Democratic and Labour Party – that took account of Fitt's attachment to the labour movement while preserving the other MPs' preference for social democracy. Some thought the name ambiguous, but it was regarded as a necessary concession to win the participation of Fitt.

Originally it had been planned to launch the SDLP in early May, but the June Westminster general election and events in Belfast caused an indefinite postponement. During the early summer months events began to favour the inauguration. Firstly, besides the success of the Catholic Unity candidates in the Westminster election, liberal unionism had realigned two months earlier with the Alliance Party. The emergence of Alliance from the structure of the non-party-political New Ulster Movement demonstrated how far post-1968 political change had created the preconditions for the rise of new political parties and served as an example to those on the Catholic side who were trying to emulate them. The apparent split between liberal and mainstream unionism heralded by Alliance also underlined a second factor conducive to the SDLP's formation. This was the fear of an imminent right-wing takeover within the Unionist Party, which, coupled with the Conservative victory in Britain, might be accepted as a *fait accompli*. The third and most important consideration was the recrudescence of republican violence which made it imperative for the Catholic community to have a united parliamentary voice to balance the activity on the streets.

In the event the SDLP was launched only after the idea of opposition unity had been taken up by the media.[7] On 15 August Hume was interviewed on Radio Telefis Eireann (RTE) by the *Irish Times* political correspondent, Michael McInerney, about the feasibility of unity. Hume discussed the issue in general terms and McInerney wrote a leader in the *Irish Times* on the subject on 17 August. He concluded that

> One of the missing pieces in the Northern pattern of events is a concerted viewpoint and guiding line from the opposition MPs. . . . One of the most important factors in any decision . . . will be the attitude of the opposition. If the British government wants to sound out opposition, where does it turn? To whom does it speak? It is a question of practical politics, not of ideological differences.[8]

Following this, and a hint in a story in the same edition that a new alignment was likely, RTE interviewed Austin Currie. Currie admitted that a new party was likely and stated that he favoured Gerry Fitt as leader. A follow-up interview with Hume brought the same response to the leadership question; and thus all that remained was the formal launching of the party.

The inaugural press conference was held on 21 August in Belfast and included the six MPs most in favour of unity – John Hume, Ivan Cooper, Paddy O'Hanlon, Austin Currie and Paddy Devlin with Gerry Fitt as leader – plus a Republican Labour Senator, Patrick Wilson.[9] Fitt announced that the party's guiding principles would be the presentation of a strong alternative to unionism, to the extent of contesting the seats of other opposition members with whom they differed, and to seek Irish reunification only by the consent of a majority in Northern Ireland. He committed the party to organise on a province-wide basis, with open membership, a central party office and a democratically organised annual conference.

Reaction from other political parties quickly followed. The NILP stated that Paddy Devlin had 'severed all links' with them by his action and accused the SDLP of representing 'the other side of the sectarian coin'.[10] In a similar vein, the Alliance Party forecast that it would result in 'a hardening of the sectarian barrier'.[11] The most aggressive condemnation came from Paddy Kennedy of the RLP. Stung by the defection of Fitt and Wilson he accused the SDLP of consolidating 'the evil of partition, instead of removing it' and alleged a link with the British Labour Party.[12] At a later meeting of the RLP Executive, Fitt and Wilson were duly expelled from the party. The banned Republican Clubs saw the rise of the SDLP in more opportunistic terms calling it a 'moderate neo-Redmondite political group . . . ,'[13] while Eddie McAteer expressed regret that he had not been consulted and claimed his thinking was 'moving along similar lines'.[14]

The only unqualified welcome came from the NDP Executive who noted that the SDLP fulfilled their major requirements for opposition unity and asked for a meeting to discuss the prospects of a merger. A special NDP conference was convened on 3 October 1970 and passed a resolution encouraging members to join and 'play a full part in the development and growth of the Social Democratic and Labour Party.'[15] The central machinery of the party was immediately dismantled. The branches were instructed to remain in existence for a limited period in order to wind up their affairs, but in practice they remained in existence to become the nuclei for the SDLP's branch organisation. Thus, almost eighteen months after the Catholic electorate had indicated their preference for civil rights candidates in the February 1969 election, the party political expression of this change was formed, although in a different manner and a wholly different shape than many might have originally envisaged.

CONCLUSION

The process by which a political party is formed helps to mould many of the party's characteristics and frequently highlights much about the nature of the political system. At its inauguration the SDLP appeared less a political party than a coalition of diverse parliamentary interests linked only by a common opposition to unionism. This apparent disunity was the result of the total absence of an indigenous tradition of Catholic parliamentary politics in Northern Ireland. The republican tradition of physical force was well entrenched and self-perpetuating, as was shown by the re-emergence of armed resistance in the form of the Provisional IRA. Yet no strong parliamentary force existed to balance it.

The lack of a parliamentary tradition meant that those parties active in the 1960s had virtually no organisation and no membership in the country: they existed only as parliamentary entities. Therefore, the only way a realignment of Catholic politics could take place was for a body to form at the parliamentary level first, rather than by initially mobilising support from a mass base. This procedure was followed even though those MPs who formed the SDLP declared themselves committed to the concept of a mass party.

In many ways the formation of the SDLP in 1970 was as much the consequence of a particular set of circumstances as of agreement among members on basic aims. It meant that many of the objectives it held to be important were taken from precedents already established by other parties and groups. For example, the idea that reunification could only come about by the consent of a majority in Northern Ireland came from National Unity, a pressure group formed in 1959 to press that very aim. The belief in organised politics was a legacy of the National Democratic Party's efforts to reform the Nationalist Party, while the commitment to radical socio-economic policies was at least partly a consequence of the influence of the Republican Labour Party. The parliamentary origins of the SDLP have had a profound influence in fashioning the framework of the party, its policy content and the manner in which it has set out to attain its objectives. Part Two analyses the organisational structure of the party.

Part Two

AN ORGANISATIONAL ANALYSIS

4 Institutional Structure

For some things individual action, as opposed to organised collective action, is clearly more capable of realising the political aims of a group or community. The use of collective action through the medium of a political party is a recognition of changing circumstances and the emergence of a new set of aims, in the attainment of which organisation becomes a vital weapon. Without a practical, realisable goal, therefore, there is obviously little to gain in maintaining an organisation. As the aim of the Ulster Nationalist Party, Irish unity, was unobtainable through normal constitutional means, they possessed no motive to organise. The shift in political priorities precipitated by the SDLP introduced the concept of Catholic participation in the running of the state as a primary political objective. In the pursuit of this end organisation was assumed to be vital to maximise the Catholic community's political strength. The SDLP's institutional structure is thus important, not only in assessing the role it has played in the party's overall impact on the Northern Ireland political system, but in gauging how the general political environment has affected the organisation's evolution and operation.

THE PARTY CONSTITUTION

A party constitution is primarily a response to the need to regularise the relationships and procedures that permeate the informal party structures. From this perspective a constitution can give important insights into the party's perception of its role in the political system and into the motivations, aspirations and general outlook of the membership. The SDLP constitution sets out the formal aims of the party in its second clause. These six aims are as follows:

1. To organise and maintain in Northern Ireland a socialist party;
2. To promote the policies decided by the party conference;
3. To co-operate with the Irish Congress of Trade Unions in joint political or other action;
4. To promote the cause of Irish unity based on the consent of a majority of people in Northern Ireland;

5. To co-operate with other labour parties through the Council of Labour and to co-operate with other social democratic parties at an international level;

6. To contest elections in Northern Ireland with a view to forming a government which will implement the following principles:

(a) the abolition of all forms of religious, political or class discrimination; the promotion of culture and the arts with special responsibility to cherish and develop all aspects of our native culture.

(b) the public ownership and democratic control of such essential industries and services as the common good requires.

(c) the utilisation of its powers by the state, when and where necessary, to provide employment, by the establishment of publicly owned industries.[1]

The aims are modelled on those of the British Labour Party, the most noticeable difference being that in place of Labour's controversial clause four, the SDLP constitution substitutes the aim of Irish unity 'based on the consent of a majority of people in Northern Ireland'. Again, the constitution adds in its sixth section the contesting of 'elections in Northern Ireland with a view to forming a government', an aim that few political parties would feel it incumbent on them to mention, but which, given the previous history of Catholic politics in Ulster, the framers held to be a necessary declaration.

The aims emphasise socialist and socialist-oriented concerns, yet only a tentative attempt is made to define the extent of this commitment. Conversely, the aim of reunification is relegated to the fourth section, reversing the predominance accorded it in other formal statements of policy by nationalist parties in the Republic and Northern Ireland. One concession to nationalist ideology exists in the object, introduced by the 1972 annual conference, of promoting 'culture and the arts with a special responsibility to cherish and develop all aspects of our native culture'. This, in fact, is the only amendment that has been made so far to the constitution's second clause.

In common with the British, Irish and Northern Ireland labour parties, both individual and corporate party members are admitted. Individual members join the party through the local branches while corporate members are affiliated via the trade unions and related bodies. To date the SDLP's membership is exclusively individual and the trade unions have not been persuaded to affiliate, although individual contacts are maintained with trade union leaders. It seems certain that for the foreseeable future no Northern Ireland trade unions will be persuaded to affiliate, given the movement's difficulty in maintaining the allegiance of two antagonistic groups of workers. The overriding need to preserve unity on economic issues thus precludes the movement adopting any formal political ties. One Ulster political party, the NILP, has gained the support of some British-based trade unions, but this has never amounted to more than approximately 10 per cent of the province's total trade union membership and may be contrasted with the 63 and 45 per cent claimed by the British and Irish labour parties, respectively.[2]

An individual member is admitted on the understanding that he subscribes 'to the principles and objects of the party and is not a member of any other political party'. The member's £1 annual subscription fee is divided equally between the branch through which he affiliates and the central organisation. No strict conditions of membership are laid down, nor is there a pröscribed list of organisations from which members will not be accepted, as there is, for example, in the British Labour Party. The power to refuse membership or expel existing members 'whose activities they consider injurious to the party or inconsistent with its principles and objects' rests in the first instance with the branch, while an appeal may be made against their decision to the Executive Committee. In the case of a corporate member the Executive Committee exercises the power to refuse or expel but the right of appeal is vested in the annual conference.

The commitment to maintain links with other socialist and labour organisations is also contained in the party constitution's fifth aim, 'to co-operate with other labour parties through the Council of Labour and co-operate with other social democratic parties at an international level.' The Council of Labour was formed in 1968 'to enable joint consultations on social, economic and political issues without reference to partition'[3] between the Irish and Northern Ireland labour parties and the Irish Congress of Trade Unions. The SDLP joined the Council in 1970, although it has been dormant in recent years. In 1976 the SDLP was granted full, corresponding, membership of the Socialist International, along with the NILP, after a lengthy process that began with an application by Paddy Devlin in 1971.

The framework of the SDLP's organisation is given in Figure 4.1. In outline the structure resembles that of the National Democratic Party, not least because members active in that party helped to initially establish the SDLP organisation. The NDP framework was itself based on those of the two major parties in the Republic, although some modifications were made and carried over into the SDLP. Specifically, a large consultative body, the Central Council, was included in addition to the annual conference. All the component parts, save for the Central Council, can therefore be found in both Fianna Fáil and Fine Gael performing comparable functions. This is especially important to note because the District Executives and Constituency Councils have no direct parallel with the parties in Britain and are a reflection of the autonomy of local units which need co-ordination from bodies more acquainted with local conditions than the central organisation.

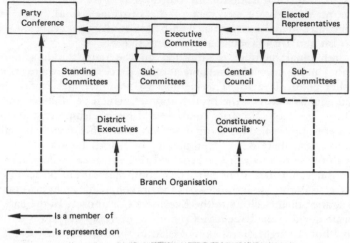

FIG. 4.1 The Structure of the SDLP

LOCAL ORGANISATION

The SDLP has managed to establish a cohesive, cross-local organisation in spite of the absence of any tradition of organised politics within the Catholic community. The Nationalist Party's organisation, for example, never surpassed that of the registration society, a form of organisation common in countries on the threshold of universal suffrage. In 1968 and 1969 the NICRA did stimulate the growth of many local civil rights associations which, although affiliated to the parent body, were largely independent of central control or discipline. This loose, federated structure aided the movement's extemporaneous growth, but became a drawback in so far as local associations were vulnerable to the influence of extremists. From an organisational perspective, therefore, the civil rights experience was harmful in acclimatising people to an undisciplined and spasmodic form of political organisation that was the antithesis of the centralised, highly structured form demanded by a political party. The National Democrats did possess such a local organisation whose resilience and commitment had been proven by successive electoral reverses, but its spatial growth had been limited by the agreement not to encroach into areas controlled by the Nationalist Party.

The SDLP's fundamental problem in initially constructing an extensive local framework covering all 52 of the Stormont single-member constituencies was thus the lack of organisational experience. In terms of the constituencies they organised in, it is possible to isolate three types. Firstly, there were the constituencies where Catholics were in a numerical

majority, mostly in counties Fermanagh and Tyrone. Here both nationalists and republicans were well established and there was an extant
electoral tradition and a core of activists familiar with the mechanics of
electoral politics. Secondly, there were the constituencies where Catholics
were in a numerical minority and hence held no incentive to contest
elections. In between these two categories there was a third type where
Catholics were numerically strong but not necessarily dominant. Constituencies in this position, like parts of counties Londonderry and
Armagh, possessed no identifiable tradition of electoral politics and what
political activity took place often encompassed a strong republican
element.

Table 4.1 indicates the spatial growth of branch organisation between
1971 and 1976 arranged by Westminster constituencies, together with an
estimate of the number of Catholics to each branch and an estimate of the
percentage of Catholics in the constituency, according to the 1971 census.[4]
The expansion of the organisation began in early 1973 in response to the
impending Assembly elections, but the growth shows no clear pattern and
is apparently unrelated to the frequency of Catholics or the previous
tradition of political activity. For example, the smallest numbers of
Catholic electors to each branch are recorded for North Antrim (where
approximately 17.9 per cent of the electorate is Catholic) and Londonderry (49.1 per cent Catholic). Similarly, East Belfast has one branch for
8327 Catholic electors, West Belfast one branch per 10,333 electors, yet the
former has only about 10.6 per cent of the electorate Catholic, the latter
48.5 per cent. The development of the branch organisation would
therefore seem to be less the result of common, quantifiable variables, than
local factors such as the activity or influence of local leaders.

Branch membership varies considerably, from a handful up to as many
as one hundred, although the optimum size has been considered to be in
the region of 30 to 50. Geographically branches may extend over any area
within the constituency boundaries, showing a greater concern for
covering territorial units than encompassing centres of population. As
branch membership passes 50, new branches are formed and the area of
responsibility sub-divided. The total membership figure for the party is
confidential, but the number may be estimated by delegate attendance at
annual conferences, since branches are permitted to send one delegate for
every ten paid-up members. This gives an approximate figure of between
5000 and 6000 members in 1976.

In theory branches are expected to perform a variety of functions,
broadly falling into four categories. Firstly, during elections they combine
with other branches in the constituency to nominate and select candidates,
and to organise the campaign. Secondly, they propagate party policy
among the membership and electorate; and, thirdly, they play a part in the
formulation of policy at a local and provincial level. Finally, at least part of
the financial burden of maintaining the party is expected to be met by

TABLE 4.1 Branch Organisation, 1971–76

Constituency	1971	1972	1973	1974	1975	1976	Estimate of Catholic electors per branch in 1976	Estimated percentage of Catholics in constituency (1971 census[a])
Antrim North	1	1	9	11	13	13	1,426	17.9
Antrim South	1	1	2	4	5	6	6,211	31.1
Armagh	1	1	4	9	10	11	3,632	44.1
Belfast East	—	—	1	1	1	1	8,327	10.6
Belfast North	2	1	2	2	2	2	8,344	23.6
Belfast South	1	1	1	2	3	3	3,370	13.8
Belfast West	2	2	2	2	3	3	10,333	48.5
Down North	—	—	1	1	2	3	6,564	14.0
Down South	2	1	14	18	19	19	2,130	45.0
Fermanagh and South Tyrone	—	2	7	9	9	9	3,534	45.2
Londonderry	2	2	17	20	24	25	1,807	49.1
Mid-Ulster	3	2	9	9	13	15	3,017	56.0
Total	15	14	69	88	104	109	3,098	32.9

NOTES [a]The 'not stated' religion category in the 1971 census has been divided according to the religious balance in the constituency in the 1961 census. Figures relate only to those Catholics of voting age in 1975 and are based on the size of the electorate in 1975.

SOURCES SDLP Executive Committee Annual Reports, 1971–76; 1971 Northern Ireland Census County Reports (Belfast: HMSO, various dates) and unpublished census tables.

branches. In practice their varying size plus the different degrees of interest shown by members results in a wide divergence between branches as to how far they go towards performing all these functions. As no limit is placed on the number of motions a branch may submit to the annual conference, this provides a tentative gauge of branch activity. By this measure branch activity is relatively low. In the four conferences between 1973 and 1976 on average only 34 per cent of the branches submitted between one and four motions for discussion, and only 9 per cent five or more. The majority of branches failed to submit a motion of any kind.

The most important power residing in the local organisation is candidate selection. For a provincial body or the United Kingdom parliament SDLP candidates are selected by a convention of delegates from the branches in the constituency. Each branch appoints the appropriate number of delegates and may mandate them to vote for a particular candidate or group of candidates. A significant change made in this procedure came in 1973 when responsibility for organising the selection convention, including the appointment of the chairman and the preparation of a list of prospective candidates, was transferred from the Constituency Council to the Executive Committee. This reform was justified by a belief that central control was essential to ensure impartiality and regularity in the selection procedure, but perhaps a more pertinent reason was that as the party came nearer to the prospect of participation in a power-sharing administration, party discipline became vital and necessitated the introduction of stronger central control.

The local framework is augmented by two bodies whose purpose is to strengthen and support the branch organisation. The Constituency Council is composed of branch delegates, in the ratio of one delegate to every 30 paid-up members, and district councillors, Executive Committee members and elected representatives who reside in the constituency. It was originally formed to direct and co-ordinate the branches, especially during election periods, but after the removal of responsibility for candidate selection, their main function has been restricted to managing the election campaign in their constituencies. Between elections Councils meet about four times a year and are mainly concerned with stimulating branch activity and, where possible, organising the formation of new branches.

The composition and functions of the District Executives are broadly similar to those of the Constituency Councils, except that their area of jurisdiction is the district council. They were not provided for in the original constitution, but introduced in 1973 to co-ordinate the work of the party's local councillors in the twenty-six district councils and to provide them with a channel of communication to the branches. Unlike the Councils, District Executives have retained the power to select candidates. They are empowered to convene 'a general meeting of party members' at which local government candidates are selected. In theory this task should be performed by branches, but as branch boundaries are rarely coterminous with ward boundaries, the procedure is conducted at District Executive level. Although no precise rules are laid down in the constitution to guide the Executives in organising a selection convention, the model of constituency selection is closely followed.

CENTRAL ORGANISATION

If a political group is primarily office-seeking, then central organisation becomes especially important in co-ordinating the activities of local groups. The mobilisation of the maximum support depends largely on the efficiency and control of the central organisation, which, in the SDLP, consists of the Executive Committee and to a lesser extent the consultative machinery, the annual conference and the central council. The Executive Committee is composed of 20 members elected annually by the party conference, plus the leader, deputy leader and one other member of the elected representatives. The constitution authorises the Executive Committee to have 'day-to-day control of the organisation and the administrative affairs of the party . . . [to] interpret the constitution and make provision for any matter not contained therein . . . [and] be responsible for implementing conference decisions and developing policy between conferences.' In practice, the Executive's responsibility is to oversee the general management of the party.

The Executive meets monthly, with twice-yearly meetings being held between the full Executive and the elected representatives to review policy and strategy. The Executive's role as a mediator between the will of the mass membership, expressed through the annual conference, and the elected representatives, has not been entirely successful. Theoretically the Executive is a superior policy-making body, but in practice the political attitudes within the party confer greater power on the elected representatives. In this context the most divisive dispute between the Executive and the representatives took place after the Ulster Workers' Council strike when, in contravention of the explicit wishes of the Executive, the SDLP ministers agreed to a phased Council of Ireland. A less serious dispute concerned proposed talks with the Ulster Defence Association, when the elected representatives took the decision to proceed, this time without reference to the Executive.[5] But inspite of these disputes, the two bodies have normally acted in unison, although it is evident that the elected representatives consider themselves ultimately answerable not to the mass membership or the Executive, but to their constituents.

A major responsibility of central organisation is to provide sufficient finance to ensure the party's smooth functioning. Political parties need money to maintain the organisation's normal operation in terms of wages and general office overheads and to mount election campaigns. The former accounts for the heavier burden of expenditure; the latter is unpredictable, but requires large sums of money to be available (or at any rate obtainable) at short notice. Finance may be raised by a variety of means. The obvious source for a mass party is its membership, but the SDLP's £1 annual membership fee, half of which is meant to be forwarded to the central office, provides only a small proportion of the annual need. Moreover, financial obligations have mounted with the proliferation of elections since 1973. The disturbances have further contributed to this by reducing personal canvassing and necessitating the expensive business of reaching the voters through advertising in the daily newspapers.

To supplement income, other sources of finance have had to be found. The traditional means of open fund-raising by local groups has had to be curtailed due to the ever-present danger of intimidation or attack. An alternative method is the door-to-door appeal and branches have been instructed to carry out a collection annually in their area, retaining 30 per cent of the money donated and sending the remainder to the central party funds. In 1974 this method produced £10,000,[6] and in the following year it was extended to the Republic in the form of a Sunday 'chapel-gate' collection.[7] An additional source of income in 1974 was an £11,000 grant to help meet election expenses from the Joseph Rowntree Trust Ltd, a charitable group that has taken an interest in Ulster politics. But the largest and most consistent source of finance has been the fund-raising activities of a small group of executive and professional expatriate Ulstermen living in Dublin. Sympathisers rather than members of the SDLP, the organisers of the 'Dublin Fund' have set themselves since 1972 the task of organising meetings and dinners to directly finance the party. The first event, a meeting in a Dublin hotel addressed by SDLP leaders, realised £2500 from the 500 invited guests.[8] But dependence on this Republic-based income has restricted SDLP freedom in commenting on politics in the South. In one instance, Gerry Fitt caused much dissension by terming Fianna Fáil the 'siamese twin' of unionism and, fearing a loss of support, the Dublin Fund asked the party to formally clarify its attitude to Fianna Fáil. The perilous economic state of the party has thus made its leaders wary of their comments on the Republic: Fitt's indiscretion, for example, was estimated to have cost the SDLP in the region of £10,000 through lost donations.[9] It has also engendered friction with the in-digenous parties, who have suspected that SDLP fund-raising activities erode their own financial bases of support.

The other major component of the central organisation is the con-sultative machinery. In a mass party the points of convergence between the membership and the elected representatives take on a special significance as the leadership are theoretically bound by the policies defined by the membership. Conceptually, the elected leadership are seen as delegates rather than representatives. Following the pattern of the mass party, the SDLP constitution confers the annual conference with 'the supreme governing authority in the party' and continues: 'it shall be the duty of each individual member and section of the party to promote the policies decided by the conference.' Powers (so far dormant) also exist to call a special conference at the instigation of the Executive Committee or if one-third of the branches demand it. The conference is composed of branch delegates in the ratio of one delegate to every ten paid-up members, elected representatives, district councillors and Executive Committee members.

While the conference's formal function is the formulation and discussion of policy, in reality the limited length of time available plus the low level of information open to delegates on specialist subjects precludes any vigorous discussion of issues and the accompanying danger that the membership reach a decision diametrically opposed to that of the elected leadership. In only one instance did such an eventuality occur: in January 1975 the fourth annual conference voted to refer a policy document on policing back to the sub-committee that drafted it and at the next conference in December 1975 an amended document was overwhelmingly endorsed. Two further factors militate against the annual conference performing its con-stitutionally defined role. Firstly, the dominant role of leadership, plus deference for authority, strengthens the passivity of the majority of the delegates. Secondly, the dichotomy between delegate and representative leadership is least acute in a mass party where, as occurs in the SDLP, the social characteristics of the membership relate closely to the usual and anticipated support within the electorate.[10]

Despite the general nature and the limited influence of conference resolutions, a breakdown of conference business in terms of motions (Table 4.2) reveals the priorities of the membership. The predominant emphasis on socio-economic policy is notable, as is the number of motions concerned with internal party matters. Together these account for slightly less than two-thirds of all motions over the period. The decline in the emphasis on internal party matters in December 1975 and 1976, combined with the renewed interest in political strategy, reflects the concern shown at the failure of the constitutional Convention to reach an agreed political settlement.

The unwieldy nature of the annual conference provides the rationale for the Central Council. As the membership of the Executive Committee is small and elected from the floor of the conference, many branches obviously fail to gain representation on it and thus lose the opportunity of projecting local opinions. The Central Council was conceived to bridge the gap between the small, pragmatic Executive and the large annual conference. The Council is required to 'meet at least three times a year . . . [to] hear reports from the Executive Committee, the Assembly party and the party organisation in the various constituencies . . . [and] provide a means of communication between the membership and the central organs of the party.' The composition of the body is similar to that of the annual conference, except that branch delegates are admitted in the ratio of one delegate to every fifty paid-up members. In practice the Council has not

TABLE 4.2 Analysis of Conference Motions, 1971–76

Subject	1971	1972	1973	Conference (Jan) 1975	(Dec) 1975	1976	Total 1971–76
Security, policing and the administration of justice	22.7	28.6	15.0	19.8	18.5	8.9	16.2
Socio-economic policy	34.1	28.6	33.1	37.1	42.6	52.2	40.8
Political policy and strategy	22.7	28.6	16.9	15.5	22.0	27.4	21.1
Internal party affairs (including constitutional amendments)	20.4	14.3	35.0	27.6	16.9	7.7	21.0
Miscellaneous	nil	nil	nil	nil	nil	3.8	0.9
Total	100.0	100.0	100.0	100.0	100.0	100.0	100.0
(N)	(44)	(14)	(160)	(116)	(195)	(157)	(686)

SOURCE Minutes of SDLP annual conferences, 1971–76.

proved to be the cohesive force originally envisaged and it meets irregularly, rarely attracting its full delegate quota. To some extent this malaise is attributable to the Council's purely consultative nature and in reality it provides only a forum for the informal, and frequently inconclusive, discussion of party policy.

ELECTORAL ACTIVITY

In a society divided into two communities of unequal size, elections possess little more than a symbolic function. So long as the government is formed by the majority, the minority receives no incentive to maximise its electoral strength. Conversely, the majority has everything to gain from maintaining a cohesive and disciplined electoral organisation. If, on the other hand, the conditions for success cease to be the attainment of a majority and become the institutionalised representation of communities, as potential governmental participation rests with *all* the parties in the legislature, it becomes advantageous for minority groups to enhance their support, no matter how tenuous or localised it may be.

The introduction of the single transferable vote (STV) method of proportional representation, based on the twelve Westminster constituencies, has considerably aided the SDLP's electoral position. By reducing the number of constituencies and lowering the threshold of representation in each, PR has given the SDLP and other minority parties an incentive to contest elections on a province-wide basis.[11] The results of the Assembly and Convention elections have been a major success for the SDLP, making them the sole elected representative of the Catholic community. In the Assembly election, for example, the SDLP won 22.1 per cent of the valid first preference vote, as opposed to 3.2 per cent for their anti-partitionist competitors.

Four main conditions are necessary for success in a PR election. Firstly, a realistic estimate of the party's strength has to be made so that the appropriate number of candidates can be nominated. With the exception of the district council elections, the SDLP nominated candidates in all the constituencies, the nominating strategy being governed by the general rule that a party should enter one more candidate in a constituency than it expects to have elected. The expertise with which this was implemented was demonstrated by the high level of successful candidatures – 67 per cent in the Assembly – and by the pattern of transfers. In both the Assembly and Convention elections, out of a total of 38 transfers involving the redistribution of SDLP votes (either through elimination or surplus), in only 11 cases was there not another party candidate still in the running to benefit from them.

The second element is the geographical fragmentation of the constituency into bailiwicks. This enables candidates to concentrate their campaign in one area. So as to gain the optimum advantage from the local forces of parochial attachment and personal acquaintance, candidates well rooted in the local community are chosen, and the instances in which candidates from outside the constituency have been selected has confirmed the strength of these forces.[12] The third element is strong central direction and co-ordination at the constituency level and in the SDLP this is provided by the Constituency Councils. In 1973 five Councils were in operation, rising to nine in 1975.

Fourthly and finally, an active membership is essential to help to maintain a vigorous campaign in the constituency. Here the SDLP has encountered problems, partly through the unwillingness of the majority of the party's paid-up members to become active in campaigning, and partly because of the physical dangers inherent in personal canvassing in a period of violence and unrest. To some extent these problems have been countered by utilising extensive publicity in local newspapers and by exploiting the postal vote. For example, although the percentage of the poll cast through the postal ballot dropped from 15.9 per cent in the Assembly to 12.3 per cent in the Convention, the latter saw a higher concentration in Catholic constituencies.[13]

The SDLP's consistently high vote has thus been due partly to their ready adaption to PR, but what part has organisation played in mobilising the Catholic vote? Table 4.3 gives an estimate of the number of Catholics in each constituency and of the number of Catholic electors to each branch in 1973, together with the SDLP Assembly and Convention votes expressed as a percentage of the Catholic electorate. The four constituencies with the lowest mobilisation figures, South and East Belfast, South Antrim and North Down, all have a weak organisation, although of the four the most active election campaigns have undoubtedly been undertaken in South Belfast, which attains the best level of mobilisation. In North Down, an active campaign was mounted for the Convention and this too appears to have improved the total SDLP vote. The constituencies with the highest levels of Catholic mobilisation possess only a modest organisation, suggesting the influence of factors other than organisation. Similarly, constituencies with extensive local organisations, Londonderry and South Down, achieve only an average level of mobilisation, again suggesting that here too organisational strength has not made a strong impact.

The use of STV permits the voter to list as many preferences, or as few, as he desires, subject only to the number of candidates on the ballot paper. An analysis of vote transfers provides a unique opportunity to discern the structure of preferences within the electorate. The major drawback in such an analysis is that transfer options are conditional upon the number and affiliation of candidates in the running at any stage of the count, and in addition transfer totals relate only to vote values and not to actual preferences.[14] Thus, although it is impossible to ascertain the *exact* ordering

TABLE 4:3 The SDLP Mobilisation of the Catholic Vote, Assembly and Convention Elections

Constituency	Estimate of Catholics in constituency (1971 census[a])	SDLP Assembly Vote as percentage of Catholics	SDLP Convention Vote as percentage of Catholics	Estimate of Catholic electors per branch in 1976
Antrim North	18,537	57.1	57.1	1,426
Antrim South	37,265	21.2	23.2	6,211
Armagh	39,958	54.4	42.6	3,632
Belfast East	8,327	22.2	15.3	8,327
Belfast North	16,689	60.7	60.2	8,344
Belfast South	10,109	32.8	30.3	3,370
Belfast West	31,000	43.7	43.7	10,333
Down North	13,129	21.6	30.4	6,564
Down South	40,461	47.1	58.4	2,130
Fermanagh and South Tyrone	31,802	71.1	66.9	3,534
Londonderry	45,171	52.0	51.4	1,807
Mid-Ulster	45,268	52.0	43.7	3,017
Total	337,716	47.3	46.2	3,098

NOTES [a]See note [a], Table 4.1.

SOURCES 1971 Northern Ireland Census County Reports (Belfast: HMSO, various dates) and unpublished census tables; Ian McAllister, *The 1975 Northern Ireland Convention Election* (Glasgow: Survey Research Centre Occasional Paper No. 14, 1975).

of preferences, it is possible to identify a pattern.

Omitting intra-party vote transfers, it is evident that in the Assembly and Convention elections the main sources of SDLP transfers were the Alliance Party and the Republican Clubs. However the distribution of SDLP vote transfers indicates that Alliance made the greatest gain, partly at least because Republican Clubs candidates tended to be eliminated early in the counts. Combining the vote transfers in the two elections, 66.4 per cent of SDLP transfers went to Alliance, 0.7 per cent to the Republican Clubs and 25.6 per cent became non-transferable.[15] Clearly, Alliance was perceived by SDLP voters as the party most nearly adjacent to their own, and the common link of power-sharing proved stronger than the link of Irish unity with the Republican Clubs.

In terms of the social composition of the SDLP vote, ecological analysis matching data from the 1971 census and the SDLP vote in the Assembly and Convention elections indicates that Catholicism is easily the strongest factor defining the constituencies in which they gained their support.[16] Socio-economic variables played little part in delineating supporters. SDLP electoral support therefore appears broadly representative of the Catholic community as a whole, and this finding has been confirmed by survey research. It is however notable that at least one survey has suggested that, in terms of social class, the SDLP tends to finds its strongest support in the clerical, skilled and unskilled manual grades, and least amongst the professional and managerial grades, who tend to favour the Alliance Party.[17]

CONCLUSION

Organisation is essential for any political party endeavouring to attain a clearly defined aim and in helping to draw together diverse sections of support. The SDLP's institutional structure is that of the mass party, based on a large card-carrying membership, with the elected representatives subordinate to the collective dictates of the mass. The reality is somewhat different. In practice the elected representatives are free to act and formulate policies without having to take any significant account of the membership; indeed, what influences them more is the response of the Catholic electorate to their policies. Preventing a potentially damaging clash between these two forces are the membership's passivity and relatively small size. The SDLP's 5000 to 6000 members compares unfavourably with the Alliance Party's estimated 10,000 members – a party the same age as the SDLP, with a similarly efficient organisation, but with less success in mobilising the vote.[18] While socially representative of the Catholic community, the membership lacks the size necessary to make it a weighty component in policy formulation.

The costs of the organisation are difficult to estimate. Politically, the cost is the risk of a clash between the membership, expressed through either the Executive Committee or the annual conference, and the elected representatives. Financially, the cost is the never-ending search for money to sustain it. This is in itself self-defeating, as the aim of the organisation, to enable the membership to participate in political affairs without dependence on outside interests, is unfulfilled. The need for money has forced them to seek funds in the Republic, and thus necessarily restricted freedom of comment, not to mention engendering suspicion among Protestants as to the party's putative Ulster orientation.

Ultimately, however, the benefits of organised collective action have shown themselves superior to that of individual action. Organised action has been instrumental in creating the circumstances possible for it to attain the political leadership of the Catholic community through support for power-sharing within a Northern Ireland administration. In addition, by absorbing and channelling dissatisfaction into various forums within the structure, the organisation has preserved party unity at times when the pressures to fragment have seemed irresistible. To a significant degree, the end of the schismatic Catholic politics of the pre-1970 era is attributable to the cohesive influence of the SDLP's institutional structure.

5 Policies

The formulation and articulation of policy is a function integral to any political party, but especially so to a party committed to socialist principles and organised on a mass basis. To hold the loyalty of its activists and maintain a large pool of voluntary workers, the party must project a coherent set of aims attractive to its supporters and with which they can readily identify. The importance of policy is further increased within a two-party system, particularly where conflict over policy is reinforced by a social structural cleavage. Policy is vital to the party in power precisely because it has the opportunity to implement its plans on behalf of its supporters; it is central to the opposition party since, without a coherent policy, it would be 'in danger of forfeiting its claim to be an alternative government.'[1]

Within the Ulster party system, the SDLP is placed in a contradictory position. On the one hand, it operates in the form of a mass party and all its structural characteristics impel it towards developing a wide range of policy objectives to maintain cohesion. On the other hand, the party's permanent minority status within the political system means that power is denied to it, unless agreement is reached on how to restructure the system to grant minority participation or an arrangement made with one or more of the competing parties to form a majority coalition. Thus, as the party is not in practice 'a government in waiting' the system provides no natural stimulus for it to undertake a programmatic function. This chapter examines the policies of the SDLP in two fields, constitutional change and socio-economic reform, with the aim of assessing the extent to which it has coped with these two contradictory influences, mass membership and the lack of direct access to political power.

POLICIES

(i) Constitutional
Traditionally, the link between all the groups seeking support from the Catholic community has been the aim of Irish unity, although the means employed to achieve this has always been a source of contention. The Nationalist Party was unconditionally anti-partitionist, while committed to non-violent means. In the 1960s the National Democrats sought unity

conditional upon the consent of a majority in Northern Ireland and further added the aim of posing as an alternative government to the Unionist Party, thereby implicitly accepting the Westminster model of government. The SDLP inherited the NDP's constructive approach to politics and the crucial condition of unity only by consent. As consent was not forthcoming, the need arose to present a constructive policy towards the system of government within Northern Ireland. Initially, like the NDP, the party aimed at posing 'an alternative to the Unionist Party'.[2] But this strategy consigned any office-seeking party representative of the Catholic minority to political impotence. Moreover, other political groups in the province were beginning to formulate their own radical proposals to end the permanent exclusion of Catholics from governmental office. The Alliance Party, for example, in its 1970 statement of principles committed itself to 'complete and effective participation in our political, governmental and public life at *all* levels by people drawn from both sides of our religious divide.'[3]

The SDLP encountered three problems in trying to restructure the governmental system to incorporate minority interests. Firstly, no serious thought had been devoted as to how the rules determining the formation of the government could be altered to achieve this aim. Secondly, even if a plan could be drawn up, the violence militated against their winning the political initiative for a sufficient length of time to enable their plans to be given serious consideration. Thirdly, the logic of Irish unity through consent dictated that they participate in the state, yet this would give it recognition and increase consensus, hence improving its longevity and making Irish unity an even more distant prospect.

The basic dilemma of recognition and participation was not completely resolved until mid-1973 when the party accepted the White Paper proposals on the Assembly and Executive. Hitherto, reticence in delineating a clear policy on the constitution had undoubtedly served to increase support for physical force, since SDLP politicians were advocating an end to the Stormont system of government without presenting a positive, attainable alternative. During this period the only constructive plan was the demand for the formation of an 'interim commission' composed of representatives from both communities to govern the province while a solution involving Irish reunification was agreed upon. SDLP involvement in such an 'interim' arrangement (the detailed form it would take was never given) avoided the question of political recognition for the prevailing constitutional arrangements naturally inherent in participation. The only extensive account of the party's thinking on the constitution at this time was the condominium proposals, *Towards a New Ireland*, [4] prepared for the Darlington conference in September 1972, which involved three distinct components: firstly, a British declaration in favour of Irish unity; secondly, an interim form of government; and thirdly, the machinery to implement unity.

The demand for a British declaration in favour of unity stemmed from the premise that the province was fundamentally unstable, due not only to the failure of the Stormont system of government, but to that of the 1920 Government of Ireland Act. From this it was agreed that 'any re-examination must . . . take place, not on a purely six-county context, but in an Irish context.' This would necessitate an immediate British declaration that 'it would be in the best interests of all sections of the communities in both islands, if Ireland were to become united on terms which would be acceptable to all the people of Ireland.' Unity would not be immediate because of the 'many problems inherent in its implementation which will take time to resolve'.

While unity was in the process of maturation, the province would be administered by an 'interim government' incorporating 'the present basic loyalties of both sections of the people' and guaranteed by Britain and the Irish Republic through a 'treaty accepting joint responsibility'. The structure would be composed of an assembly elected by proportional representation and an executive elected by the assembly, also by PR. All legislation passed by the assembly would have to be ratified by two commissioners representative of the sovereign powers. To expedite unity, a 'National Senate' was envisaged, composed equally of members from the Northern Ireland assembly and Dáil Eireann apportioned by party strength. The Senate would 'plan the harmonisation of the structures, laws and services of both parts of Ireland.'

Despite their ingenuity, the condominium or joint sovereignty proposals were impractical. In the first place, they would be obviously unacceptable to most Protestants, and significantly, while the proposals stated that the ultimate phase of Irish unity would only be realised with 'the agreement and consent of the people of Ireland, North and South', nowhere in the document was it unequivocally stated that it would need the consent of a majority within Northern Ireland. Secondly, the proposals were, strictly speaking, not a pure condominium, since they envisaged an extra form of association between the Ulster Catholic community and the Irish Republic. In fact the form of this association, the National Senate, differed only in name from that of the 1920 Council of Ireland which had been empowered 'by mutual agreement and joint action to terminate partition'[5] but which had never operated. Thus, while the party asserted that the three components of the plan were interdependent, the only part likely to find favour with Westminster were the plans for Catholic participation in government.

That the SDLP obtruded such radical plans reflected their belief that Westminster was reappraising the whole Irish problem, and that some form of unity was at least a medium-term possibility. The policies of the centre groups, the New Ulster Movement, and the Alliance and Northern Ireland Labour parties, were all aimed at ensuring a Catholic presence in the executive level of government. The SDLP extended the logic of this by saying that if it was acceptable for the new system of government to encompass representatives of the two communities, then it was also right to grant the legitimacy of their aspirations through the constitutional device of joint sovereignty. The application of the condominium concept to Ireland was not new and had found a contemporary advocate in Ritchie Ryan, a Fine Gael TD.[6] Not surprisingly, the SDLP plan was well received in the Republic, the only discordant note coming from the Irish Labour Party's spokesman on the North, Conor Cruise O'Brien, who asserted that 'to insist on unity or nothing, while the majority of the people of Northern Ireland are opposed to unity, is to push towards the terrible nothing of anarchy and civil war.'[7]

The condominium proposals were important because they represented the first serious attempt by the SDLP to set out a coherent policy on the constitution. But they were innately incapable of realisation in the political context of the time. The manifesto prepared for the 1973 Assembly election, *A New North, A New Ireland*,[8] represented a more realistic set of constitutional goals, but since the document followed in the wake of the White Paper which outlined at length the form the new structures of government would take, the SDLP plans lacked the detail of the condominium proposals.

A New North, A New Ireland emphasised the twin aims which would remain the core of party policy on the constitution: power-sharing and an institutionalised link with the Irish Republic. The more abrasive aspects of the condominium concept were dropped and replaced by the idea of 'partnership in government'. Within Northern Ireland this partnership would be reflected in a system of administration 'seen to be fair and just to all sections of the community and to which all can give their loyalty.' Partnership with the Republic would take the form of a Council of Ireland, with wide powers to bring about Irish unity 'by planned and agreed steps' within the context of the European Economic Community. In essence the dilemma of recognising the regime through participation was resolved by setting the price of that participation as the formal association with the Republic provided for by the Council of Ireland.

The fall of the power-sharing Executive in May 1974, and with it the whole system of government constructed by the British, resulted in a reappraisal of the political roles of many participants. The Protestant community's antipathy towards the Council of Ireland dictated that this aspect of policy at least be dropped. Although the party's manifesto for the Convention election, *Speak With Strength*,[9] continued to emphasise the interrelationship between power-sharing and a formal link with the Republic, Catholic participation in government was projected as the main goal. The partnership concept was re-emphasised but not defined, and left as a base from which the new institutions could evolve.

Symptomatic of the political malaise following the collapse of the Executive and the loyalist rejection of power-sharing in the constitutional

Convention was the emergence of the independence debate within the SDLP. The concept of negotiated independence for Northern Ireland has always attracted some loyalist support as a means of reasserting their majority without British interference, but the emergence of limited support within the SDLP is indicative of a belief held by some that a *quid pro quo* renunciation of each community's political aspirations could possibly provide a means of delivering power-sharing.[10] Although the 1976 SDLP annual conference voted to 'undertake an immediate study of negotiated independence',[11] it is unlikely that the concept will gain any significant support within the party as a practical policy option in the absence of any fundamental change in the constitutional relations between Ulster and Britain. Even in such an eventuality, it would be only one of a number of constitutional alternatives and not necessarily the most attractive for Catholics. Summing up the basic objection against independence common among the majority of SDLP members, one party member commented: 'what common political ground can there be between one group who sees independence as a means of maintaining loyalist supremacy, and another group who see independence as a means of ending that supremacy?'[12]

In the last analysis, some form of power-sharing is certain to remain at the centre of party policy in the constitutional field. Originally the formulation and evolution of the power-sharing concept was made possible by the British government, which was in 1972 and 1973 reaching similar conclusions about the composition of governmental structures in the province. But since May 1974 Westminster's power to impose a system of government has been negated by the loyalist veto. Hence the SDLP's plans have remained consistent but essentially impractical, so long as the problem remains one of persuading Protestant politicians to accept a Catholic presence in government. In continuing to articulate this central aim of power-sharing, SDLP policy on the constitution is best seen as an *aspiration*, like Irish unity, since it posits a future set of circumstances in which the outlooks and attitudes of others will change to accommodate the present demands of one group.

(ii) Socio-Economic

The structure and aims of the SDLP mark it out as a socialist party. In the socialist pattern the party is structured around a mass membership which, at least in theory, dictates formal party policy through an annual delegate conference. The party's aims, enshrined in the party constitution, are, among other things, 'to organise and maintain in Northern Ireland a socialist party', to implement 'the public ownership and democratic control of such essential services as the common good requires', and 'when and where necessary, to provide employment, by the establishment of publicly-owned industries.' Why did the SDLP adopt this socialist commitment at its inception? There are two reasons: firstly, in order to maintain an independent political stance within the party system; secondly, in response to the constraints of the social structure.

The tradition of social reform has been well entrenched in anti-partitionist politics. In the 1920s, for example, the social policies of the Nationalist leader, Joe Devlin, were aimed at limited reform, although in general many Nationalists were attracted to socialism more in response to the need to oppose the conservative philosophy of unionism. In the 1960s the attempts of more socially radical Catholic groups to stimulate political discussion on economic issues forced a deeper thinking. The commitment was fostered by the existence of a tradition of anti-partition labour in Belfast which was largely kept alive in the post-war years by Harry Diamond, the voluble MP for the Falls constituency at Stormont from 1945 until 1969. This tradition of social reform within the Catholic community meant that the politicians who came to form the SDLP were already imbued with socialism. The adoption of socialist symbols and aims served to create another dimension of cleavage with the unionists, and helped to promote the role of a credible alternative to the prevailing conservative economic policies. A complementary consideration was that as socialist policies are necessarily non-sectarian and non-religious, they were able to further emphasise SDLP political independence within the party system. In addition, such policies provide a natural point of contact with other socialist parties outside Ulster.

The second main reason is attributable to the social structure of the Catholic community, which has always possessed a higher level of unemployment and general social deprivation than the Protestant community. Thus socialism, with its emphasis on full employment, social welfare and the amelioration of bad housing conditions, was a natural choice for the political representatives of a community with a large working class. The adoption of socialist objectives and ultimately programmes was therefore the consequence of, on the one hand, the necessity of impelling the party towards an independent political stance within the Ulster party system, and on the other, the alternatives offered by the province's social structure. Moreover, as has been pointed out, 'nationalists in Ulster have been little aware of any conflict of interest between nationalism and social reform', and thus anti-partitionism in the North is in many ways comparable with pre-independence nationalism in the South.[13] Given this socialist commitment, how extensive is it, and to what extent is it reflected in the policy output?

By-passing the emphasis in the party constitution on state intervention and public ownership, the evolution of policy has largely concentrated on reform in specific but peripheral areas such as education, housing and agriculture. Beginning in 1974, small policy sub-committees have examined various topics in depth, and this strategy has filled numerous gaps in the policy framework, but tended to reflect the proclivities of individual members in the choice of topics. Thus, for example, discussion papers have been produced on such socially diverse topics as the role of women in society, the problems of alcoholism, and community relations.[14] The scope and imbalance in the socio-economic programme is exemplified by examining three specific areas, all of particular relevance to Ulster: employment and industrial development, housing and education.

Although in retrospect the post-war years now stand out as a period of relative prosperity, the underlying weaknesses in the Ulster economy persisted and demanded direct governmental action to reduce unemployment, guarantee the future of those concerns already operating, and to stimulate growth. In line with this policy capital grants and other financial inducements were offered to industry to commence operations in Ulster. In *A New North, A New Ireland* this approach was seen as too costly, perpetuating the regional imbalance by favouring the east of the province, and encouraging capital-intensive, rather than labour-intensive, industries. The SDLP response was 'the radical alternative' of developing 'the infrastructure of the province' to attract labour-intensive industries, and establishing 'industry directly sponsored by public funds'. Coupled with cross-border schemes under the auspices of the EEC, it was envisaged that this would create a more balanced industrial base by promoting growth in the Catholic rural areas.

This policy was augmented in 1976 by a substantial and well-researched document, *Economic Analysis and Strategy*,[15] which replicated in advance the major recommendations of an in-depth government report. The document foresaw a reduction in unemployment through injections of finance into 'normally profitable' industries which, 'because of Northern Ireland private enterprise's inhibitions have not been developed here.' It advocated a radical and widespread policy of public ownership not as a short-term palliative, but as a permanent feature of the province's economic life. Among other measures, it envisaged the creation of investment facilities in Northern Ireland to ensure that capital channelled into local banks and building societies would be redeployed in local business and industry.

The second area, housing, illustrates how detailed party policy can become if time and interest are devoted to it. Initially a set of principles laid down in *A New North, A New Ireland* were expanded upon in a discussion paper prepared for the January 1975 annual conference.[16] The general requirement of the housing industry was seen as rapid growth 'guaranteed by state enterprise', although the encouragement of other house-building agencies, private and co-operative, was also seen as of importance. The central element in the drive to double annual house building would be a 'Building Corporation' to co-ordinate the groups involved, including the Housing Executive and the construction industry. In addition, the Corporation would provide training facilities, encourage rationalisation within the industry and conduct research into building methods. The problem of land availability would be eased by public ownership, and in the private sector public control of privately rented accommodation would be instituted. Overall, the ideal of the policy would be that 'everyone should own their own home, [but] realism dictates that for the foreseeable future greater emphasis must be put on public authority housing.'

The third area of policy, education, has also been developed in considerable detail, as befits a political party with a large teacher membership. A long and detailed paper, *Education: the Need for Reform*, [17] outlined the main points of policy. This involved, principally, the implementation of free nursery education, an end to the eleven-plus examination and the introduction of comprehensive education, and a reorganisation of higher education to make it more responsive to the community in which it was set up. On the contentious question of integrated education, which is vociferously opposed by the Catholic hierarchy, the paper agreed that the concept should be seriously examined, but believed that it was being used as a 'scapegoat for political and religious divisions, by the same politicians who have supported the institutional sectarian structures of Northern Ireland . . .' Any adoption of integrated education would have to respect 'the primacy of parental rights in education and the ideal of equality in educational opportunity.'

This policy of leaving the question of integration open is dictated by electoral expediency, for, on the one hand, segregated education is clearly unpopular with many Catholics,[18] but to advocate its replacement would risk a clash with the Catholic hierarchy. Thus the SDLP solution to the problem is to emphasise a high standard of education coupled with 'the primacy of parental rights', a device that effectively removes the onus for seeking a change in the system back to the Catholic community as a whole.

It is instructive to examine SDLP policy in these three areas because it demonstrates the imbalance in the overall socio-economic programme. The reasons why the central issues of employment and public ownership are relatively under-developed and indirect social areas so detailed are perhaps a function of the constraints that operate on the policy-making process within any political party. It is possible to isolate five limitations of particular concern to the SDLP that restrict the evolution of policy and serve to explain the anomalies.

The first and most obvious constraint is the predominance of the constitutional issue in political debate and the parallel tendency to relegate discussion of socio-economic matters to a secondary role. Institutionalised power-sharing is visualised as an objective which once attained will create a new climate of opinion conducive to the resolution of all other questions. Thus, for example, the question of integrated education is left open because it would need to be 'part of an overall strategy of community harmonisation and community integration.' Similarly, policing is an issue that must be seen 'not in isolation but as part of an overall political settlement'.[19] A second, complementary, constraint is the recognition that if the SDLP again achieved participation in a power-sharing adminis-tration, it would only be one component of a coalition and hence unable to enjoy the prerogative of a sole governing party: the ability to fully implement its own policies. SDLP policies would thus be subject to the general approval of the coalition.

Thirdly, the party membership lacks strong doctrinal views on socio-economic matters. There are no sectional groups or factions operating within the party to press their own particular demands on the leadership. Related to this is the fourth constraint, the fact that since the party draws its support from a whole community rather than from a single class, to define policy too closely would be to risk narrowing electoral appeal. Maintaining the support of diverse social groups is facilitated by the projection of a 'catch-all' appeal, restricted by a positive policy position only on issues that are unanimously endorsed by the potential reservoir of supporters.

Fifthly and finally, there is the constraint of the Roman Catholic Church. The Church applies a subtle influence, for although the clergy have withdrawn from active participation in politics, and indeed the SDLP is a secular party, those formulating policy must take into account the attitudes and possible reactions of the Catholic hierarchy since, if nothing else, the bulk of the party's members and supporters pray as well as vote together. In recent years the Church has relaxed its traditional opposition to any form of public ownership, nationalisation or co-operation in economic life, but still retains, with dogged enthusiasm, its influence on education. The view of the Catholic Church that education should be a matter of parental choice, and that Catholic religious instruction is the major factor militating against any form of integrated education in Northern Ireland, is also the view that is put forward in the SDLP policy on the topic.

THE COMPARATIVE CONTEXT

It is difficult to make any direct comparison between the socio-economic policies of the SDLP and those of other labour and social democratic parties as the SDLP has to operate within a system where no agreement has been reached on the form of political institutions, and has to draw its support exclusively from one section of a deeply divided society. However, it is useful to contrast the programmatic content of the SDLP and two other parties, the Irish and British Labour parties.

The problem for the Irish Labour Party is its role as 'a class-based party in a system dominated by two large national parties divided along a constitutional axis that cuts across social, economic and religious divisions.'[20] The lack of a class cleavage plus the absence of an urban proletariat has stunted the party's growth and the evolution of distinctive policies, although the party constitution does proclaim a commitment to ensuring 'that when the common good requires, essential industries and services shall be brought under public ownership and democratic control.'[21] To examine the practical exposition of the party's policies, it is useful to look at the manifestoes for the 1969 and 1973 general elections.

The 1969 Irish Labour manifesto was characteristic of a reformist approach, seeking amelioration of social conditions by a limited degree of state intervention in the economy. The manifesto advocated a new department to promote full employment, aided by a development corporation to assist the expansion of private firms. The public ownership of housing land was suggested to help remedy the housing shortage, and the formation of a state construction company to speed building growth. All this was underpinned by a banking policy geared to 'make financial institutions serve the people.'[22] For the 1973 election, Labour formed a coalition with Fine Gael and as might be expected the objectives of the joint manifesto were less radical but more clearly defined. The immediate aim was 'to stabilise prices, halt redundancies and reduce unemployment under a programme of planned economic development.' The one concession to Labour ideology was the pledge to introduce 'worker participation in state enterprises'.[23]

In formulating socio-economic policy, the British Labour Party has been in the more advantageous position of having won six of the ten post-war elections. Thus, while emerging initially as a class-based party, Labour has widened its appeal sufficiently to gain inter-class support and the years in power have led to the evolution of detailed, practical policies. In 1970 the party manifesto laid much stress on the formation of corporations and boards to stimulate development and the rationalisation of industry. The February 1974 manifesto extended this by advocating limited public ownership of a number of selected areas such as the North Sea oil resources and mineral rights, as well as public holdings in such areas as the chemical industry and road haulage 'to enable the government to control prices, stimulate investment, encourage exports, create employment . . .'[24]

The common feature of the policies of all three parties, the SDLP, Irish Labour and British Labour, is the belief that 'particular conditions . . . can be reformed without the alteration of the system as a whole; hence the grievances of one group can be remedied while the grievances of others remain.'[25] But within this general commitment to reformist political methods, the policies of British Labour, limited in scope but well-defined, contrast sharply with those of Irish Labour and the SDLP which are ill-defined in major areas, well-developed in peripheral areas. Although all three favour state intervention in the economy, nowhere it is more succinctly laid out than in the socio-economic programme of British Labour; furthermore, public ownership is promoted sparingly, in areas of the economy that are depressed and inefficient. By contrast, both Irish Labour and the SDLP promote state intervention and public ownership as the major panacea for deficiencies in the political system, yet fail to carry through the plans for defining their scope or the means of their implementation.

Perhaps the major deciding factor in the depth and extent of socio-economic policy is that of power. While the British Labour Party has access to power, neither the Irish Labour Party nor the SDLP have the ability to attain a majority on their own and are hence dependent on others to form a coalition. Both exist in political systems in which the salient cleavage is not socio-economic and thus lack the stimulus to develop a coherent programme. But while there is no advantage to formulating a detailed policy in the major field of economic concern – industrial development and employment – more advantage accrues to formulating policies in indirect social fields, such as housing, education and the social services, where practical reforms can expedite the creation of a fairer system but not challenge the economic *status quo*.

CONCLUSION

The analysis of the SDLP's policies illustrates how well developed these are in the constitutional field, yet how ill-defined is the socio-economic programme. The inability to evolve consistent socio-economic policies was also noted in the Irish Labour Party and attributed there, like the SDLP, to the lack of direct access to political power, which serves both as an impetus towards maintaining a programmatic function and as a disciplining force in determining the scope of change envisaged. Without the crucial prospect of imminent power, the party's socio-economic policy will continue to be vague on the central issues of public ownership and the limits of state intervention in the economy, and the emphasis maintained on formulating detailed plans in social aspects that do not challenge the *status quo*.

Given the importance of a coherent policy towards sustaining the support of a mass membership, how has the party managed to maintain cohesion? The answer lies in the party's proposals for constitutional change, and in particular, to the undoubted support both the Catholic electorate and the party membership have accorded the demand for power-sharing. In 1968, for example, Rose's survey found that one third of Catholic respondents disapproved of the Northern Ireland constitution.[26] By contrast, two surveys carried out by National Opinion Polls in 1974 and 1976 found that 94 per cent and 91 per cent of Catholic respondents, respectively, endorsed institutionalised power-sharing between the two communities.[27] Thus a large minority withholding consent from the regime has been transformed into a majority in favour of maintaining the union, through power-sharing, in 1974 and 1976. This popular backing for the SDLP's policies for constitutional change is the major reason why the party continues to enjoy the support of its membership without adequately developing a socio-economic programme.

6 Personnel

Recent studies of political elites have done much to uncover information about how political groups, communities and political systems function. Numerous arguments have been employed to justify elite analysis and particularly those aspects of it which concentrate on the social composition of the elite and the patterns by which members are recruited into it. In examining the elite of an elective institution, the main justifications are four-fold. Firstly, knowledge of how a society 'selects' a particular set of persons who hold common social attributes can tell us much about the values and biases of that society. Conversely, the manner in which a political party states a preference for a certain type of candidate for elective office can convey similar conclusions about that party. Thirdly, if the study is extended over time, change in the collective characteristics of an elite can reflect change within the social structure of the society. Fourthly, if the study is placed in a comparative context, inferences may be drawn about the relationship between the party's organisational structure and that of the social system.

As a method of social and political inquiry, elite analysis has never been fully exploited in Northern Ireland, partly because of the limited size of the political elite and partly because of the lack of accurate information on its members. Its explanatory power has however been developed in the Republic where a number of comprehensive studies have focused on the link between the social composition and recruitment of the elite and the structure of the social and political system. By drawing on the framework provided by this research, this chapter examines the social characteristics of the elite representative of the Ulster Catholic community, the SDLP elected representatives, and for comparative purposes includes Unionist and Nationalist elected members, as well as Dáil Deputies.

A NEW POLITICAL GENERATION?

The membership of a political elite normally undergoes change through a gradual evolution, rather than a rapid transformation. As members move out of the elite through death, retirement or the failure to gain re-election, new members are recruited to replace them, usually from the younger sections of the population. Thus the elite perpetuates itself, replenishing its ranks and ensuring continuity of leadership. When, however, a radical disjuncture occurs and the old elite is replaced *in toto* by a newer elite, then a comparison of the two serves to indicate much about the nature of that change.

The decline of the Nationalists in Northern Ireland and their replacement by the SDLP has provided such a break in political leadership for the Catholic community. One frequently mentioned explanation is that of generational change, or the displacement of one older political generation by a newer and younger generation, imbued with a different range of attitudes and aims from those of its predecessor. This hypothesis can be tested by comparing the older Catholic elite, the Nationalist MPs at Stormont, with the new Catholic elite, the SDLP Assembly members, over four basic variables: age, education,occupation and extent of localism. In addition, Deputies elected in February 1973 to the Republic's twentieth Dáil and Unionist Assembly members are also included in the analysis. As the main criterion for selecting the units of comparison has been that of a popularly elected legislative body, this precludes consideration of both Stormont Senators and members elected to the 1975 constitutional Convention.[1]

(i) Age

Age is often cited as a principal determinant of political outlook. Its effect is most meaningfully related to generational concepts of political change, as opposed to the simple theory of political senescence, since, as Butler and Stokes have demonstrated, an individual's age is rather less important than 'the issues and events that dominated the political scene when [he] entered the electorate.'[2] The validity of the intergenerational change model is at least nominally born out by an examination of the ages of Nationalist and SDLP representatives. At every post-war election, the average age of the Unionist elected representatives gradually declined, in line with a general tendency among members of elected bodies, from 56 years in 1945 to 50 in 1969. An opposite pattern occurred among the Nationalists, where there was a gradual increase, from 53 years in 1945 to 55 in 1969. By contrast, the average age of the six SDLP elected representatives in 1970 was 34 years, or 21 years younger than their Nationalist counterparts. Even in the 1973 Assembly, the average age of the 19 SDLP members was 39, still substantially lower than any other major political group.

This difference in age is significant in relation to political socialisation. If socialisation is defined as having its greatest impact when the individual first entered the electorate (taken here as age 21), then up to 1962 the average Nationalist was socialised in the decade immediately prior to partition. The period in which the average SDLP member entered the electorate is in the 1950s, a decade of relative prosperity and communal peace in Northern Ireland. In the absence of further research relating age to attitudinal variables, it would be wrong to base any firm conclusions on this difference in age, but it is reasonable to posit the proposition that partition can have had a greater impact on the Nationalists than their SDLP successors, and that the generational concept of political change would seem to have some bearing on the process.

Table 6.1 gives the age structure of the three Ulster political groups, the Unionists, SDLP and Nationalists and the members of the Republic's 1973 Dáil. Results for all four show a variety of differences. The Unionists and Dáil Deputies are comparable with the highest concentration in the 40 to 49 age group. As previously noted, the largest variation is to be found between the Nationalists and the SDLP, the former heavily concentrated in the 50 to 59 group and the latter in the 30 to 39 group. Representatives under 30 are relatively few in all the groups except the SDLP. This in itself may be indicative of intergenerational change, although more likely attributable to the fact that while the young are influenced by their social environment, they are generally not yet committed to a political outlook. Moreover, it is doubtful if a person under 30 could have won the deference and status in the local community essential to the successful attainment of a leadership position.

TABLE 6.1 The Age Structure of Irish Elected Representatives

Age	Political Group			
	Unionists[a] (1973)	SDLP (1973)	Nationalists[b] (1945–69)	Dáil Deputies (1973)
70 or over	nil	nil	19.6	2.8
60 to 69	20.0	5.3	17.4	12.1
50 to 59	28.9	5.3	28.2	24.1
40 to 49	31.1	26.3	21.7	34.8
30 to 39	17.8	42.1	10.9	24.1
Under 30	2.2	21.0	2.2	2.1
Total	100.0	100.0	100.0	100.0
N (missing)	45(5)	19	15(4)	141(3)

NOTES   [a]Includes unofficial, official, Vanguard and Democratic Unionists and other loyalists.

[b]To improve the total number of observations for the Nationalists, their ages have been recorded for the seven post-war Stormont elections. This results in 46 observations with nine missing, although the data was based on a total of 15 individuals with data on four others missing.

SOURCES Ted Nealon, *Ireland: a Parliamentary Directory, 1973–4* (Dublin: Institute of Public Administration, 1974); John Harbinson, *The Ulster Unionist Party, 1882–1973* (Belfast: Blackstaff, 1973); Dr Patrick McGill.

(ii) Education

Education is at least as important as age, and indeed it has been argued that often 'levels of education are a better indicator of real generational change than mere age categories.'[3] Table 6.2 gives the level of educational attainment for the four political groups. Again the strongest similarities are between the Unionists and the Dáil Deputies, while substantial differences are to be found between the Nationalists and the SDLP. Only the SDLP possess a majority in the higher educational category and one third of the Nationalist members have only primary education. This pattern might to some extent be expected, as the large majority of post-war Nationalist MPs were educated in the 1920s or earlier and therefore unable to benefit from opportunities offered by the post-1945 educational expansion.

It is notable that the SDLP representatives have a greater propensity than the Nationalists to undertake higher education in Ulster. Out of the five Nationalists with degrees, all but two obtained them in the Republic: Austin Currie, later to join the SDLP, took a degree at Queen's, Belfast, as did James McSparran, who continued his studies at the National University of Ireland. Of the eight SDLP graduates, four obtained their qualifications in Ulster, while a fifth, Aidan Larkin, took a primary degree at University College, Dublin, and a second at Queen's. The tendency for the SDLP to attract a high percentage of graduates is reflective of a trend that has been noted occurring in other socialist parties. For example, 32 per cent of British Labour MPs in 1945 had a university education, a figure that had risen to 51 per cent by 1966.[4] In the Irish Labour Party the level of university educated TDs increased from 22 to 30 per cent between 1944 and 1965, respectively.[5]

TABLE 6.2   The Educational Attainment of Irish Elected Representatives

Educational Attainment	Unionists (1973)	SDLP (1973)	Political Group Nationalists (1945–69)	Dáil Deputies (1973)
University/Higher[a]	44.9	57.9	27.8	39.6
Secondary/Grammar	46.9	31.6	38.9	52.1
Primary/Elementary	8.2	10.5	33.3	8.3
Total	100.0	100.0	100.0	100.0
N (missing)	49(1)	19	18(1)	144

NOTES   [a]Includes teacher training.

SOURCES   As for Table 6.1

TABLE 6.3 The Occupational Structure of Irish Elected Representatives

| Occupation[a] | Political Group | | | |
	Unionists (1973)	SDLP (1973)	Nationalists (1945–69)	Dáil Deputies (1973)
Professional	38.0	63.2	50.0	34.7
Commercial/ Business	24.0	21.0	16.7	29.2
Clerical/ Administrative	4.0	nil	5.6	12.5
Skilled Manual	4.0	10.5	5.6	4.1
Semi- and Un- skilled Manual	8.0	5.3	nil	1.4
Farming	18.0	nil	22.1	17.4
Miscellaneous	4.0	nil	nil	0.7
Total	100.0	100.0	100.0	100.0
N (missing)	50	19	18(1)	144

NOTES [a]Where occupation is listed as full-time politician, classification is according to previous occupation.

SOURCES As for Table 6.1

(iii) Occupation
The third variable used for comparison is occupation. Table 6.3 gives results for the four groups over seven occupational categories. Again, as in the case of the previous two variables, the Dáil and Unionist figures are similar and it is left to the SDLP and Nationalists to provide a contrast. While the differences are not as marked as those in education, the classifications tend to mask important variations in the type of occupations pursued. The post-war Nationalists count five barristers or solicitors among their number, the SDLP only one. Again, the Nationalists possess four farmers (three following other occupations on a part-time basis) and four publicans, while the SDLP have no farmers and only two publicans. On the other hand, eight of the 19 SDLP Assembly members list their previous occupations as teaching, an occupation that only one Nationalist, Austin Currie, had taken up.

In general the occupations of the Nationalist MPs are the orthodox ones indulged in by the Catholic community, such as farming, law, insurance and the managing of public houses. Many of these occupations respond 'to the felt need of [the] religious group to have certain services provided by their co-religionists'[6] and have the added advantage that they can often be passed on through a family guaranteeing the status of each succeeding generation and lending stability to the social structure. On another level these occupations can all be interpreted as being connected with brokerage and mediating roles, a pattern endemic to the political structure of Irish rural areas.[7] Thus, for example, the large number of barristers and lawyers among the Nationalists may have been attributable to their negotiating role within the local community, a function that adds an 'element of flexibility and the attitude of compromise necessary to multi-group politics.'[8]

This pattern of occupation is manifestly absent from the occupational structure of the SDLP Assembly party. With urban as well as rural support they more closely resemble a nascent urban middle class, a social group fundamentally different from the traditional hierarchic structure from which the Nationalists were drawn. The preponderance of teachers in the SDLP underlines this aspect and has its parallel in the British Labour Party. After the February 1974 election almost one quarter of the Parliamentary Labour Party listed their previous occupation as teaching. The comparable figure for Conservative MPs was a mere 2 per cent.[9]

(iv) Localism

Studies in the Irish Republic have shown how elected representatives tend to be predominantly local men. This fact has been much commented upon in recent years, particularly in regard to its consequences for the political culture and the operation of the electoral system.[10] The only period when localism was not strong was during the Anglo-Irish War of 1919 to 1921, when the dominant issue of political independence submerged even the power of personality. At all other times national issues have been refracted by the salience of local interests. The origins of the phenomenon stem from the traditional rural communities which have always enjoyed little intercourse with one another and perpetuated local customs dating from feudal times. As one observer commented of nineteenth-century pre-famine Ireland, there were 'different districts in Ireland almost as unlike each other as any two countries in Europe.'[11] In recent times the adoption of multi-member constituencies has intensified the trend of local representatives providing personal services to constituents.[12]

Ulster has been no less subject to the power of parochial loyalty and influence. Table 6.4 gives the percentage of representatives born and/or living in their constituency, plus the percentage bearing some family relationship to another representative, a further measure of the strength of local forces. Unfortunately data are not available for post-war Nationalist MPs. The figures are strictly comparable across the three groups, with the SDLP showing slightly more local attachment than the other two. On the other hand, no SDLP representative is closely related to a sitting or previously elected member, demonstrating the break in continuity with their political predecessors. Familial relationship is not obviously a route of entry into politics for the SDLP, as it is in the Dáil and to a lesser extent within Unionist politics. It will, however, be interesting to see if, when the

TABLE 6.4 Localism in Irish Politics

Extent of Localism	Political Group			
	Unionists (1973)	SDLP (1973)	Nationalists (1945–69)	Dáil Deputies (1973)
Born in constituency[a]	52.0	73.7	dna	61.0
Living in constituency	70.0	84.2	dna	76.4
Related to another elected representative	17.5	nil	dna	31.2
(N)	(50)	(19)	-	(144)

NOTES [a]In calculating the Ulster figure, the Belfast constituencies have been amalgamated. The figure for Dáil Deputies relates to 1969 and is taken from Brian Farrell, 'Dáil Deputies: "the 1969 Generation" *Economic and Social Review* 2:3 (1971) p. 314.

SOURCES As for Table 6.1.

present SDLP members begin to relinquish their seats, they adopt the pattern in the Republic and are succeeded by their relations.

To return to the hypothesis originally raised, the extent to which the emergence of the SDLP represents intergenerational political change, it has been shown that there are distinct and important differences between the Nationalists and the SDLP. In comparative terms these two elites occupied the two extremes while the Unionists and Dáil Deputies together tended to occupy the middle ground. The main conclusion must be that the Nationalists represented a particularistic rural community and the SDLP, while retaining strong local attachments, are reflective of a broader, urban-oriented community. The variation in age, supported to a lesser degree by education, suggests that intergenerational change may be the main motivational force in this shift.

It may be more rewarding to examine the differences in the structure of the elites, not from the perspective of the generations from which they were recruited but by delimiting the boundaries of the social groups available for recruitment. In other words, the structure of the two political parties and the manner in which they recruit their leaders may be a determining influence. Without political organisation, the Nationalists recruited their MPs direct from the Catholic community and all its members were theoretically eligible. The introduction of local organisation by the SDLP has had the consequence of making only party members eligible for nomination. While potential aspirants to office may circumvent this by joining the party solely to seek a nomination, such is the nature of party organisation that those who work for it are unlikely to nominate anyone less than energetic in his commitment to the party. It could therefore be argued that the differences between the two elites are a consequence of the fact that the Nationalist MPs emerged from a process of selection that encompassed the whole Catholic community, while the SDLP Assembly members are reflective only of a small social group inclined to participate in party politics.

A further point of interest is the degree of social heterogeneity or homogeneity to be found among SDLP and Unionist Assembly members. Political groups have the perpetual problem of reconciling the need for group solidarity and the conscious selection of members with a wide social representation and unrestricted entry. A political party must thus attain a balance between these two factors sufficient to give it a coalition 'just as large as they believe will ensure winning and no larger,'[13] without forfeiting some of its original support by diluting its appeal. As Eldersveld has concluded, parties are 'prone to be very tolerant and least exclusive where their status is that of a minority.'[14]

In terms of the religious cleavage in Northern Ireland, the Unionists and the SDLP adopt different strategies. The Unionists are exclusive on religious membership so as to ensure the permanence of their majority, because to invite Catholic membership would necessitate a reassessment of the very aims that unite the Protestant majority. By contrast, the SDLP tends towards religious inclusion. No bar has operated on membership, and although the vast majority are Catholic it is notable that the party had one Protestant Assembly member and two Protestant Convention members. In order to try and mitigate their minority status, the SDLP makes the nominal effort to recruit members from deviant political groups normally outside its universe of support.

INITIAL RECRUITMENT

The initial recruitment of political activists is important because it demonstrates something of how the individual views politics and how the collective party outlook may be shaped by the political origins of its leadership. Recruitment is contingent on the existence of opportunities to indulge in political participation. Once recruitment takes place, then it is normally possible to discern a common career pattern or 'ladder' and isolate the main routes of entry into politics.

Political opportunity is central to the recruitment process. While it is feasible to construct a comprehensive set of 'thresholds' that define the levels of involvement and, ultimately, recruitment, it is more useful in the Ulster context to define political opportunity as consisting of two factors, theoretical opportunity and opportunity afforded by the Catholic community's attitude to politics and politicians. Firstly, what opportunity exists to enter politics in a theoretical sense? Ulster politics has always revolved almost entirely around the single issue of the constitution and consequently the political colour of elected representatives has been predetermined. Defining the two tendencies, unionism and anti-partitionism, in their broadest sense, the marginal seat has been virtually unknown. In the post-war Stormont parliament only three seats changed hands in any of the seven general elections (out of a total of 216 electoral contests). At every election the average number of seats open to anti-partitionists was 11, and the remainder, 41, to unionists.[15]

The figure of 11 anti-partitionist seats hides another consideration. Compared to Unionists, Nationalist MPs tended to retain their seats for a longer period. The average post-war Nationalist MP spent 16.2 years in Stormont and participated in 3.6 parliaments, while his Unionist counterpart spent 13.1 years in Stormont in 2.9 parliaments. If a Catholic seat fell vacant a new candidate would often be selected by a closed meeting of the local community's leaders and frequently returned unopposed. An unopposed return was not necessarily indicative of any general consensus in the choice, but showed that the Unionists considered the seat not worth contesting and that Catholics felt the need to rally round the new candidate and avoid a split vote. This made the actual number of theoretical opportunities open to potential aspirants in provincial elections extremely small. Between 1958 and 1965, for example, the percentage of new members entering Stormont was considerably less among anti-partitionists than unionists.

The second factor from which to gauge the rate of political opportunity is the Catholic community's perception of politics and political service. The esteem in which political office is held among the community 'constitutes a fine mesh filter, determining which potential politicians seek elective office and which remain aloof.'[16] Prior to 1969 the Catholic community held politics in poor regard and it was not considered a prestigious occupation. Most Stormont MPs rarely deemed the job full-time and many retained their jobs and business connections in the manner of local councillors. This low opinion of politics altered after the first civil rights experience of 1968 when political action was seen to have made material gains. Politics and political service became, if not a totally respectable occupation, at least one that was accepted as an important integral part of the community. To some extent this was reflected in the fact that the SDLP, unlike their forebears, treated it as a full-time occupation: only four of the 19 Assembly members continued to work at their previous jobs.

Despite the same level of theoretical political opportunity, by 1969 more practical encouragement was forthcoming for those wishing to participate in electoral politics. What were the main routes of entry into politics to be found among the new SDLP representatives? Successive studies of Dáil personnel have isolated four major routes: firstly, through participation in the Anglo-Irish War of 1919 to 1921; secondly, family succession; thirdly, through prominence in sport; and fourthly, by involvement in local government. The first of these routes is not applicable to Ulster and the second has already been demonstrated not to be a factor. This leaves sport and local government.

The major sporting activity in the Republic and for Ulster Catholics is Gaelic football, institutionalised in the Gaelic Athletic Association. The GAA was formed, with clerical help, during the Gaelic revival at the turn of the century. In post-1921 Ulster the GAA has evolved as an influential social organisation within the Catholic community but avoided the prominent political role of its southern counterpart. Of the 19 SDLP representatives, nine (47 per cent) are GAA members, compared to 35 per cent of Dáil Deputies recorded in a recent study.[17] The influence of the GAA as a political ladder largely results from prominence in the sport as a player rather than as a member. Among SDLP GAA members, only one played the game seriously and as this was in the early 1960s it cannot be considered to have contributed significantly in his election.

An examination of experience in local government as a route of entry is more rewarding. Table 6.5 details prior local government experience among the four political groups. The results show the highest percentage among the SDLP and Nationalists, the lowest among the Unionists and Dáil Deputies. In fact the Dáil figure has been constant since 1961,[18] but hides significant differences between the parties. Local government experience appears to count most in the Labour Party where upwards of 70 per cent have experience and least in Fianna Fáil where less than 50 per cent have served in local authorities prior to election to the Dáil. Mackenzie has noted a similar trend within British party politics: in an analysis of the 1951 parliament he found that 22 per cent of Conservative

TABLE 6.5 The Local Government Experience of Irish Elected Representatives

		Political Group		
	Unionists (1973)	SDLP (1973)	Nationalists (1945–69)	Dáil Deputies (1973)
Percentage having local government experience prior to national or provincial election	27.3	57.9	72.2	53.5
N (missing)	50	19	18(1)	144

SOURCES As for Table 6.1

and 53 per cent of Labour MPs had served on local authorities.[19] A pattern emerged of long-serving local government men getting safe seats, particularly in the Labour Party and specifically among trades union sponsored MPs.

While the SDLP figure is inflated by the fact that the majority were elected to the new district councils in May 1973 just one month before the Assembly election, both the SDLP and Nationalist figures are significant. The large numbers involved in local government point to the necessity of such activity in gaining a local power base and becoming known and respected within the local community for public service before standing for provincial office. This was especially the case in the local councils as they existed before the changes recommended by the Macrory Review Body in 1970 and accomplished with the elections of 1973. These councils managed and dispensed a wide range of resources likely to enhance a local councillor's importance. At the very least, in a multi-member constituency where a candidate must compete not only against his political rivals but also against his fellow party candidates, retaining a place on a local authority reduces 'the opportunity for potential rivals to build up a local base'.[20]

The main route of entry into politics for SDLP Assembly members has no parallel in the Republic and is wholly unique to Ulster: the NICRA. The NICRA was a vital link in moulding new Catholic attitudes towards politics and to the concept of political change. All of the six MPs who initially formed the SDLP in 1970 were prominent in it and able to directly capitalise on its success. In the Assembly party twelve (63 per cent) belonged to the NICRA or a related group.[21] Participation in the civil rights movement makes it comparable as a route of entry to involvement in the 1919 to 1921 Anglo-Irish War for Dáil Deputies. Both were ephemeral events and thus of declining importance with the passage of time.

Local government experience and involvement in the civil rights movement would therefore appear to be the two main qualifications needed for potential SDLP election candidates. Within the Assembly party only one member did not fall into either of these categories. Both qualifications overshadow the degree of prior party political involvement. Only eight of the 19 had a previous party political affiliation, of which three belonged to the National Political Front or the National Democratic Party, two to the Nationalist Party and one each to the Northern Ireland Labour Party, the Republican Labour Party and the Unionist Party. Of the eight, half had their political affiliations eclipsed by their leading roles within the civil rights movement.

In order not to overestimate participation in the civil rights movement as a route of entry into politics, it is important to note that it marked a growing political awareness, but it did not guarantee a party nomination. The general pattern of group membership and organisational involvement suggests that no single affiliation or qualification can dramatically increase the chances of nomination and subsequent election. The determining factor is how far the membership of these bodies gives the individual a strong local base and a wide circle of personal acquaintances. This is consonant with the fact that a political party is in essence bureaucratic and recruits from within its own ranks only those who have demonstrated a willingness to work to further its aims. For example, within Unionist politics a high office in the Orange Order is a guarantee of an equivalent position in the Unionist Party. No such parallel organisation exists beside the SDLP and whatever influence the Catholic equivalent of the Orange Order, the Ancient Order of Hibernians, may have had on the Nationalist Party, no SDLP Assembly member belongs to the organisation.

CONCLUSION

The change in the nature and composition of the Catholic political elite, exemplified by the demise of the Nationalist Party and the emergence of the SDLP, is thus extensively reflected in the social background of the two groups. Clear differences were perceived between SDLP and Nationalist representatives in age, occupation and education. Both groups were drawn from separate and wholly different social groups, particularly with regard to age and occupation. At least part of this disjuncture in political leadership can be attributed to the effects of intergenerational political change and to the influence of political organisation, which refined the social groups from which the respective parties were recruiting their leaders.

Organisation was also seen to be of importance in the initial recruitment of elected representatives. While involvement in the civil rights movement was a pervasive element in the elite, its influence was perhaps secondary to that of local government experience. As in all political parties structured around a mass membership, service to the local community and commitment to the party emerge as the central characteristics likely to facilitate nomination. Ultimately, the only route of advancement in the party is through the party structure. The importance of organisation cannot be underestimated, particularly in view of the organisational weakness of former and contemporary political groups. It also emphasises the extent to which the SDLP is a deviant from the other political parties in Northern Ireland in so far as it operates as a parliamentary entity only: it is not a movement, in that is has no extra-parliamentary links with other bodies.

Part Three

EXPERIENCE

7 Constitutional Opposition (August 1970–July 1971)

In most Western democracies, oppositions which seek to alter the fundamental framework of the political system have flourished only in the initial stages of nation-building. The disaffected minority represented by this type of opposition gradually comes to use and identify with the institutions of the political system and there is a corresponding decline in the proffering of 'sweeping alternatives to the basic framework of the political system, for . . . it would endanger rules and institutions now familiar to oppositions, without promising successful change.'[1] Where a society is fundamentally divided and, in effect, in a perpetual condition of nation-building with the form and existence of the state continually in question, the options that a permanent minority can exercise are limited.

If it is assumed that the minority's primary aim is a change in the structure of the political system and not the territorial boundaries of the state (although the latter would also have the desired effect), the opposition can have only two options. Firstly, it can work within the prevailing framework seeking to put the case for reform at all levels and at every available opportunity. Secondly, the opposition may absent itself, withdrawing the consent implicit in its participation and canvassing change with more unorthodox means. The two options are by no means exclusive, but represent different *sites* on which the political conflict may take place. The sites chosen for political conflict have been consistently fluid throughout Irish history. Groups and parties have often arrogated the means of a parallel but separate opposition, or even simultaneously employed a number of means. This is determined not by the political rules, but, on the contrary, by the likely prospect of success. Hence, as Dahl has pointed out,

> An opposition will adapt its specific tactics to its resources and to the most vulnerable site or sites. This kind of strategy is encouraged by a system in which constitutional rules and practice prevent any site from being decisive and where opportunities for preventing or inhibiting government action are numerous.[2]

Although a constitutional political party, the SDLP consistently altered the site on which it chose to press its demands. For example, in 1970 it was advocating gradualist political change, in 1971 it was acting as an abstentionist opposition, while by 1974 it was a component in a governmental coalition. Part Three examines the period 1970 to 1976 to see how the party behaved in its approach to the political system. This chapter is concerned with the attempt at reform from within and SDLP's experience as a constitutional opposition between August 1970 and July 1971.

THE FAILURE OF REFORM

In the wake of the initial agitation for civil rights, the Unionist government announced a series of reforms on 22 November 1968. The list included reform of the system of housing allocation, the appointment of a parliamentary ombudsman for central government, the replacement of the gerrymandered Londonderry Corporation by a development commission, the reform of local government, and finally, when it could be done 'without undue hazard', the repeal of the Special Powers Act.[3] The Downing Street Declaration of 19 August 1969 reaffirmed the joint commitment of the Stormont and Westminster governments to implement these reforms and asserted that 'every citizen of Northern Ireland is entitled to the same equality of treatment and freedom from discrimination as obtains in the rest of the United Kingdom . . . '[4]

In reality, these Westminster-inspired reforms were part of a policy of 'neutralisation', since they withdrew powers from local elected representatives. Thus the reforms proceeded through the Stormont parliament without deference to the majority or to the opposition, on whose instigation the train of events leading to Westminster's intervention had originally started. While law may create a framework within which government imposes its priorities on society, even in the most auspicious circumstances law can only have a very gradual effect on individual and group attitudes. In the case of the Northern Ireland state, 'discrimination was a structural problem created over a period of many years of decision-making affecting both individual job appointments and the allocation of public resources. The imbalance . . . could not have been corrected overnight by any form of judicial or quasi-judicial supervision or control.'[5] Thus, whatever image the reforms gave to the Unionist government, their attitudes were still determined by the traditional antipathy towards Catholics.

In September 1971 a group of prominent Catholics published a booklet assessing the extent and progress of reform.[6] Whatever objective conclusions the booklet reached, it plainly illustrated the authors' lack of confidence in seeing the amelioration of their position under a Unionist administration. Changes that had been hailed as genuine steps forward, such as the Hunt Report on the police, were marred by doubts as to whether the will existed to carry them through. For example, Hunt recommended that 'the RUC should be relieved of all duties of a military nature' and that 'the general issue and carrying of firearms should be phased out . . . ,'[7] but the decision on when and where arms were to be carried resided with senior RUC officers themselves.

Perhaps the most notorious example of a reform that failed was the Prevention of Incitement to Hatred Act, which became law on 2 July 1970. The Act imposed penalties for incitement to hatred and was designed to curb the more blatant sectarian manifestations. But as the Attorney-General himself admitted in Stormont, the Act was virtually impossible to apply. For a successful prosecution, it would have to be shown that the accused were

> Likely to stir up hatred . . . not against an individual or a number of persons but against a section of the public in Northern Ireland. This hatred must be hatred against people, not against a religious de-nomination or church or a society . . . A person may use abusive language which is likely to stir up racial and religious hatred but the circumstances may show that he had no intent to stir up racial or religious hatred.[8]

Only one prosecution has ever been attempted under the Act. In May 1971 a leading loyalist, John McKeague, was charged with two others under the Act in connection with the *Orange Loyalist Songbook 1971*. Despite the crude sectarianism of the book, all the defendants were acquitted on a re-trial in December 1971. As the first Catholic chairman of the Community Relations Commission commented, 'such failed reforms, by throwing doubt on the sincerity and reforming zeal of the government, spread cynicism among minority groups . . . '[9]

Despite the reforms, then, attitudes had altered little. The SDLP found themselves in a position where, on the one hand, they were passive spectators to a reform programme that was not, with the notable exception of housing, radically improving the standard of Catholics in Ulster society. On the other hand, since the electoral system and parliamentary rules had not been reformed, they could neither initiate nor amend legislation with even a remote chance of success.[10] Other political groups were only too well aware of the SDLP's problem and had been manoeuvring themselves into a position where, following the discrediting of constitutional politics among the Catholic community, they could wrest the political initiative. There were three political groups who remained in the shadows after the 1969 election: the rump of the Nationalist and Republican Labour parties; the Northern Ireland Civil Rights Association; and the republican movement.

The remaining Nationalist and Republican Labour MPs in Stormont had been relegated to secondary positions by the vigorous parliamentary performances of the SDLP MPs. Many of the Nationalists failed to attend with any regularity and only one, James O'Reilly, had struck up any rapport with the members of the new party. The lone Republican Labour

MP, Paddy Kennedy, was by contrast a frequent attender and participant in debates, but his party still suffered from the split caused by Fitt's departure and those remaining members tended to sympathise with militant republicanism.

After the 1969 election NICRA's ability to influence the political situation had also declined and the movement had suffered several splits between the more conservative professional members and the ideologically-motivated activists of the People's Democracy. This, coupled with the widely held belief that the search for reform had entered a parliamentary phase, contributed to the prevailing view that NICRA had outlived its usefulness. After 1970 most SDLP MPs ceased active involvement in the movement, fearing the violence that demonstrations might provoke. Many NICRA activities during this period attracted SDLP criticism, notably the decision to re-activate street protest which was called 'the wrong type of protest at the wrong time'.[11]

The third and most important group in a position to challenge the SDLP for political leadership was the republican movement. After the August 1969 debacle had demonstrated the Official IRA's inability to defend the Catholic community, military considerations once again became dominant. Many IRA members helped to form citizens' defence committees, *ad hoc* community groups autonomous from the IRA organisation, but nevertheless containing a core of activists who would support more militant tactics. The Provisional IRA was formed in January 1970 after a core of dissidents walked out of the Official Sinn Féin Ard Fheis in Dublin.[12] Although a more militant role in the North was only one of their stated reasons for leaving the organisation, it was by far the most important. In a situation where communal violence was only just being held in check, the need for a defensive organisation was obvious since many Catholics distrusted the ability or commitment of the British army to protect them and regarded the RUC as wholly partisan. This was the fertile ground on which the Provisionals began to recruit and attract support, both lay and clerical, in early 1970. The strength of the new IRA, noted Conor Cruise O'Brien, lay in 'its simple relevance to the situation. Any ordinary, patriotic Catholic, clinging to the dual pieties of his community, could identify with the Provisionals.'[13]

In a defensive role the new organisation had no need to justify its existence: it was only when an offensive strategy was adopted that a coherent policy was published, combining orthodox physical force republicanism with Catholic conservatism.[14] Throughout 1970, and particularly after the Falls Curfew of July 1970, IRA members became active in fomenting street disturbances and carrying out individual bombings and shootings, largely in and around Belfast. In their defensive role the Provisionals posed only a minimal threat to the SDLP. Catholics could support constitutional politics and physical force at the same time: it was, after all, sensible to back peaceful political change, but not to the extent of ignoring the consequences of its failure. This seemingly ambiguous duality of allegiances has appertained in the relations between nationalists and republicans and the Catholic community for many years and is not new. But an aggressive IRA policy courted SDLP condemnation and would obscure constitutional politics as the focal point for Catholic hopes of change. Not least, it would attract more stringent security measures and make the threat of a Protestant backlash more explicit.

Thus the constitutional opposition at Stormont, led by the SDLP, was under the constant threat of being eclipsed by street violence. This in turn rendered almost impossible the political dialogue they felt held the best promise of a solution. With this prospect every day becoming a reality, it is not surprising that the party's parliamentary behaviour in 1970 and 1971 was volatile. During the second session especially, they exhibited an undue concern for issues of minutiae that only illustrated the lamentable failure to produce a comprehensive and coherent body of policy. Table 7.1 gives a summary of the SDLP's voting record in the House of Commons, and shows the party's consistent tendency to abstain in about one-fifth of all divisions. The decline in the number of divisions in which they abstained in the third period, 18 May to 8 July 1971, is matched by a corresponding increase in divisions against the government.

TABLE 7.1 SDLP Voting in the Stormont House of Commons, 20 October 1970–8 July 1971

Percentage of divisions in which the SDLP	20 October 1970 to 3 December 1970	Period 8 December 1970 to 13 May 1971	18 May 1971 to 8 July 1971	Total
Abstained	17.9	20.0	12.5	17.6
Voted against the government	69.3	80.0	87.5	76.5
Voted with the government	12.8	nil	nil	5.9
Total	100.0	100.0	100.0	100.0
(N)	(39)	(30)	(16)	(85)

SOURCE HC Deb (NI) 77–82.

At least some of this malaise must be attributed to the lack of organisation, save that which existed in the constituencies of the six MPs. No attempt was made to recruit members outside these areas or to set up a permanent framework incorporating a constitution with regular procedures for consultation. Perhaps most significantly, the party had not yet been tested at the polls. The overall result was frustration with the parliamentary process as it functioned in Stormont. The behaviour of the MPs became erratic. On one occasion they 'boycotted' John Taylor after his appointment to the post of Minister of State at Home Affairs on 2 September 1970, because they considered him too right-wing for the job. The boycott was discontinued on 20 October 1970 after a meeting between Chichester-Clark and Gerry Fitt, but the incident left a residue of bitterness that extended beyond the government benches. On another occasion, the opposition walked out following a clash between Austin Currie and the Speaker on a point of order. And in yet another clash, the normally restrained Hume withdrew from the chamber rather than retract his description of Faulkner as a liar.

In terms of evolving a policy towards the future shape of the province's political system, some attempt was made by Hume and Currie to stress the view that the 1920 Government of Ireland Act had failed, but this was little more than the Nationalists had said for half a century. The main panacea became the direct representation of the Catholic community in government, although how this was to be effected was never expanded upon. In February 1971 Hume rejected coalition government or the idea of opposition ministers filling government appointments. This, he asserted, would only be 'a patching-up operation.'[15] In not formulating any plans for the future government of the province the party implicitly recognised that any change in the system would not come through their own volition. Fundamental change could only come from Westminster, but it was evident after Maudling's visit in March 1971 that he had no new initiatives to offer.

Maudling's visit, coming as it did after the renewal of street violence in Belfast and a revival of loyalist demands for stronger security measures, created the hope among Catholic politicians that Westminster was at last about to follow what they saw as the logic of the British intervention in 1969: direct rule and the abandonment of the Stormont system of government. When these hopes were crushed it became apparent to all that it was they themselves who would have to undertake the role of catalyst in trying to force political change. Abstention began to be mentioned as a practical option. Its constant invocation informed the government that the SDLP considered it a valid tactic in any future situation and let their supporters know that they were not entirely impotent, albeit ephemerally. Withdrawal was often threatened in connection with the use of internment. As Ivan Cooper forecast in December 1970, 'some opposition MPs will be prepared to turn their backs on parliament if this measure is introduced. In other words, we consider this a crunch issue . . . '[16] The single event that temporarily arrested the inexorable drift towards abstention was Faulkner's offer of opposition participation through the committee system.

THE COMMITTEE PROPOSALS

After the summer of 1970 the deteriorating security situation affected not only the relations between the Unionist Party and the Prime Minister, but also those between Stormont and Westminster. To placate his Unionist critics, Chichester-Clark endeavoured to glean more stringent measures from Westminster, or at least a public affirmation of their will to restore order in Catholic areas. The changing relationship between the two governments and the realisation that Westminster was not going to unconditionally back the Unionist government forced Chichester-Clark to resign. His resignation statement implied that the reason for his departure was the failure to persuade the Unionist MPs to support the existing security policy or to persuade Westminster to change it. Chichester-Clark was succeeded as Prime Minister by the late Brian Faulkner, a more astute and versatile politician than any of his predecessors, and a man to whom balancing the conflicting pressures of politics was second nature. Although the idea of 'minority participation' – a euphemism for Catholic presence in government – had been mooted several times before, it fell upon Faulkner to crystallise the idea into a concrete plan.

The joint communique of 29 August 1969, issued after Callaghan's visit to the province, first hinted at the possibility of Catholic participation. It asserted that 'proper representation of minorities [is] to be assured at the elected levels of government by completely fair electoral laws, practices and boundaries, and at nominated or appointed levels by a recognition that such minorities have a right to an effective voice in affairs.'[17] Little was said about this in government circles until Chichester-Clark remarked during a debate on cross-border relations in February 1971 that he accepted

> That any man is likely to say: let me be a first-class citizen in a poorer community rather than a second-class citizen in a richer one . . . This means something more than mere fairness. It means a chance to participate at every level of society and in every aspect of our institutions . . . We accept that the health of this society depends on the creation of new opportunities for participation by all.[18]

Chichester-Clark's remarks received widespread publicity, but the idea was not followed up and it is impossible to know whether he possessed any clear plan or whether he was merely testing Protestant reaction. In any event it was left to Faulkner to give the concept practical shape.

Speaking in the opening debate of the new parliamentary session, an occasion that was also by chance the fiftieth anniversary of the opening of the Stormont parliament, Faulkner outlined his proposals. He noted that exchanges in the House had become 'increasingly bitter and sterile. If that trend, with all its disastrous implications for the future of this community, is to be reversed, all members have a contribution to make.' Emphasising that Westminster would have to approve any possible changes as the sovereign authority under the Government of Ireland Act, he suggested the setting up of three functional committees covering the social services, the environment, and industry. Without executive powers, the committees would review and consider government policy and provide 'a means of expressing legitimate parliamentary interest in the overall quality of government proposals and performance.'[19]

The committees would be composed of 'not more than nine members each, broadly representative of party strengths in the House.' Adding the three new committees to the already existing Public Accounts Committee, 'the opposition should provide at least two chairmen', the posts being salaried and having 'real status and importance in the new scheme of parliamentary operation.' Summing up the proposals, Faulkner said:

> Our proposed scheme of functional committees is designed, first, to allow the House as a whole to perform more effectively its functions of scrutiny and control; second, to permit genuine and constructive participation in the work of parliament by all its members; and third, to encourage the development of much greater specialisation and expertise.[20]

As a final enticement, he hinted that other constitutional changes, such as the introduction of proportional representation, could be considered in the future.

Immediate SDLP reaction was muted, the more so since no reference to the new committee system had been made in the Queen's Speech. In reply, Fitt promised to 'read his remarks with great care and we hope we shall be able to co-operate with him in the new departure he has announced.'[21] Speaking on the second day of the debate, Hume's response was more considered. He saw the proposals as ' . . . very fine words and we will match them with equally fine words. But we will want to see fine actions following these words . . . ' Moreover, Hume doubted whether the will existed in the Unionist Party to implement the proposals, and particularly how the Orange Order would react. This connection, he continued, 'must make us all on this side of the House cautious about any promises that come from the government.'[22]

The strongest speeches in favour of the proposals came on the third day of the debate. Currie praised Faulkner for speaking of 'genuine and constructive participation', a phrase, Currie remarked, 'which I doubt if I could have bettered myself.' Moving an amendment for the setting up of a select committee to recommend more far-reaching 'institutional and procedural changes' in the Stormont system, he gave a 'guarded welcome' to the proposals but regretted that 'they do not go far enough.'[23] Paddy Devlin's response was even more laudatory of Faulkner. The proposals, he said, 'showed plenty of imagination. It was his best hour since I came into the House.'[24] In contrast to this optimism, the Nationalist MPs did not refer directly to the proposals, but dealt with the lost opportunities for reconciliation and the iniquities of Unionist government. The only wholly discordant note came from Paddy Kennedy who claimed that Stormont had lost 'any credibility as a parliament . . . this is an attempt . . . to bolster its credibility by trying to work the committee system.'[25]

In a parliament famed more for the mediocrity of its speeches the opening debate was a memorable event, for it produced a consistently high level of discussion. Whatever doubts SDLP MPs harboured about the new system, it is clear that they were prepared to participate in it. They unreservedly accepted the need for such a system; indeed some opposition MPs had made similar proposals to the Macrory Commission to cope with the centralisation of local government functions and Hume had made a submission to the Kilbrandon Commission along almost identical lines. Faulkner pitched his offer in exactly the right tone and hinted at the possibility of just enough future change to make the SDLP more than eager to respond. Faulkner's closing remarks highlighted the two elements of concrete proposals and future change that so entranced the SDLP: 'we say, start with three committees; see how they go, learn from our experience, but above all let us trust one another.'[26] The success of his speech was shown by the SDLP's decision not to press their amendment to a division.

Why did Faulkner make the proposals? There are three possible answers to this. Firstly, from the perspective of Westminster he judged that if Catholics were seen to be involved in the legislative process Westminster would find it difficult to refuse him more stringent security measures. Secondly, within Ulster party politics Faulkner had become an exponent of balancing the various forces ranged against him, in this case the right wing of the Unionist Party and the Catholic opposition. He had included in his cabinet the traditional Unionist Harry West – an appointment that had caused dismay even outside the opposition – and David Bleakley of the NILP. Bleakley was not however a Catholic nor from an anti-partitionist party and was, because he was not an MP, limited to six months in cabinet office. Opposition involvement at the lower levels of government, via the new committees, would provide a sufficiently weighty long-term balance to the presence of right-wingers in his cabinet.

The third and perhaps most important reason was that Faulkner's strategy was not only to balance the forces confronting him, but to try and split them. In the case of the Unionist right wing he had effectively neutralised it by the inclusion of Harry West, hence breaking the axis between the hard-line but still acceptable West and the more charismatic figure of William Craig who, starting in the early 1960s as a promising Unionist minister, had become so much associated with the threat of Protestant paramilitarism that he had been dismissed by Terence O'Neill. Faulkner's strategy towards the Catholic opposition was similar. He realised that the SDLP were ready to participate in any regional government and that the issue of participation could easily drive a wedge between the nationalists and republicans on the one hand, and the SDLP on the other. Once the SDLP were firmly ensconced within the constitutional framework, Faulkner hoped that they would not risk all their gains by joining the inevitable walk-out, if and when more repressive security measures were introduced.

In essence, the committee proposals were Faulkner's long-term strategy for preserving a degree of Catholic involvement in constitutional politics, while at the same time enabling him to stave off right-wing pressure by the use of stronger security measures. For their part, the SDLP were prepared to accept the proposals at face value and use them as a basis for further reform of the system. By the end of the opening debates, initial reticence had given way to almost wholehearted approval.

On the Monday following the end of the debate, an event occurred which could have had disastrous consequences for Faulkner's plans. In the company of five cabinet ministers he travelled to meet leaders of the Orange Order, the Royal Black Preceptory and the Apprentice Boys of Derry at Brownlow House in Lurgan, Co. Armagh. The government delegation had apparently little to discuss since they were in a strong position, both politically and in the security field. It was unlikely that the committee proposals were discussed and it seems more plausible that, as Faulkner claimed, the government were merely making their views known on the advisability of holding traditional parades. But if that was the case, why did Faulkner travel to Lurgan to see the Protestant leaders rather than they to him? And more important, why did he find it necessary to take half his cabinet with him?

The most tenable answer is that the meeting was a balancing gesture, necessitated by the offer to the opposition the previous week. The meeting could easily have jeopardised government plans in reopening long-standing Catholic mistrust of the connection between Unionist politicians and the Orange, Order; but, significantly, there was only a muted response to it from the opposition. In the first of a proposed series of meetings between Faulkner and MPs from all parties, held on 7 July, it was left to a former Unionist cabinet minister, Phelim O'Neill, to raise the question. He criticised Faulkner for devaluing parliament by deferring to a secret, sectarian society.[27] It is inconceivable that the SDLP MPs accidentally missed the opportunity of mounting a major attack on the government over the Lurgan meeting. The only conclusion that can be drawn is that at this time the party was heavily committed to pursuing the new initiatives and that the Orange Order meeting was deliberately ignored so as to preserve the conciliatory atmosphere.

As it turned out, the committee system proved to be of only academic interest. With great prescience, Austin Currie anticipated during the opening debate the circumstances that could negate all the attempts to reform Stormont: 'in a way it is unfortunate that the Prime Minister's speech had to wait until 22 June . . . The month of June . . . is not usually a good time for serious consideration of issues such as those in the Prime Minister's speech. I hope that other events will not overtake us.'[28]

THE WITHDRAWAL FROM STORMONT

By the early summer of 1971 the violence on the streets, both organised and spontaneous, had begun to take its toll. Even so, relatively few people had died as a result of action by the security forces and most of those had been the subject of intensive inquiries. Samuel Devenney, for example, had been beaten in his house by RUC officers on 19 April 1969 and died three months later. An exhaustive inquiry confirmed that the assailants were RUC officers, but was unable to identify them. Another death thoroughly investigated was that of John Gallagher, who was shot in Armagh on 14 August 1969. The subsequent inquiry by the Scarman Tribunal considered itself satisfied that he had been killed by members of the Ulster Special Constabulary.[29]

It was against a general background of spreading violence, but relatively few civilian deaths caused by the security forces, that Faulkner announced in Stormont on 25 May 1971, in the course of a reply to an adjournment debate, that 'any soldier seeing any person with a weapon or seeing any person acting suspiciously may fire either to warn or may fire with effect, depending on the circumstances and without waiting for orders from anyone.'[30] While events had rendered obsolete the rules governing the occasions on which soldiers could fire, the conditions Faulkner laid down placed virtually no restrictions on soldiers' use of their guns. The statement was significant because it seemed to supply an open political justification for any future contentious shooting involving the army. Although the army appeared to qualify the conditions after the announcement, in any incident the army would support the actions of their own men and in turn be fully endorsed by the Stormont government. The significance was not lost on either Currie or Devlin (the only SDLP MPs in the chamber at the time), both of whom threatened to withdraw over the issue. 'If authority is now being put into the hands of soldiers', commented Devlin, ' . . . we will withdraw from parliament.'[31]

In Londonderry the situation had been quiet since the intervention of the army in August 1969 and the withdrawal of the RUC. While 1970 witnessed a worsening relationship between Catholics and the army, no one had been killed since the death of Devenney. Tension, however, gradually increased and culminated in the early hours of 8 July 1971 when, after four successive nights of rioting in which stones, petrol bombs and gunfire had been directed at the troops, Seamus Cusack was shot in the leg by a soldier and died through loss of blood shortly after being admitted to Letterkenny Hospital in Co. Donegal. The army claimed that Cusack had been aiming a rifle when shot; this was refuted by rioters and bystanders, all of whom insisted that he had been unarmed. Intensified rioting followed and during renewed disturbances Desmond Beattie was shot dead by troops. Once again a basic conflict of evidence arose: the army stated that Beattie had been about to throw a nail bomb when shot; local people asserted that he was unarmed.

The immediate response to the two deaths was the most sustained and systematic violence that the city had seen since August 1969. Behind this stood the fundamentally different versions of the deaths from the army and local authorities. After inquiries John Hume announced on 9 July that he would 'personally, publicly challenge the British army to face an inquiry, which will prove that they are telling lies about these deaths . . . Those of us who are urging moderation are doing so against an impossible background.'[32] Occurring on the day that Stormont rose for the summer recess, the only government response to the deaths came from Faulkner who gave support to the troops and blamed the cause of the trouble on 'evilly disposed persons.'[33] Eddie McAteer characteristically appealed to Dublin for help: 'protocol be damned, either directly or indirectly Dublin must take effective action in the protection of their Northern people.'[34]

On 11 July Hume conferred with three other SDLP MPs: Currie, O'Hanlon and Cooper (the latter having been in the city throughout the crisis). After the meeting in Hume's house the decision was taken to withdraw from Stormont if an inquiry was not held into the deaths. A Labour TD, Michael O'Leary, was also present and counselled the idea of an alternative assembly to retain the political initiative they hoped to gain by abstention. Paddy Devlin was contacted by phone and assented to the decision if the withdrawal issue could be broadened beyond the deaths in Londonderry. Fitt was at his holiday home in Cushendun, Co. Antrim, and could not be contacted.

At a press conference on 12 July the statement outlining the party's stance was released. It pointed out that they had continually urged restraint on their supporters and tried at all times 'to give responsible leadership'. But, it continued,

There comes a point where to continue to do so is to appear to condone the present system. That point, in our view, has now been reached. . . . The British government must face up to the clear consequences of their intervention of August 1969 and reveal their determination to produce a political solution which will be meaningful and acceptable to those present. Without such evidence we cannot continue to give our consent to a continuation of the present system. . . . If our demand is not met . . . we will withdraw immediately from parliament and will take the necessary steps to set up an alternative assembly of elected representatives to deal with the problems of the people we represent, and to become the authoritative voice to negotiate a political solution on their behalf . . .[35]

The statement was unambiguous in committing the party to abstention and the setting of their minimum demand as the abolition of the Stormont system. The growing tide of violence had swamped constitutional politics and made the tentative steps towards Catholic participation in government irrelevant. As Hume put it, 'there is no role we can usefully play within the present system.'[36]

Hume and his colleagues must have known that Westminster would not accede to an inquiry, least of all one seen to be granted under duress. Replying to a question from Bernadette Devlin in the Westminster House of Commons, the junior Defence Secretary, Lord Balniel, rejected the call for an inquiry into the deaths, but agreed that the army would co-operate in 'any proceedings that may be appropriate under civil law.'[37] Meanwhile, Fitt, who had not participated in the withdrawal decision and privately viewed it as ill-judged, met Maudling and members of the Labour Party in London. Maudling still refused to institute an inquiry but the idea of an immediate inquest with wider powers of investigation was discussed. Fitt hinted that this might avert the SDLP walk-out: 'whether or not the request for an inquiry is acceded too, it is of paramount importance that an inquest be held at the earliest possible moment . . .'[38] This possibility was also raised by Conor Cruise O'Brien, who discussed with Labour shadow ministers 'the possibility of a speeded-up inquest which would explore the circumstances in detail . . .'[39]

By this time it must have been patently clear to Fitt that his colleagues were intent on abstention and would not accept a compromise. He thus fell in line with the rest of the Stormont opposition (save Vivian Simpson) who had all affirmed their support for the SDLP stand. The Nationalists decided to abstain after a meeting in Armagh on 14 July, withholding any decision about participation in the proposed alternative assembly until they had been convinced of the merits of the idea. The Republican Labour Party went further by saying they would withdraw whether an inquiry was granted or not. The party's Stormont MP, Paddy Kennedy, suggested that abstentionist MPs be given seats in the Dáil, which, he claimed, would be more effective than the proposed 'Derry Parliament'.[40]

At a press conference on 16 July the SDLP formally confirmed their intention to withdraw. The reasons were substantially the same as those given earlier in the week, but the statement did appeal to Westminster to end their 'irresponsibility and negligence' with regard to the province and strive for a meaningful political solution. The abstentionist MPs would not resign their seats and would continue to draw their parliamentary salaries.

No detailed plans about the alternative assembly were given, the practical reason being that no thinking or planning had been devoted to the idea beyond the basic intention to set up 'a voice of anti-unionists'.[41]

In general, all anti-partitionist groups supported the withdrawal, while unionist bodies, from the NILP and the Alliance Party to the extreme loyalists, condemned it. The withdrawal did not however leave Stormont without a constitutional opposition: three Protestant Unionists crossed the floor of the House to join the single NILP member who remained. As Paisley put it, 'if the non-constitutionalists withdraw from Stormont, we would feel it our duty to see that there was a loyal opposition.'[42] But parliament was without the balancing influence of a non-unionist opposition (though not for the first time). Other periods of abstention had in the past originated with relatively trivial events, as this had done, but a comparison of Nationalist and SDLP abstention is deceptive, for the former were inherently abstentionist, the latter participatory.

In this context, the SDLP decision is of considerable interest. It was accepted that if internment were introduced then the opposition would withdraw *en masse*, but it was wholly unforeseen that the deaths of two civilians, however tragic and contentious, would provoke such a serious reaction. An equally disputed army killing, that of Daniel O'Hagan in Belfast in July 1970, had produced only a mild political response by comparison, so why were the Londonderry deaths different? One reason was that in July 1970 the security situation was generally calmer. Cusack and Beattie were shot after a period in which the SDLP had shown evident frustration with Stormont politics. Moreover, increasing pressure was being put on them to relieve, or at least to try and mitigate, the army activity in Catholic areas, which was growing in proportion to the IRA campaign. Thus, as the party statement of 16 July 1971 admitted, withdrawal was provoked by 'a whole series of issues and events of which the Derry deaths were but the culmination.'[43]

A second reason that made the deaths different was their impact on the Catholic community in the city. Both socially and geographically it is immensely more cohesive than that in Belfast. Perhaps more important, the city has always symbolised the Catholic sense of grievance; and in the small orbit of Londonderry politics, Hume was aware of the danger that constitutional politics could at any time be threatened by the IRA and was equally alive to the tactical fact that the IRA happened to be not particularly strong in the city just then. The possibility that the future leadership of the Catholic community could be lost by the SDLP was also considered in the Belfast context and was undoubtedly a major factor in the decision. The fact that not only the remainder of the SDLP but the rest of the anti-partitionist opposition publicly and privately supported the move (save Fitt and the three Nationalist Senators), illustrated the widespread Catholic frustration with Stormont. Indeed, Paddy Kennedy had advocated withdrawal since 1969. All followed Hume's lead and whatever misgivings they harboured were swept aside by the overriding need for Catholic solidarity.

Another question raised is how the SDLP's attitude to Stormont could have swung so dramatically in the three weeks from a very overt desire to seek reform within the system, shown by the response to Faulkner's committee proposals, to outright rejection of it. The answer to this lies partly in the growing radicalisation of the Catholic community and the fear that participation in Stormont would result in a loss of support. Fitt elaborated on this point in a BBC interview:

> The unnecessary killings in Derry are the end of a long road for the SDLP. We have tried since our formation to bring responsible influence into the political arena. We have co-operated at every level with the government at great political sacrifice to ourselves. People thought that we were half Unionists and that we had forgotten the people who voted for us . . . [44]

But essentially, withdrawal was the logical extension to the simple reaction to events. No attempt had been made to formulate an overall strategy or a comprehensive party policy to cope with the rapidly escalating situation. Events were making political action more difficult, but the duty of a political party lay in trying to lead and present a constructive alternative to all-out communal violence. This was not done; and the primacy of personality over policy led inescapably to the only dramatic gesture the SDLP MPs could muster to match a traumatic event.

CONCLUSION

The period from August 1970 to July 1971 is easily divided into three parts. The first consisted of the failure of the reform programme to capture the confidence of the Catholic community. Frustration and political indecision about the direction in which the SDLP was to go gave way to temporary optimism with the offer of opposition participation in the committee system. The second stage, the committee system, produced optimism, not because it appeared as an acceptable solution but because it seemed to show a change of heart on the Unionist side. At the very least, it provided a basis for discussion. But throughout this time organised violence on the Catholic side was growing and as pressures began to be exerted on the SDLP MPs, so their attitude to Stormont altered. The brittleness of June's optimism was shown by the Londonderry deaths, resulting ultimately in the third and final stage, abstention.

In June 1971 the SDLP had been a participatory political party; by July it was abstentionist. There were three immediate consequences of this.

Firstly and most obviously, the SDLP appeared to be in the same position as the Provisional IRA in that they demanded an immediate and unconditional end to the Stormont system of government. Whatever the party's protestations about non-violent intent, their rejection of Stormont could only aid physical force republicans and give their campaign respectability. The second consequence was that in terms of seeking a solution, Westminster and not Stormont had become the focus for SDLP action. Not once during the July crisis was Faulkner asked to do anything, make any concessions or enter any negotiations: the role of the Unionist government had been vicariously filled by the sovereign power. From July on, Stormont became an increasing irrelevancy, not just because anti-partitionists were absent from the opposition benches, but because Westminster had emerged as the centre of lobbying and attention. The impact of events was now gauged by Westminster's reaction to them.

A third consequence was a closer relationship between the Nationalists and the SDLP. With other groups they were now working in concert to set up the alternative assembly. On another level the idea of an alternative assembly implied that at least moral support would have to be sought from Dublin. The withdrawal of the whole opposition created problems for the Dublin government themselves, with the prospect of embarrassing encounters in carrying out their normal relations with the Stormont government. The denial by a constitutional party of the focal point for constitutional action, whatever its shortcomings, can only forebode ill for any society. But significantly, no mention had been made at any time throughout the crisis that opposition politicians would cease to talk to government and the channels for working out a compromise were still theoretically open, even if the will was noticeably absent. That was, until the introduction of internment without trial less than a month later.

8 Abstention (August 1971 to March 1972)

For a constitutional political party, parliamentary abstention is always an available option when normal procedures for bringing change fail to match expectations. The difficulties in making it a successful tactic are obvious, for the constitutional party becomes a revolutionary party in that what it seeks is nothing less than a change in the structure of the system on its own terms. As abstention by-passes the normal channels of debate and compromise, the two remaining alternatives both encompass the actual or threatened use of force. One means is that of the armed revolutionary force, using explicit violence to challenge the state on the party's behalf, the second a mass civil disobedience campaign orchestrated by the party or its supporters and deploying the implicit threat of violence. Neither is likely to be effective in isolation: co-ordination by a central body that will also disseminate propaganda is crucial.

In Ireland, North and South, abstention has a long history. It was used most successfully between 1919 and 1921 when the political representatives of the physical force movement in the South established Dáil Eireann, accorded it legitimacy and refused to recognise British institutions or law. This policy was twice ratified by the electorate, in 1918 and 1921. Any political party that does reject established channels of change but retains an ultimate commitment to constitutional procedures and electoral politics must, however, end abstention at some stage, whether or not its demands have been met. This chapter examines the period of SDLP abstention, from August 1971 to March 1972, and endeavours to evaluate the success of the tactic in Ulster and more generally, the conditions needed to promote and sustain it.

INTERNMENT AND ITS AFTERMATH

Faced with a threat to the existence of the state, a regime may either use conciliation by removing the grievance (or grievances) motivating its opponents or coerce them with any (or all) of the means at its disposal. Undoubtedly disappointed by the lack of response on the part of the Catholic community to the series of reforms conceded under pressure between 1969 and 1971, the Unionist government, faced in 1971 with the additional menace of an incipient IRA campaign, chose the latter path of coercion. Coercion involved both security measures designed to apprehend the subversives and judicial powers to ensure that they remained within the custody of the state. It may seem strange that the ultimate executive answer to subversion – internment and sweeping emergency powers of arrest, search and seizure – was adopted without a full appraisal of the other, less contentious, devices that make the securing of a conviction easier. But in reality the activation of the internment powers, embodied in the Special Powers Act, had become the traditional Unionist response to IRA activity, although it is significant that, with the possible exception of 1922, Catholic reaction to their implementation was notably apathetic. The markedly divergent responses of the Catholic community in 1938 or 1956 and 1971 are bound up with the reasons why the present circumstances differ fundamentally from those of past years.

In the first place, while sharing a common title and evoking similar emotions, the IRA of the 1970s was a different organisation in nature and outlook from its parent. In previous decades members were motivated by a deep, almost theological, republican conviction. Now activists were inspired more by the sectarian environment of post-1969 Ulster. Perhaps most important, the IRA was now an urban phenomenon, emanating directly from the working-class areas of Belfast and Londonderry. The corollary to this was that the organisation was now almost indistinguishable from its habitat, a situation that imposed severe limitations on the effectiveness of the security forces.

Secondly, the troubles had evolved in a novel manner. The 1930s and 1950s had witnessed IRA 'declarations of war' on the British 'occupation forces' in the province. Now the disturbances had stemmed from a respectable movement of largely middle-class Catholics seeking equal rights with their Protestant fellow-citizens. In the course of this they provoked a sectarian loyalist response, which in turn produced a counter 'defensive' force, the Provisional IRA. Catholics viewed the course of the post-1968 period as an attempt to attain reform, to achieve justice within the context of the prevailing constitutional and legal system. An assault by the government on the IRA would be taken as sidestepping the real issue and an implicit rejection of their demands for reform.

Thirdly, as the IRA was now an urban force, it had few direct links with the Republic, at least in the early stages. Successive Fianna Fáil governments had been as harsh as their Unionist counterparts in dealing with the IRA , and internment in Ulster had almost always been quickly followed by its imposition in the Republic. But this time the continuance of IRA violence did not appear contingent on aid from Southern sympathisers. When a pattern of active Southern support did emerge, general hostility towards the British army and the Unionist government made the activation of internment impossible for Jack Lynch's Fianna Fáil administration. On the one occasion Lynch threatened internment, on 4 December 1970, the almost universal condemnation must have left him in no doubt that its use in the Republic would be both counter-productive and politically dangerous.

It is not known at what stage the final decision to introduce internment in Ulster was made, but in the period immediately prior to 9 August Faulkner made a number of trips to London to confer with Heath and Maudling. Maudling himself denied that he was holding up its introduction and indicated that he 'would not shrink from introducing it if necessary.'[1] Faulkner had repeatedly asserted that its use was a security, as opposed to a political, decision, although the British army opposed it. On 23 July the security forces mounted dawn raids to gather intelligence for the impending round-up. This, coupled with widespread newspaper speculation and Faulkner's surreptitious trip to London on 5 August, convinced many (and all of those who mattered) that internment was imminent.[2]

The operation was carried out on the morning of 9 August, a day earlier than planned. The advance was necessitated by the disturbances that followed in the wake of the shooting of a Catholic driver whose van backfired while passing a Belfast army post. In all, 342 men were arrested from throughout the province, all but a handful Catholics. Worse, many were merely members of NICRA or fringe political groups such as the People's Democracy and in even a few cases, relatives were lifted in lieu of the wanted person; 116 of those arrested, or 34 per cent, were released within 48 hours.[3]

The reaction in Catholic areas was immediate, violent and strengthened by the very obvious fact that the military capacity of the IRA had been left unimpaired. To many Catholics internment appeared not as a carefully planned and executed military operation against the IRA, but a punitive expedition against their community. As the stories of ill-treatment began to filter back, Catholics closed ranks around the single issue of internment. The raw statistics of violence before and after internment have been frequently quoted, but they attest directly to its failure. In the six months preceding August there were 288 explosions; in the succeeding six months, this increased three-fold. In the same two periods, shooting incidents multiplied six-fold, security forces deaths four-fold and civilian deaths over eight-fold, respectively.[4]

Opposition politicians, particularly the SDLP, appeared to be impotent for they were already abstentionist and had declared their intention to set up an alternative assembly. But the circumstances dictated that they make a major gesture of defiance, but without seeming to condone IRA violence. Meeting in Dungannon, SDLP, Nationalist and Republican Labour MPs announced that they regarded internment 'as further proof of the total failure of the system of government in Northern Ireland' and condemned 'the British government's action in clearly taking a course of repression'. Their response was to have two distinct aspects:

> We call on all who hold public positions in Northern Ireland, whether elected or appointed, to express their opposition by immediately withdrawing from those positions and to announce their withdrawal publicly and without delay . . . We call on the general public to participate in this protest by immediately withholding all rent and rates. We expect one hundred per cent support from all opponents of internment . . .[5]

Catholic withdrawal from public life was adjudged a symbolic gesture, but the rent and rates strike was aimed at materially damaging the financial viability of the regime.

The call for Catholics to withdraw from public life was the logical extension to parliamentary abstention. Until internment, no SDLP thinking had been devoted to whether or not to involve local government representatives in their plans for an alternative assembly. This was compounded by the fact that at that time the SDLP had few local councillors in the party. However, at a meeting in Coalisland on 22 August, 130 councillors from 20 councils unanimously agreed to withdraw immediately from their elected positions.[6] In Londonderry, 30 prominent Catholics, including the vice-chairman of the Londonderry Development Commission, withdrew from their offices in protest against internment and the 'inhuman treatment' meted out to Hume and Cooper, who had been arrested during a sit-down demonstration the day before.[7] Withdrawals by Catholics impinged on other fields, notably the part-time Ulster Defence Regiment, where in all approximately 200 Catholics left the force.

While the attendant publicity surrounding the withdrawals magnified the impression of widespread dissatisfaction, it was by no means total. The legal profession, for example, has always contained a large proportion of Catholics and many retained their government posts. Sixty-six Belfast lawyers did however sign a petition protesting against internment 'and the circumstances and manner in which it has been carried out',[8] as did 425 priests, or 80 per cent of all priests in Northern Ireland, who condemned it as 'immoral and unjust'.[9]

The rent and rates strike was the second plank in the civil disobedience campaign. The mounting of a strike on a large scale combined many organisational problems and the omnipresent risk of intimidation. The strike was consistently and consciously over-represented in the impact it was thought to have in order to increase support. For example, at one point Paddy Devlin forecast that it could rob Stormont of £100 million within months.[10] By October, the NICRA was claiming that in excess of 40,000 households were participating.[11] Table 8.1 indicates the true extent of the

TABLE 8.1 The Extent of the Rent and Rates Strike

Date	Number of households on strike	Estimated percentage of Catholic council households[b]	Amount owed per quarter (£m.)	Cumulative debt (£m.)
1971 September	21,613	22.9	dna	dna
December	23,190	24.9	dna	dna
1972 March	22,404	23.7	dna	dna
May	21,413	22.7	1.5	dna
August[a]	21,229	22.5	dna	dna
November	19,936	21.1	dna	dna
1973 April	17,150	18.2	1.7	1.8
June	15,704	16.6	1.6	1.9
September	13,794	14.6	1.6	2.4
December	12,012	12.7	1.3	2.1
1974 March	10,953	11.6	1.3	2.2
June	6,108	6.5	1.0	2.9
September	5,343	5.7	0.9	3.3
December	5,051	5.3	0.9	3.4
1975 March	3,922	4.1	0.7	3.8
June	3,739	4.0	0.7	4.0
September	3,602	3.8	0.7	4.7
December	3,728	3.9	0.6	5.3

NOTES [a]Estimated figures.

[b]Based on the religious composition of council house tenant given in Richard Rose, *Governing Without Consensus* (London: Faber, 1971) Table IX. 5. The total number of such houses in 1971 was 167,000.

SOURCE Press Office, Northern Ireland Department of Housing, Local Government, and Planning.

strike. Although the numbers involved were substantial, at their highest they represented only about one quarter of all Catholic council households. Where figures are available, the debt incurred is hardly large by government standards. The real value of the strike lay, firstly, in the embarrassment it caused to Stormont, who were forced to ask Westminster to defray the debt; and, secondly, as a tangible expression of the virtual secession of many Catholics from the state. Its strength was the creation of a non-violent alternative to the IRA. In this it found the right level of opposition: it was not illegal but participants were brought into conflict with authority. Moreover, participation did not presuppose a party-political commitment and a striker could be apolitical and still play a part in opposing internment.

The problem with the civil disobedience campaign was that once in motion, the SDLP lost control of it. They were unable to exercise any influence on the numerous *ad hoc* local committees that sprang up to co-ordinate the strike. In many areas these committees attracted a pre-ponderance of republicans and the strike became a complement to violence rather than an alternative. And from this stemmed the problem of intimidation. Unionist ministers, for obvious reasons, characterised the strike as one large exercise in intimidation, and although only a small factor in the overall picture, it was nevertheless a constant theme. That the SDLP was aware of the problem but unable to deal with it was shown by their initial reluctance in lending support to the periodic one-day shut-downs that took place in towns all over the province.

The other problem was that some SDLP MPs urged people not to save their unpaid rent and rates. Plans had existed, drawn up by the NICRA and the Republican Labour Party, to collect and debit the money to a central fund for eventual payment, but these were never activated. MPs must have been aware that no government would wipe out such a debt even if a solution were found and internment ended. Not to warn people of this, particularly working-class Catholics, many on social security and who would be caused real hardship by repayments, was gross irresponsibility.

The government could do little to counter the wave of withdrawals from public life, other than replace them and make provision for the running of defunct local authorities. This it did in the Local Bodies (Emergency Powers) Act, which became law in October. The Act authorised the Governor, if convinced that a local authority had failed to 'exercise its functions duly and effectively', to 'authorise the Minister of Development to appoint a person to take over the functions of that authority.'[12] In fact four councils ceased to function: the urban district councils of Strabane, Newry, Keady and Warrenpoint were all suspended through non-attendance in the autumn and winter of 1971. The functions of the councils were transferred to a commissioner; but, rather than appointing a group of local people to act for the council, the unusual course was taken of appointing a senior civil servant to administer the duties of all four councils. The civil servant conferred with the local authority officials, who then sat with the powers of the full council.

To counter the rent and rates strike, the Payment for Debt (Emergency Provisions) Act was passed, granting retrospective powers (from 1 April 1971) to government departments, private landlords and even building societies to recoup debts from state benefits and wages. If, in the latter case, an employer refused to make the deduction, he himself became liable for his employee's debt. The Finance Ministry, which was to administer the scheme, was only required to accept a statement by a government department, public or local authority, that the amount specified was due. Undoubtedly the Act suffered from the haste in which it was drafted and indeed Professor Peter Townsend of the Child Poverty Action Group saw it as 'a candidate for the worst piece of social legislation passed in the United Kingdom this century.'[13] It is however difficult to imagine what other measures could have been introduced. Catholics, invariably, regarded it as purely punitive in design and intent. Opponents pointed to the steady rise in the cumulative debt (confirmed in Table 8.1) and the cost of administering the whole operation. The NICRA co-ordinator of the strike, Kevin Boyle, claimed that if a striker wished to restart payments, it took two weeks to stop the deductions during which time normal rent had to be paid.[14] Psychologically, the effect of the Act was clearly counter-productive and rather than break the strike or substantially reduce the debt, it only increased Catholic solidarity.

From any point of view internment was a disaster. In military terms it left the IRA's capacity untouched but with a wider base for support and recruitment from which to escalate their campaign. Politically, the Catholic community was more united and disaffected than at any time since 1921, with moderate Catholic elected leaders engaged in a campaign of civil disobedience. In a real sense, though both differed on means, they were united in seeking Stormont's abolition. To the Catholic community in 1971, a difference in means was a political luxury few could afford and even fewer heed; and in the collective psyche the two strategies merely augmented one another.

A survey conducted in 1973 and 1974 among Northern Ireland men demonstrated the polarity of views on internment and its effect on the Catholic community. Of the Protestant respondents, 19 per cent agreed that internment was a strong cause of the troubles, compared to 67 per cent of Catholics.[15] Similarly, only 3 per cent of Protestant respondents were recorded as having had a member of their family or a close friend interned, compared to 34 per cent of Catholics. Activity by the security forces was also more widespread in Catholic areas: for example, only 3 per cent of Protestant respondents had had their home searched by the security forces, compared to 24 per cent of Catholics.[16] Given both the cohesion of the Catholic community and the frequency of inter-familial relationships, internment and its aftermath thus had a vastly wider impact than the immediate family circle.

A further survey, this time carried out in 1972 and focusing on working-class Catholic political activists, found that only two of the 259 respondents interviewed failed to express an opinion on internment. Of the remainder, 'dissidence about the decision to use this power completely submerged divisions . . . economic differences, levels of education, attitudes about the desirability of the unification of Ireland, none of these mattered at all. Internment was seen as morally unjustified . . .'[17] When questioned about political disobedience, 80 per cent approved of parliamentary abstention, although most popular was the rent and rates strike: nine out of every ten interviewed supported it and 89 per cent of those who occupied council housing (or 41 per cent of the total sample) claimed to be a participant.[18]

THE ALTERNATIVE ASSEMBLY

Throughout August persistent violence and the internment issue clouded all political debate with a welter of recrimination. SDLP political activity concentrated on organising the civil disobedience campaign and publicising their case against internment in London and Dublin. After this initial period of confusion, thought began to be devoted to the alternative assembly, which, it may be recalled, had been posited as the opposition's answer to Stormont following their withdrawal in July. In the two weeks preceding 9 August scarcely even rudimentary planning had gone into the idea. Nationalist and SDLP MPs had met in Belfast on 29 July and 6 August but little agreement had been forthcoming other than on the principle that an assembly should indeed be set up.

Internment altered the status of the proposed assembly and gave it a much-needed fillip. With the daily withdrawals of prominent Catholics, it achieved a degree of relevance and immediacy impossible in previous circumstances. It was hoped that the new assembly could become the definitive political mouthpiece for Catholics and a focal point for co-ordinating the civil disobedience campaign. After two false starts, one caused by the refusal of the Londonderry Development Commission to let the city's Guildhall and the other by the refusal of the Ministry of Development to permit the letting of Strabane Town Hall, the Assembly held its inaugural meeting in the inauspicious surroundings of the Castle Ballroom, Dungiven, on 26 October 1971. The structure of the new body, given the pretentious and misleading title 'the Assembly of the Northern Irish People', had two main components.

The guiding body was the Executive Council, composed of the abstentionist Stormont MPs and Senators. The Council elected a President and a Chairman for two years, the latter appointment being subject to ratification by the full Assembly. John Hume and Senator J. G. Lennon were elected to these two positions, respectively. The second component was the Assembly itself, but as only the ex-officio members could be the Stormont-elected representatives, a crucial function for the Executive Council, acting as a Membership Committee, was to determine admissions. The Committee's function was to vet applications for membership from any 'organisation which feels that it is representative of a wide section of opinion'. In addition they were empowered to 'co-opt other members . . . having regard for the need to ensure that the Assembly is representative, both politically and geographically, of as wide a spectrum of non-Unionist opinion as possible.' Co-option was not direct, but by means of a convention. In constituencies without an abstentionist Stormont representative, a convention of local councillors was to be convened 'to appoint one of its number to represent the constituency in the new Assembly . . .'[19]

A major condition of membership, and one which sets the tenor of the whole body, was a written assent by each prospective member that he accepted the first three articles of the Assembly's Constitution. The articles were:

Article One: the Assembly of the Northern Irish People is the principal representative body of the non-Unionist community in Northern Ireland.

Article Two: pending the peaceful reunification of the country, the Assembly shall work towards the objective of obtaining equality of treatment for everyone in Northern Ireland, irrespective of political views or religion.

Article Three: the Assembly shall pursue this objective by non-violent means.[20]

These conditions were obviously intended to exclude militant fringe groups who might threaten the equanimity of the debates. This aim was also seen in the reliance on local elected representatives to form the bulk of the membership. The rigidity of these requirements was tempered slightly by Article Five (*b*) which stated that assent would not 'preclude a member from holding and advocating any political, economic or social policy that is not in conflict with Articles Two and Three.'[21]

Despite the elaborate detail embodied in the constitution and rules, no unequivocal statement of function was given. This was the crux of the problem, for the Assembly had no powers to exercise other than to debate motions proposed by the membership. It was merely, as a speaker at the first meeting affirmed, 'a forum for non-Unionist opinion', although it could, he warned, 'if the situation deteriorated, become an administrative Assembly.'[22] The Assembly's failure to make a significant impact was shown by the fact that it held only two plenary sessions. At the second meeting, on 4 December (and again held in Dungiven), a resolution was passed which floated the idea of the Assembly assuming responsibility for the administration of law and order in Catholic areas, 'until such time as a satisfactory political settlement of the current community problems is arrived at.'[23] How this policy was to be implemented was never elaborated, perhaps wisely, nor was Ivan Cooper's suggestion that the Assembly supervise the running of the public services.

Whatever parallels were consciously or unconsciously drawn between 1971 and the experience of Dáil Eireann between 1919 and 1921, the belief that the Assembly could at any time exercise power was never tenable. In the first instance, it possessed no coercive powers to enforce its decisions and as no positive decisions were ever taken, the anomaly between potential (or threatened) influence and real power was never tested. In so far as a commitment to non-violence was adhered to, it could never hope to exercise the powers of a state, nor, by implication, make a claim to be the legitimate government as the first Dáil had done. Secondly, widespread support for it was patently lacking. Two of the 17 opposition politicians, Dr Patrick McGill and Tom Gormley, refused to participate on the grounds that it was a meaningless exercise, while the participation of the remaining Nationalist MPs and Senators was contingent on Unionist policy necessitating that Catholics present a united front.

The division within Catholic ranks in this respect was also illustrated by the decision of the Provisional IRA's Army Council in August to encourage the establishment 'of a provisional parliament to exercise jurisdiction over the historic province of Ulster.'[24] The efforts to construct this Dáil Uladh (Parliament of Ulster) met with as conspicuous a failure as that of the Assembly of the Northern Irish People and gave the whole concept of creating bodies to cater for abstentionist minorities something of a farcical note. Neither Dáil Uladh nor the Assembly managed to mobilise any degree of support beyond their immediate political supporters.

Whatever long-term aim the Assembly was intended to fulfil, it was a moderately successful, though ephemeral, propaganda exercise. As such it played a part in the overall objective of the civil disobedience campaign, which was, in Hume's words, to 'demonstrate clearly that a large section of this community has withdrawn its consent from the system of government. No system of government can survive if a significant section of the population is determined that it will not be governed. . . .'[25] But even as a propaganda exercise it largely failed. It met only twice and was overshadowed by the more tangible successes of the rent and rates strike. What the Assembly did show was the extent of political polarisation in Ulster, for opposition politicians, meeting in a ballroom in a small rural town, were comparable in their myopia only with that of a Unionist government presiding over a parliament that boasted a three-member loyalist oppostion. The only conclusion to be drawn from this was that some system of government would have to be sought to accommodate both of these seemingly irreconcilable interests.

A SOLUTION WITHOUT DIALOGUE?

By December 1971 relations between the two communities in Northern Ireland were as polarised as they had ever been. The SDLP and Nationalist MPs were viewed by the Unionist government as being, in the words of Faulkner, 'under the thumb of the men of violence' and 'playing the IRA game by staying out of parliament.'[26] Whatever assertions were made about the common intent of the IRA and SDLP, it was evident that most Catholics were in accord with any tactics that sought to oppose the regime. The lack of dialogue between the two sides led to a political vacuum that was substantially filled by the war between the IRA and the British army. Violence and counter-violence spiralled, serving only to exacerbate communal divisions. Not surprisingly, the Stormont and Westminster governments interpreted Catholic support for the IRA as a consequence of intimidation and from this they concluded that the answer was a military, not a political, solution. But military action only brought the IRA fresh support and made constitutional politics, as propounded by the SDLP, an irrelevancy.

Grass-roots pressure on the SDLP forced them to delineate four basic conditions that would have to be met before they engaged in political dialogue. These were first enunciated by Austin Currie at an anti-internment rally in Keady, Co. Armagh, on 31 August 1971:

> Firstly, the SDLP is not prepared to enter into negotiations with anyone in government until the last detainee or internee has been released or has been charged with a specific offence. Secondly, when this necessary pre-requisite has been met we are prepared to negotiate on the basis of the suspension of Stormont; [thirdly] the appointment of a commission representative of the two main sections of opinion in the North as an interim measure; [fourthly] quadripartite talks embracing Westminster, in order to establish a long term solution to the Northern Ireland problem.[27]

After the original withdrawal in July, the main condition for their return was the abolition of Stormont. Now the added condition of 'no dialogue before the end of internment' – one which Westminster could not meet without undermining the Stormont government – had the effect of further encouraging Westminster to seek a military solution. Both Westminster and the IRA realised that the latter could not win the conflict, but, as in the 1919 to 1921 campaign, could try to make 'regular government impossible, and the cost of holding the country so great that the British would be compelled to withdraw.'[28] The strategy of the IRA, in the classic pattern of the urban guerrilla, was 'not to win battles, but to avoid defeat, not to end the war, but to prolong it, until political victory, more important than any battlefield victory, has been won.'[29]

The political thinking of the SDLP, formulated in the main by Hume, also invoked historical parallels. His argument maintained that the Unionist threat to Westminster since 1912 had been nothing less than a bluff and so long as this was left unchallenged a veto was placed on all efforts towards a permanent solution. 'There will be no permanent peace in Ireland', Hume declared, 'until that threat has been faced and its power broken and to do so is a lot less painful way of solving the Irish problem than the policies of the past or present.'[30] Although Hume's thesis appeared to be borne out by Protestant quiescence at the imposition of direct rule, the subsequent loyalist campaign of sectarian assassinations plus, ultimately, the Ulster Workers' Council strike, demonstrated its hollowness.

During this period the maintenance of internal unity among the SDLP MPs was a major problem. Two issues of dissension were paramount. Firstly, there was the question to what extent, if any, their conditions for dialogue should be relaxed to match a change in British policy. Gerry Fitt and Paddy Wilson, neither of whom fully endorsed abstention, made a two-minute return to Belfast Corporation in January to save their seats from becoming declared vacant through six months' consecutive absence. The rest of the party saw this as breaking the spirit of their withdrawal, and pointed to the fact that four councils had already been dissolved through non-attendance. Fitt's reply was that he had returned in order to save his safe ward from becoming Unionist, as had occurred when Paddy Kennedy's seat had fallen vacant the previous month.

The second issue concerned the party's relations with Dublin. The Taoiseach, Jack Lynch, had on a number of occasions publicly aired the opinion that the SDLP's terms were unrealistic. In the course of one press conference he had seemingly implied that the SDLP's refusal to talk with the British government gave him a mandate, by default, to negotiate on behalf of the Catholic minority. This was compounded by the suspicion, harboured by Paddy Devlin for one, that Lynch's regular consultations with them were merely attempts to display his hegemony over the Ulster opposition MPs. A more conciliatory faction led by Hume viewed it as misguided to antagonise Fianna Fáil politicians at a time when they needed all the moral support they could muster.

While the SDLP exhibited a facade of unity, the Unionist Party's unity was, if anything, more tenuous. Despite persistent rumours of defections by moderate Unionist MPs the party appeared unanimous in opposing the radical restructuring of Stormont. Throughout Faulkner defended internment, insisting on its success and scotching all suggestions that it would be phased out. A Green Paper was issued in October that substantially reiterated the committee proposals announced the previous June, but with explicit references to the enlargement of the House of Commons and Senate. At the executive level the paper rejected the inclusion in cabinet of anyone not from the majority party, except 'in times of grave national emergency' or when the Prime Minister himself decided to bring in 'an eminent figure who has not hitherto been engaged in active politics.'[31] Such a person would have to fulfil three conditions: firstly, to accept the constitutional position of the province; secondly, be dedicated to the preservation of democratic politics; and thirdly, be committed to constitutional politics.

The stringency of these conditions appeared to explicitly exclude Catholics, but not apparently to tax Faulkner's ingenuity, as he recruited Dr G. B. Newe to the post of Minister of State in the Prime Minister's Office and that of the first (and as it turned out last) Catholic ever to serve in a Stormont cabinet. Faulkner did not forgo the opportunity of making capital out of the appointment. Newe's brief, according to Faulkner, was nothing less than to tell him 'how best to establish and maintain contact with the various elements of the Catholic population . . . I am recognising the importance of letting it be clearly seen that the point of view of the religious minority in Northern Ireland is adequately taken into account by the government.'[32]

The poverty of ideas among the Unionists, aptly illustrated by the Green Paper and the gimmickry surrounding Newe's appointment, highlighted more than ever the need for a radical formula to break the political deadlock. As the first round of tripartite talks involving Lynch, Faulkner and Heath in August demonstrated, there could be no progress to a solution without the participation, and ultimately the acquiescence in an agreement, of the SDLP. The SDLP could point to the fact that if Westminster refused to make concessions on internment and hence bring them into talks, then, as Fitt commented, 'if we talked now we would be representing nobody.'[33]

By the end of the year it was evident that Westminster was at last considering plans to bring Catholics into government. Various groups had already posited the idea of community government. In September the NILP produced a plan for an 'inter-community government charged with the task of social reconstruction.'[34] The New Ulster Movement published a pamphlet by John Whyte in June which tentatively suggested that some form of power-sharing between political representatives of the communities should be considered 'at least as a long-term possibility.'[35] The SDLP were themselves thinking along similar lines. In the course of an *Irish Times* article, Hume said that Stormont was too elaborate a structure for the task in hand. 'The standards of a sub-ordinate regional council would be much more accurate and much more applicable', he asserted, 'and there is no reason whatsoever why it should not be administered by the community as a whole.'[36]

In his efforts to entice the SDLP into discussions, Maudling indicated the direction of Westminster thinking. In a Commons debate in September, he saw it as 'reasonable and desirable to see how it is possible to broaden the basis of government in Northern Ireland.' 'We must try,' he continued, 'to find agreed ways whereby there can be assured to the majority and minority communities alike an active, permanent and guaranteed part in the life of public affairs of Northern Ireland . . .'[37] Further evidence of rethinking was shown by Maudling's statement, made during a trip to Ulster in December, that he could foresee a situation in which the IRA would 'not be defeated, not completely eliminated, but have their violence reduced to an acceptable level.'[38] These two phrases, 'an active, permanent and guaranteed' role and 'an acceptable level of violence' became recurrent themes in the utterances of Westminster ministers. They indicated that the emphasis on a military solution was being replaced by a political one.

The activities of Harold Wilson proved an important stimulus in forcing the proposed political initiatives. Following Labour's reversion to the opposition benches, Wilson, and to a lesser extent Callaghan, had taken a close interest in the province. After a number of trips to both Dublin and Belfast, during one of which he met IRA representatives, Wilson announced his 15-point proposals for a solution, envisaging 'a united Ireland, to be reached by agreement . . . to come into effect 15 years from the date agreement is reached . . .'[39] Although illogical in some respects, the proposals represented a political success for the SDLP. A number of meetings had been held between the Northern Ireland, British and Irish Labour parties and the SDLP, and Wilson's adoption of Irish unity as an ultimate solution was indicative of the dominance of SDLP influence on the British Labour Party over the more cautious (and pro-union) attitude of the NILP.

Despite their intentions, the Westminster government was markedly slow in formulating its initiative. For one thing, Heath was embroiled in steering the Common Market legislation through parliament, for which the votes of the eight Ulster Unionist MPs who were regular attenders were on one occasion crucial. The other retarding factor surrounded the uncertain Protestant reaction. The catalyst that finally brought the initiatives to fruition was the killing of 13 civilians in Londonderry on 'Bloody Sunday', 30 January 1972. The action in shooting the marchers was in fact the logical extension of a military policy designed to extirpate the IRA, but when faced with this, and an adverse press abroad, Westminster backed away. An investigative commission was promptly set up under Lord Widgery, although it could be argued that his subsequent exculpation of the army further harmed British credibility.

While the IRA embarked on renewed violence, Catholic politicians intensified their withdrawal campaign. Many of the Catholics remaining in public service withdrew, particularly in the legal profession. As one barrister commented, 'many of us stayed on even after internment, but for nearly all of us Sunday in Derry is the end.'[40] The Community Relations Commission chairman, Maurice Hayes, resigned on 9 February in protest against the prevailing security policies. In Dublin the political response was more frenetic. A national day of mourning was called and a huge crowd burnt down the British embassy in Dublin. Lynch announced that his cabinet had decided 'to provide out of public money, finance through suitable channels for political and peaceful action by the minority in Northern Ireland, designed to obtain their freedom from Unionist misgovernment . . .'[41] Previously Lynch's support for SDLP had been only moral, and even then noticeably explicit about lending support only to 'passive resistance' and not 'civil disobedience'.[42] In the event little money reached its intended source, the alternative Assembly, and within three weeks the Assembly's Executive was appealing for money to mount 'a vigorous research and publicity campaign . . . to combat the propaganda launched nationally and internationally by both the Unionist and British governments.'[43]

With the EEC vote concluded, Heath took personal charge of constructing the long-awaited initiative. The key to a solution was still obviously the SDLP refusal to talk while internment lasted. Moreover, little contact had been made between the two sides and in essence, Heath had only the impression conveyed to him by Lynch that the party would enter into dialogue if responsibility for security were transferred from Stormont to Westminster and some public commitment given about the phasing out of internment.

As it turned out, security proved to be the central proposal in Heath's initiative, put to Faulkner and his deputy, J. L. O. Andrews, in London on 22 March. Two of the proposals referred to the introduction of a periodic plebiscite on the border and the phasing out of internment. Faulkner agreed to these in principle, but he and his cabinet unanimously refused to accept the security transfer, 'an indispensable condition for progress' as Heath called it.[44] This, Faulkner maintained, 'would leave the government of Northern Ireland bereft of any real influence and authority by removing the most fundamental power of any government. I said clearly we were not interested in maintaining a mere sham or a face-saving charade.'[45] With the resignation of the Ulster cabinet, Heath was left with 'no alternative to assuming full and direct responsibility for the administration of Northern Ireland . . . the parliament . . . will stand prorogued but will not be dissolved.'[46]

The radical nature of the move was without doubt. Given that Heath's interpretation of 'security powers' included not only the police, but the criminal law and its procedure, public order, prisons, borstals, the probation service, and the creation of new penal offences, it is reasonable to suppose that he was counting on Faulkner to refuse, since no self-respecting government could have surrendered such a wide range of essential functions. Thus the move was a ploy to force resignation on the Unionists and make direct rule appear their responsibility and not his own. With the divergence of opinion between the two Ulster communities over the future of Stormont, Heath was worried about a violent Protestant reaction. A poll published just four days before clarified the extent of the division. Of those interviewed, 90 per cent of Catholics and 48 per cent of Protestants said they agreed that security should be transferred in order to get peace talks underway. Seventy five per cent of Catholics, but only 25 per cent of Protestants, said they would accept a new kind of government involving the abolition of Stormont and the imposition of direct rule.[47]

The response in the province was relatively peaceful, despite Faulkner's claim that many would 'draw a sinister and depressing message from these events – that violence can pay and that violence does pay.'[48] Loyalist reaction was confined to a two-day strike, and a mass rally at Stormont.

Both wings of the IRA unconditionally rejected the moves. In spite of attempts by Paddy Devlin and Ivan Cooper to secure a cessation of Provisional hostilities by meeting their chief of staff, Sean MacStiofain, in Dublin, MacStiofain saw 'only one attitude to the British government's proposals . . . concessions be damned, we want freedom.'[49]

The SDLP welcomed the initiative and called on the IRA to cease their campaign so as to enable progress towards a political solution to be made. They considered the proposals

> The first serious step on the road to peace . . . we welcome them and will give our fullest co-operation in their implementation. . . . We have given a public commitment on the question of internment. We fully intend to deliver that commitment for we consider it neither right nor proper that any citizen held without trial should be a hostage to political bargaining. We therefore ask those engaged in the campaign of violence to cease immediately in order to enable us to bring internment to a speedy end, and in order to make a positive response to the British government's proposals.[50]

The party was obviously hoping that the new Secretary of State for Northern Ireland, William Whitelaw, would rapidly end internment and enable them to enter negotiations. The statement was notable for its recognition that, by virtue of their military campaign, the Provisional IRA had, as Conor Cruise O'Brien noted, 'acquired a veto over all meaningful political initiative and dialogue in Northern Ireland.'[51] In the period of debate and compromise leading up to the Assembly elections in June 1973, this factor was of central and continuing concern to the SDLP.

CONCLUSION

The period of abstention that began in July 1971 spanned the introduction of internment, the killings in Londonderry on 30 January 1972 and the introduction of direct rule in March 1972. Direct rule, in fact, marked the lateral extreme of SDLP abstention and thereafter ways were sought to bring it to a speedy conclusion. Throughout the period the SDLP opposed the regime by civil disobedience in an attempt to provide an alternative to the violent opposition of the Provisional IRA. From an analytic perspective, however, as both shared a common aim – the end of Stormont – they acted in a parallel yet complementary manner. Moreover, in the virtual war situation that prevailed, the group least likely to distinguish between the two means was the Catholic community. The introduction of direct rule brought a practical end to this harmony of aims.

In hastening the fall of Stormont, IRA violence rather than SDLP civil disobedience had the greater impact. While civil disobedience proved ineffective in making the governmental machine unworkable, violence severely disrupted the province's economic life, although not to the extent where it threatened its very existence. In the event, the disturbances influenced Westminster's thinking on Ulster and in the final outcome it was the sovereign power and not the IRA that precipitated Stormont's demise. Westminster's attempts to find a solution were undoubtedly retarded by the SDLP's refusal to talk until internment ended, but this did ensure that the solution, when it came, was more radical than it otherwise might have been. Another consequence was the continuance of a military policy until an alternative political plan could be formulated. This led to tragedies like 'Bloody Sunday' and the strengthening of loyalist and republican paramilitary bodies.

The SDLP refusal to talk increased their importance in the evolving political situation. The IRA had created the need for a political group representative of the Catholic community to negotiate with Westminster on their behalf and the SDLP, without having fought a general election, emerged to fulfil this role. The truculent attitude towards talks enhanced their potential importance to the British government and effectively eclipsed the IRA's formal political expression, Sinn Féin, who were ready to negotiate but not recognised by either Westminster or the Catholic community as a sufficiently responsible or representative authority.

The *de facto* position of the IRA as the community's military force and the SDLP as its political mouthpiece underlines three conditions necessary for a successful abstentionist policy. Firstly, there must be grave dissatisfaction with normal parliamentary methods, coupled with, secondly, a simple and attainable goal uniting the people. Thirdly, as abstention implies the construction of an alternative system of government, 'the abstentionist party must have the means to defend this from the existing system naturally seeking to destroy their new rival.'[52] Although parliamentary methods were undoubtedly discredited, the people were not united around a single goal since the nature of the Ulster conflict is that it is a society at war with itself, not with an external enemy. Again, without control of the IRA, the SDLP were unable to exercise coercive powers that would have transformed their alternative system into an embryonic state.

The SDLP's experience in abstention made it the sole political representative of the Catholic community. After March 1972, efforts became directed at developing this role by detaching itself from the more militant groups with which it had been in formal alliance, and on releasing itself from the pledge not to negotiate while internment remained.

9 Office-Seeking (April 1972–June 1973)

The degree of political allegiance shown to a regime is never constant, and the political environment at any one time helps to determine its extent and depth. Shortly before the advent of the disturbances in 1969, about one-third of Ulster's Catholic community were recorded as withholding consent from the province's constitution, although the overwhelming majority were prepared to comply with its basic political laws.[1] Up until mid-1973 the disturbances emphasised the regime's lack of consent, but in addition exposed the small number of Catholics willing to pursue violent non-compliance and the larger number ready to endorse non-violent protest. In 1971 and 1972 the SDLP's policy of parliamentary abstention gave expression to this lack of consent, but it also prevented them from fulfilling their self-defined role of negotiating on behalf of the Catholic community. The inability to carry out this function, plus the activities of Catholic paramilitary groups, served to eclipse the SDLP and emphasise their impotence while existing policies and institutions remained unaltered.

With the end of the Stormont system of government and the introduction of direct rule the circumstances for re-entering political negotiation became more favourable, despite the party's pledge not to talk while internment persisted. This pledge had, while it was honoured, left the Provisional IRA with the power to determine whether or not negotiations took place, as the continuance of internment was contingent on the level of Provisional violence. SDLP participation in a solution was central to the series of consultations proposed by Westminster and it was also of prime importance for the party themselves in order to consolidate their leadership role within the Catholic community. This chapter focuses on the period between April 1972 and June 1973 when the SDLP were attempting to extricate themselves from the abstentionist policy and seeking to act as the natural office-holders in the new form of community government being devised by Westminster.

THE RETREAT FROM ABSTENTION

Following the imposition of direct rule and the appointment of the Leader of the House of Commons, William Whitelaw, as Secretary of State for Northern Ireland, the various political groups in the province began to readjust their positions. As the Unionist Party began to show a greater toleration for their erstwhile loyalist critics the SDLP began to edge towards a position where they could, with good grace, withdraw support from civil disobedience and relinquish their abstentionist policy. Contrary to many fears, direct rule did not signal the immediate beginning of the long-awaited Protestant backlash. The dilemma was that Protestants had not decided when they would fight and against whom; and the fall of Stormont did not resolve this, although it did see the birth of two significant developments. Firstly, there was a two-day strike, which would have been desultory but for the participation of the largely loyalist power workers, who drastically cut industry's supply of electricity. Secondly, the strike was enforced in Protestant areas by the Ulster Defence Association, a paramilitary body which increased in numbers and influence throughout 1971, to become the most dramatic expression of Protestant frustration and militancy.

The Unionist Party refused to co-operate with the new Whitelaw regime, although Faulkner's government did agree to remain in power for a few days after 23 March in order to facilitate a smooth administrative transition. The incisive effect of the boycott was lost by the continuing allegiance of the Northern Ireland Civil Service (which it had been feared might also withdraw co-operation) and by the formation of the Advisory Commission. The Advisory Commission was composed of 'persons resident in Northern Ireland' appointed by the Secretary of State 'to advise and assist him in the discharge of his duties'.[2] In the event, no mainstream unionists were appointed and thus the embarrassment of a refusal to serve never arose. In essence Protestant reaction to the new situation was negative; they were numbed, confused and largely leaderless. Faulkner's support, tenuous at the best of times, had now evaporated: he, as much as Whitelaw, was the object of Protestant anger. In addition, the newly-formed Vanguard Party was unable to lend cohesion to the disparate threads of unionism by adequately articulating a constructive response to direct rule.

Considered Catholic reaction to direct rule was harder to define. SDLP MPs were privately enthusiastic and expected to see the simultaneous end of internment and the IRA campaign. All the groups were now equal and merely individual competitors for the ear of the Secretary of State. A political conflict that had been concerned with power was now one of arguments. In such a situation, the SDLP reasoned, the possibilities for radical changes in the structure of the province's political institutions were almost limitless. More than the Unionists, the SDLP accurately perceived the shift in the locus of power with the departure of Stormont. Whitelaw himself was now the focal point for politics and his emollient approach appeared to favour them. His overall strategy was to play off the extremes against one another while attempting to halt the violence, a subsidiary effect of which would be to split the Unionist Party (or hasten the split within it) and hence, he hoped, to strengthen the centre. The political centre, as defined by Whitelaw, encompassed the SDLP, NILP, the Alliance Party and the liberal wing of the Unionist Party. These were the groups with whom he sought to build a political *modus operandi*.

The rundown of internment resulted in the release of 703 men between the beginning of April and mid-August, leaving 243 still held without trial. The prison-ship *Maidstone* was closed and the rules for internees' parole relaxed. In April the unenforceable ban on parades was lifted and over 300 people convicted of breaking it since Christmas (including the six SDLP MPs) were granted an amnesty. In general, Whitelaw's new approach was welcomed by Catholics and opposed by Protestants. A June opinion poll found that 73 per cent of Catholics, but only 21 per cent of Protestants, thought that he was doing a good job.[3]

The SDLP began to gradually institute steps to end abstention. At the end of May they announced that it was time for them to make a positive response 'as a gesture of our confidence that meaningful political progress is now possible'. 'Accordingly', their statement continued, 'we now call on all those who have withdrawn from public life to return to their positions, whether elected or appointed, in local government or statutory bodies. We ask them to give their fullest co-operation to the Whitelaw administration. . . . Every major step forward taken will be matched by a positive response from us.'[4] Early next month another apparent step towards normalisation was the agreement to meet Stormont civil servants to discuss ways of obviating the likely hardship to be caused by the ending of civil disobedience. This latter step was merely symbolic, as SDLP MPs had been in close contact with civil servants throughout the months preceding direct rule.

The SDLP's central problem was still IRA violence, for so long as it lasted internment would continue and the party bound by the pledge not to talk. To renege on this commitment would lose them support and respect throughout the Catholic community. Within the Catholic areas witnessing the bulk of the violence – Londonderry and West Belfast – there was a nascent groundswell of feeling against the IRA campaign. The failure of the IRA to respond to this led to the rise of the 'peace movement', assiduously cultivated by both Whitelaw and the SDLP. As an SDLP MP asked rhetorically, 'what possible justification can there be for any future loss of life when we can achieve the objectives that the people desire by peaceful means?'[5] What neither Whitelaw nor the SDLP took into account was the political myopia of the Provisional leaders and their inability to translate military capacity into political advantage.

In May the Official IRA, the intractable opponents of the Provisionals, called a ceasefire after the inopportune killing of a young Bogsider who was a British soldier. In recognising that 'the overwhelming desire of the great majority of all the people . . . is for an end to military actions by all sides,'[6] the Official's apparent concession effectively headed off criticism. Against this background of increasingly strident demands for a cessation of violence, the Provisionals called a press conference in Londonderry on 13 June, at which MacStiofain reiterated their peace demands—Irish self-determination, a withdrawal of British troops and a general political amnesty—and invited Whitelaw to meet him to discuss these points. If he agreed to a meeting, a seven-day ceasefire would ensue, providing that there was a corresponding de-escalation in British army activity. Not unexpectedly, Whitelaw refused the offer within hours.

A meeting of the SDLP parliamentary party in Dungiven the next day, chaired by Hume, concluded that the IRA peace plan was 'a sincere attempt to produce an atmosphere for a peaceful settlement . . . and . . . evidence of their willingness to engage in peaceful political activity.'[7] Most important, MacStiofain's offer excluded any reference to the ending of internment before talks could commence, and the SDLP seized on this vital omission to temporarily suspend their own pledge. On this basis, Hume and Devlin met Whitelaw on 15 June to discuss the possibility of a bilateral truce. In the course of the following week, the two MPs became engaged in a direct mediating role between the government and the IRA, rather than the 'public dialogue and public appeal' claimed by Devlin.

After a second meeting between Whitelaw and the two MPs, 'special category' or political status was granted to republican and loyalist prisoners, some on hunger strike, as a gesture of good faith demanded by the IRA. On 22 June the IRA announced the beginning of a ceasefire from midnight on the 26th, 'provided that a public reciprocal response is forthcoming from the armed forces of the British Crown.'[8] In the House of Commons Whitelaw averred that 'if offensive operations by the IRA in Northern Ireland cease on Monday night Her Majesty's Forces will obviously reciprocate.'[9] In the event the ceasefire lasted only until 9 July, breaking down over the proposed re-housing of 16 Catholic families in West Belfast. Two days previously Whitelaw had met six IRA leaders in a private house in London. The muted SDLP response to the news of the meeting, which implicitly devalued their own status as elected representatives, indicated that they were, as intermediaries, probably privy to the terms of the negotiations. The ceasefire defied all attempts to resurrect it, including a meeting between a number of IRA leaders and Harold Wilson in London on 18 July, conducted, it is alleged, with the full knowledge of both Heath and Whitelaw. Whitelaw was unable to again risk his credibility by directly entering into the discussions and in any event, the IRA were by now intensely suspicious of him.

The instrumental SDLP role in the ceasefire preliminaries enhanced their standing in Catholic eyes. Their ability to successfully negotiate, hitherto untested, had been publicly demonstrated and validated. The IRA had now thrown away what was unarguably their strongest position since 1921 and their political acumen, always suspect, had been shown to be non-existent. They had negotiated with the British government while internment continued and thus freed the SDLP to emulate them. In essence, they had proved themselves incapable of adapting to, or exploiting, the new political realities and left the onus with the SDLP to fulfil this role. The implicit harmony of aims that had reigned between the SDLP and the IRA during the post-internment and pre-direct rule period now gave way to direct competition for Catholic support.

Just twelve days after the collapse of the ceasefire, on 21 July, the IRA launched their largest attack on property to date. Within the space of one-and-a-half hours, 22 bombs exploded in and around Belfast city centre, killing eleven people. As 'Bloody Sunday' had been the logical extension to the then prevailing military policy of the government, so 'Bloody Friday,' as it became known, was the logical extension of the Provisional's terrorist activities. The key factor enabling the IRA to mount such a highly planned and co-ordinated attack was the continuing existence of the 'no-go' areas within which the security forces rarely, if ever, encroached. These working-class areas of Belfast and Londonderry had been difficult for the security forces to operate in since 1969, but following the intense hostility shown to them after internment their incursions eventually ceased. As a consequence, these areas, having an inclination for independence even in peaceful times, became virtually self-governing: resources were allocated by local community organisations, elections were held and the all-important (and symbolic) function of maintaining order became the prerogative of the IRA. In these areas the IRA operated openly and without hindrance, planning and organising their campaign against the commercial centres of Londonderry and Belfast.

Whitelaw's policy for subduing the no-go areas was to gradually de-escalate the activities of the British army and hope that the improved climate of local opinion, reflected in the peace movement and the SDLP, would force the IRA to respond. He repeatedly and explicitly ruled out the use of force. 'Bloody Friday', plus threats from the rapidly growing UDA to institute their own no-go areas if action was not taken, forced a reversion of this policy. On the morning of 31 July, British troops occupied the former no-go areas without the massive loss of life frequently predicted. The clinical nature of the operation, accompanied by a still lingering Catholic revulsion against the IRA after 'Bloody Friday', guaranteed little adverse SDLP, or even general Catholic, response.

In fact 'Operation Motorman', as it was code-named, failed to have the detrimental social and political impact of internment and did not result in the recrudescence of by now waning Catholic support for the IRA.[10] The SDLP thus appeared to be in a stronger position *vis-à-vis* the Catholic community and the British government. Overt IRA influence, whether voluntary or through intimidation, had been reduced and they were now forced into the clandestine mobilisation of support, thus giving the SDLP a definite advantage. 'Motorman' was not a reversal of the British government's long-term policy of finding a political solution, and the SDLP hoped that Protestant jubilation would supply a *quid pro quo* for the swift ending of internment. This perpetually anticipated event would free the party to enter the political negotiations that Whitelaw maintained to be the essential prerequisite for a solution.

THE DARLINGTON CONFERENCE

In the wake of Operation Motorman, the demand for political talks to end the crisis increased. Having broken their self-imposed pledge of not talking while internment lasted, the SDLP were put in a quandary: should they follow this precedent by maintaining contact with Whitelaw or respond to 'Motorman' by renewing their pledge and risk the initiative again falling to the IRA? The attitude of the Dublin government was unequivocal. Lynch recognised that IRA activities had made 'Motorman' inevitable and significantly no formal protest about it was lodged at Westminster. Dublin's policy towards Northern Ireland now concentrated on persuading the SDLP to enter negotiations and resulted in a dramatic move. On 1 August a helicopter was dispatched to Lifford, Co. Donegal, to carry Hume, Cooper and Devlin to Dublin to confer with two government ministers, Patrick Hillery and George Colley, both of whom asserted after the talks that 'no opportunity must now be let pass to achieve political progress. . . . talks must be held quickly between the interested parties.'[11] That Austin Currie was able to attend the meeting after travelling to Dublin by car indicated the influence the government was exercising in order to propel the SDLP into talks.

Whatever influence was exerted on the SDLP, the party condemned 'Motorman' but decided to commence negotiation. Meetings were held with the Secretary of State on 7 and 8 August, without any of the preconditions that so exasperated Whitelaw having been granted. Six of the seven hours of talks were taken up with internment, the party demanding a firm date for its ending and arguing that with Protestant satisfaction at the ending of the no-go areas, the time was ripe to abolish it without risking Protestant wrath. Moreover, with the security forces in all areas, they contended that the ex-internees would have little opportunity or incentive to return to violence. The general SDLP strategy envisaged 'gestures' being made to each side and a 'systematic de-escalation' until political talks could be held in a harmonious atmosphere.[12]

Whitelaw had already announced his intention to hold a conference of the province's political parties 'to see what common ground can be found in the working out of a solution.[13] The conference would enable the parties

To put forward their proposals for the future government of Northern

Ireland and to report thereon to Her Majesty's Government . . . it will not be the object of the conference to reach decisions. It is the Government's intention, when we have heard the views of the delegates to the conference, to draft firm proposals for the future.[14]

Both the Repulican Labour and Nationalist parties quickly declared their non-attendance, but the SDLP were placed in a more subtle dilemma: their obvious penchant was to talk and confirm their role as the political voice of Catholic opinion, but to do so in such a manner would place their constituency support at risk. Some magnanimous gesture was sought from Westminster, but after a meeting with Heath on 12 August no concessions were forthcoming, save the introduction of a tribunal system to review internees' cases.

The SDLP considered the new system of detention unacceptable. Paddy Devlin referred to it as a 'non-runner . . . a blatant ruse'[15] and the tribunals were in fact not properly constituted courts but merely a review procedure that shifted the onus for the decision to detain from the executive to a quasi-judicial body. Much to the chagrin of Heath and Whitelaw, the SDLP did not attend the conference and broadened the justification for their action by arguing that participation would imply an acceptance of the principle of a purely Ulster solution. The imminence of the conference, accompanied by the uncertainty surrounding their attendance, did provide the necessary stimulus for the party to produce a plan for the political future of the province. Apart from some inchoate declarations of intent at their inaugural press conference in August 1970, the party as a whole had hitherto failed to present a constructive, detailed plan for the future. Published as a pamphlet entitled *Towards a New Ireland*, the plan filled this vacuum.

Towards a New Ireland advocated a British declaration of intent to withdraw from Northern Ireland, and in the interim period prior to Irish reunification a provincial government representative of both communities. A 'National Senate', composed of elected representatives from both parts of Ireland, would facilitate unity by 'harmonising' the institutional structure of their respective countries. Finally, until Irish unity came to fruition, the province would be a condominium, with the British and Irish governments jointly responsible for political sovereignty.[16]

The conference was formally convened at Darlington between 25 and 27 September 1972. Only three of the seven parties entitled to attend participated. Besides the SDLP, Nationalist and Republican Labour parties, the Democratic Unionist Party abstained in the absence of a judicial inquiry to investigate the deaths of two civilians shot by the army. The three parties who did participate—the Unionist and Alliance parties and the NILP—made little progress, with all refusing to compromise on their pre-conference policy documents. From this perspective the Darlington conference was a failure, in so far as it 'did no more than define the area of disagreement'[17] between the contending parties. But the exercise was not totally unproductive. Although inevitably attenuated by the absence of four of the seven invited parties, it did extract from all (except the Nationalist and Republican Labour parties) a vision of the province's political future. In the case of the SDLP this was something that had not been done and would not have been done but for this catalyst. As the only anti-partitionist party to submit a plan, and one acknowledged to be ingenious if impractical, the SDLP were, in the absence of electoral verification, affirmed as the authoritative representative of Catholic opinion in Ulster.

A later outcome of the conference was the publication in October of a Green Paper, *The Future of Northern Ireland*. Westminster's post-war relations with Ulster had been governed by Attlee's commitment, enunciated on 28 October 1948, that there would be 'no change . . . in the constitutional status of Northern Ireland without Northern Ireland's free agreement.'[18] Heath renewed the pledge through the periodic border plebiscites and the Green Paper used this to refute the condominium plan. 'If adopted without consent', the paper commented, it would be incompatible 'with the express wording of . . . the Ireland Act 1949.'[19] In delineating a number of broad principles around which an ultimate solution would have to mould itself, the Green Paper further maintained that, although the union would only be terminated by consent, 'insistence upon membership of the United Kingdom carries with it the obligations of membership including acceptance of the sovereignty of parliament as representing the people as a whole.'[20] Coupled with this statement was the elucidation of what the paper termed 'the Irish dimension' or the recognition that 'whatever arrangements are made for the future adminis-tration of Northern Ireland must take account of the province's re-lationship with the Republic of Ireland.' The aim of the Irish dimension was to promote co-operation in the fields of the economy and security and also, within the commitment given on the province's status, to allow the possibility of 'subsequent change in that status'.[21]

In another crucial section of the paper the government outlined the essential prerequisites for a regional administration. The structure would have to be

> capable of involving all its members constructively in ways which satisfy them and those they represent that the whole community has a part to play in the government of the province. . . . Real participation should be achieved by giving minority interests a share in the exercise of executive power. . . .[22]

Although the essence of the SDLP's condominium proposals had been rejected, the objective of executive level power-sharing had been accepted. Westminster's view of the Irish dimension also implied a close identification with the SDLP plan as both envisaged a consultative and advisory body to facilitate cross-border co-operation which could, if circumstances arose, be an embryonic all-Ireland parliament.

The Darlington conference and the Green Paper represented a not inconsiderable political success for the SDLP. They had maintained their policy of not talking while internment lasted, but managed to deliver their plan to the conference *in absentia*. September and October had witnessed a plethora of plans, pamphlets and policy documents, many of doubtful practicality, from a wide variety of political groups and organisations. A survey conducted in late January 1973 indicated what potential support existed in the province for some of these. Of the total sample, only 23 per cent of Catholics and 3 per cent of Protestants expressed themselves in favour of a condominium solution. On the total integration of Ulster with the United Kingdom, 7 per cent of Catholics and 20 per cent of Protestants said they supported the idea, while only 1 per cent and 2 per cent, respectively, favoured the concept of an independent Ulster. The emphatic endorsements were reserved for the solutions more rooted in history (and indicated how little direct rule had changed basic attitudes): 39 per cent of Catholics supported Irish unity and 41 per cent of Protestants the full restoration of the old Stormont system.[23]

The energetic round of talks between Whitelaw and the Ulster political groups caused many local politicians and observers to lose their perspective. Many, including the SDLP, tabled their plans not as bases for discussion, but in the manner of non-negotiable political demands. But while Westminster was going through the motions of seeking their views, the prescribed form of government would ultimately be decided by the British government. And this solution, when it came, would not be a matter for debate and compromise; it would be imposed on the province.

THE WHITE PAPER AND THE ASSEMBLY ELECTIONS

The absence of the SDLP from the Darlington conference did not seriously harm their bargaining position, but, if anything, enabled them to exert more influence than if they had participated. This fortuitous outcome would not necessarily be repeated at any future conference. Such talks would be charged with detailed discussions and only an SDLP presence could ensure an adequate and lucid presentation of their case. At the party's second annual conference in November 1972 a motion was passed by a large majority urging that 'the parliamentary party enter into immediate discussions with the British Secretary of State and all interested political parties.'[24] The motion formally marking the end of the refusal to talk was proposed by Cooper and seconded by Hume, the latter declaring that 'the time has come for us to come out and say frankly that we are prepared to talk to anyone and talk now.'[25]

Armed with this mandate, the two MPs met William Craig and John

Taylor in Taylor's Co. Armagh home in December. The purpose of the meeting was to discuss the idea of an independent Ulster state, which the two loyalists were in the process of canvassing among their supporters. This reflected a developing feeling within the SDLP that it was likely to prove impossible to find an acceptable solution that would incorporate some form of association with the Republic. On the other hand, the two radical solutions, independence and condominium, might prove compatible by creating an autonomous state capable of accommodating the dual allegiances of its citizens. After Craig delivered a speech in February unequivocally advocating independence if loyalist objectives could not be extracted from Westminster, the SDLP made a public overture to the Ulster Loyalist Council, of which Craig was the titular head. The invitation met with a refusal, on the grounds that the only place to negotiate was the Northern Ireland parliament. But this decision failed to prevent Craig and Taylor meeting Devlin and Cooper in early March, shortly after the SDLP had taken a full-page advertisement in the Protestant *Belfast News-Letter* to publicise their concept of a condominium.[26]

By all accounts little agreement was found between the two sides. The talks worked to the political advantage of the SDLP, who were seen to be pursuing the stated objective of political negotiations with all shades of opinion. What political risks existed were run by Craig and Taylor, who participated in the face of clearly expressed Protestant disapproval. The talks fizzled out because of the divergence of attitudes between the two sides in relation to the White Paper, published in March; and the intransigence of the loyalists forced the SDLP to seek a common basis for agreement with the Alliance Party and the Faulknerite Unionists, both supporters of the Paper's proposals. The loyalist-SDLP détente, though short-lived and unproductive, was however redolent of the more dramatic reconciliation between Craig and the SDLP in the latter stages of the 1975 constitutional Convention.

In the wake of the speculation about the independence solution came the border poll, the device originally promised by Heath in March 1972 'in the hope of taking the border out of day-to-day politics . . .'[27] All the anti-partitionist parties condemned the exercise as divisive and unnecessary. Both the Nationalists and Republican Labour called for a boycott, the gravamen of their case resting on the fact that it was to be held only 'upon the six sundered counties . . .the national issue is not to be decided by any section of the Irish people.'[28] The SDLP reinforced these criticisms, seeing it as 'a futile exercise with a result that can be readily forecast'.[29] They had initially agitated for the publication of the White Paper before the poll, in order to let the Protestant electorate see the political price of continuing the union and to enable the asking of questions 'meaningful in the present context'. This course of action was supported at Westminster by Merlyn Rees, the shadow Northern Ireland Secretary, who put at risk the bipartisan policy of the Westminster parties by referring to the poll as 'foolish' and the outcome predetermined.[30]

The result of the poll was that 98.9 per cent of those that voted, or 57.4 per cent of the electorate, supported the union with Britain and the exercise therefore served its purpose of giving 'an added assurance to the Protestant community'.[31] The call for anti-partitionists to ignore the poll appeared to have been generally heeded. The effects of the campaign were not as divisive as had been predicted, especially when it is recalled that virtually every election in the province since 1921 has been concerned with the border. With a majority in favour of the constitutional *status quo*, the British government was now free to proceed to the next step in their policy, the refining of the Green Paper's broad principles into a workable system of government.

Twelve days after the border poll the White Paper, *Northern Ireland Constitutional Proposals*, was published, laying out the government's plans for the future administration of the province.[32] The paper's central proposals outlined a unicameral assembly of 80 members elected by the single transferable vote method of proportional representation from the twelve Westminster constituencies. This assembly would determine its own regulations, but form itself into a committee system 'to create a strong link between the Assembly and Executive, to involve the majority and minority interests alike in constructive work', and the committees would reflect 'as far as possible, the balance of the parties in the Assembly'. The Office of the Secretary of State would remain and he would initially play a central role in the formation of the Executive by determining 'how an acceptable basis for the devolution of powers may speedily be achieved.'

Compared to the Stormont system, the powers of the new regional administration were severely reduced, although it did retain legislative and executive functions. The crucial powers incorporating control of the judiciary and security were reserved to the Secretary of State. In regard to the relationship between the new administration and the Republic, the paper committed the government to setting up some form of Council of Ireland 'to consult and co-ordinate action', although the exact details were left to await 'discussions involving all the parties'.

In general, the White Paper proposals did not significantly deviate from the outline laid down in the Green Paper. Not surprisingly, therefore, the responses to it were stereotyped, with conditional approbation from SDLP, Alliance, NILP and liberal Unionists and unconditional opposition from loyalists and republicans. Reserving judgement until after they had retired to a remote hotel in Co. Tyrone to consider the document in depth, the SDLP gave it a guarded welcome, but demanded amplification on the future of internment, the Council of Ireland and the formation of the Executive. In addition, the absence of any reference to police reform was seen as 'a glaring omission'.[33]

The feared SDLP rejection of the paper because of the guarantee on the province's constitutional position proved ill-founded. They did contend that this constitutional guarantee was 'not a secure basis for constitutional stability since an Act of Parliament can be changed at any time', but noted in mitigation that the structure and election of the proposed assembly was 'largely in keeping with our own recommendations'. Finally, they concluded that 'as a party committed totally to the solution of our problems by political means', they would 'willingly accept the opportunity offered to us to sit at the conference table.' This favourable response was apparently endorsed by the Catholic community; in an April poll 64 per cent of the Catholics interviewed said they wished to make the proposals work while only 9 per cent voiced unequivocal opposition.[34]

Political attitudes for and against the White Paper were important not just in relation to the new system of government, but because they crystallised the emerging political themes that would dominate Ulster politics in the next two years. In its last year the old Stormont parliament had presided over an abstentionist Catholic minority bent on its destruction and a Unionist majority equally committed to its survival. With the new assembly in prospect, only the liberal elements in the Unionist Party remained stationary, although subject to continuous erosion. Now the Catholic minority's aim, enshrined in the SDLP, was to participate and make the system function, while the loyalist minority (ultimately to capture a majority) was pledged to its total destruction. The roles had been reversed.

The elections to the new assembly were scheduled for June but were preceded by the election to the new district councils, repeatedly postponed since their original planned date of 1971. Both were conducted under PR, a move Westminster hoped would maximise electoral support for the moderate centre. The district council elections were the first province-wide election of any kind since 1969 and thus a major test for many of the political parties that had come into existence since then. The SDLP manifesto dwelt on the reasons for participating in the local elections. As Denis Haughey, the party vice-chairman, stressed at a press conference to launch the document, participation was the only way to counter the Unionists' abuse of power in local areas: 'those who either refuse to fight these elections or who have declared their intention not to take their seats if elected must bear the responsibility of making it easy for the old Unionist establishment to maintain and even accentuate the familiar, vicious, discriminatory practices.'[35] Branches nominating candidates were left to produce their own policy statements and fight the election on local issues.

The fragmentation of the political groups in both communities was illustrated by the number of candidates contesting the 526 seats in the 26 district council areas: eight major loyalist and unionist groups nominated 449 candidates; and six anti-partitionist groups, nominated 418 candidates. In the Protestant community the result of the election confirmed this fractionalisation by giving the bulk of their 297 seats to the official and unofficial unionists, and to the loyalists. In the Catholic community, however, the SDLP won 83 of the 103 anti-partitionist seats with 13.4 per cent of the first preference vote, confirming their role as the major minority group.

In the Assembly election, held on 28 June, the fragmentation of unionism was again reflected in the diversity of candidates. In the Catholic community, however, the divisions were not so great. Three distinct political groups sought to influence the anti-partitionist vote. Firstly, the Provisional IRA and its supporters adopted the orthodox republican stance of refusing to nominate candidates and urging their supporters not to vote. Secondly, the Nationalist, Republican Labour and Republican Clubs parties all nominated candidates but announced that if elected, they would not take their seats until internment and special powers were abolished. The SDLP constituted the third group, advancing the view that participation in the election and the working of the White Paper proposals presented the only possible way towards a solution.

As in the district council elections, the SDLP emerged as the dominant anti-partitionist group, but this time the clearly defined party lines, plus the lack of variegation in the vote enabled them to win 22.1 per cent of the first preference vote, compared to 1.8 per cent and 1.4 per cent for the Republican Clubs and Nationalist parties, respectively. Moreover, the election boycott advanced by the Provisionals proved of no significance. The 19 seats the party gained in the Assembly not only made them the sole electoral representative of the Catholic community for the first time, but in the Assembly as a whole second only to the divided Faulkner Unionists, with 23 seats. These 23 seats, coupled with the 19 SDLP, eight Alliance and the single NILP seat gave the pro-White Paper groups a majority of 24 over the unionists and loyalists opposed to the White Paper, although during the remainder of 1973 the realignments within the official Unionist Party and the shift of opinion within the Protestant community slowly eroded this majority.

CONCLUSION

The period that began with the imposition of direct rule and ended with the Assembly elections is notable for two changes in the SDLP's role. Firstly, they began to seek a way to withdraw support from the civil disobedience campaign while simultaneously seeking office within any future regional administration. Secondly, the elections confirmed what had been suspected: that they were representative of the overwhelming majority of Catholic opinion in Ulster; and that, in the electoral sphere, the other anti-partitionist groups posed no serious challenge to them. Henceforth, their sole political rival from within the Catholic community was the Provisional IRA and its political counterparts.

The apparent success of the Assembly election was however indicative of failure in another respect, for it demonstrated that the party had no Protestant support of consequence. After direct rule many Protestants began to reappraise their position and the fragmentation of the loyalist community, for a few crucial months largely leaderless, presented an opportunity for the SDLP to make contact with their more liberal members. This was not done and the only contact across the sectarian divide came in the impractical, short-lived détente with the extreme loyalists.

Thus, one element in the failure of the centre groups to provide a bulwark for a new form of politics was the SDLP's inability to come to grips with the sectarian problem. Although more Catholics than Protestants have always been willing to cross the divide, leaving the pro-union Alliance Party in a better position to capture support from both sides than the anti-partitionist SDLP, this is hardly the point. If the SDLP had striven to gain Protestant support they would have lost some of their own more republican-inclined supporters but at least tried to allay Protestant fears and vitiated the loyalist attack on them when it came. Placing an advertisement in a Unionist daily newspaper was not sufficient for a party proclaiming non-sectarian aims.

The condominium plan prepared for the Darlington conference merely reinforced Protestant suspicions. Whatever appeals were made to rationality and logic, it appeared unnecessarily convoluted, as indeed would any plan that envisaged, for example, a state with three official flags. From this perspective the joint sovereignty proposals were merely a distraction, and, after their explicit rejection in the White Paper, they were gradually dropped from party policy. The two central features that remained, power-sharing within an Ulster administration and a strong North-South body, were consonant with the plans that the British were themselves formulating for the province. The inability to gain a foothold in the Protestant community has been a constant theme in helping to shape the SDLP's outlook and has meant that the party has devoted more energy towards consolidating a power base within the Catholic community. The consequences of this strategy had no greater detrimental impact than during the period of the Assembly and Executive.

10 Power-Sharing (July 1973 to May 1974)

For a competitive democratic system to function normally over time requires consensus on the transference of political power from government to opposition. The acceptance of the right (and duty) of the opposition to accede to power if it can obtain a majority on the floor of the legislative body depends not only on that party acting at all times in a constructive constitutional manner, but on widespread agreement that it is a legitimate opposition. A peaceful shift of political power is indicative of the maturity and stability of a political system. Correspondingly, inability to sustain the transition is a direct expression of political instability and dissensus.

In Ulster the question of whether or not the SDLP has the right to be regarded as a legitimate opposition has centred on the issue of whether or not it has recognised the province's constitutional *status quo*. If, as opponents claim, the party was an 'opposition of principle' and 'bent . . . on ending once and for all the system on which the government rests,'[1] then its presence in power would indeed forebode the destruction of the system. If, on the other hand, it accepted the constitutional position then it should have the right to participate in government, if and when the opportunity was to arise, in the meantime acting as a constitutional opposition. This chapter deals with the period immediately following the Assembly elections, up to the Ulster Workers' Council strike which brought down the power-sharing Northern Ireland Executive in May 1974.

THE SUNNINGDALE AGREEMENT

Two opposing groups dominated the Northern Ireland Assembly: those supporting the White Paper proposals and those against them. The pro-White Paper group consisted of the SDLP (with 19 members), the Faulkner Unionists (23), Alliance (8) and NILP (1), making a total of 51 members. The opposing bloc was made up of the Democratic Unionists (8), Vanguard Unionists (7), anti-White Paper Unionists (10) and unaligned loyalists (2), making a total of 27 members. The group in favour of Westminster's plans for the future administration of the province therefore possessed an apparently unassailable majority of 24 over its opponents. But a basic question mark surrounded the allegiances of the

Faulkner Unionists. As in previous elections, Unionist constituency associations were able to nominate their own candidates without reference to the central party organisation and with many associations openly hostile to the policies of the leadership, considerable confusion developed over the loyalties of individual candidates. Faulkner himself attempted to maximise electoral support by being suitably imprecise about the official party policy on the White Paper.

The Unionist manifesto stated that they would not 'share power with any group whose primary aim is a united Ireland.'[2] The use of the word *primary* was an attempt by Faulkner to increase support and to maintain room for manoeuvre in the forthcoming negotiations with Westminster. The statement apparently included the possibility of sharing power with the SDLP, as their *primary* aim was a community administration within Northern Ireland rather than Irish unity. In any event, a group harbouring the primary aim of a united Ireland would undoubtedly have been unwilling to share power in a purely Ulster context. But the crux of the problem was that the Protestant electorate interpreted the manifesto as explicitly excluding the possibility of sharing power with the SDLP, while Faulkner's shrewd use of words included it.

To clarify the allegiances of official Unionist candidates Faulkner introduced a pledge to let 'the people of Ulster know the policies of those for whom they will vote on election day.'[3] The list of signatories committing themselves to party policy, 23 of whom were elected, was published on 14 June 1973.[4] Ten official Unionist candidates who refused to sign the pledge were also elected, declaring their complete opposition to the White Paper proposals. This attempt by Faulkner to win the support of a majority of his party rebounded on him, for 'the pledge had the effect of formalising a rift within the party, resulting in two separate and clearly identifiable factions.'[5]

Despite, then, the relative numerical weakness of the anti-White Paper group, the schisms within Faulkner's party plus the group's ability to disrupt the Assembly's proceedings gave them power in excess of numbers. The initial strategy was to try and halt progress towards the formation of the Executive until March 1974 when the Northern Ireland Constitution Act would lapse, at which point they would muster support for a new parliament 'with powers which will enable it to be the custodian of the constitutional position of Northern Ireland.'[6] To this end they obstructed the normal legislative functions of the Assembly. As Craig put it, 'it is not just a question of us adopting an abstentionist attitude, we will use our position to prevent anything being legislated for in the Assembly . . . if we have to be there to obstruct something, we will be there to obstruct.'[7] In practice, however, obstruction frequently spilled over into disorder. On 28 November and 5 December 1973 and 22 January 1974 violent scenes erupted and police had to be called to clear the debating chamber.

To break the impasse surrounding the Executive's formation, the SDLP proposed a meeting of the parties willing to participate to discuss a socio-economic policy. The other two parties, Unionist and Alliance, agreed. Faulkner's previous stipulations that the SDLP should accept the Northern Ireland Constitution Act (and hence the province's status) and the Republic's Taoiseach, Liam Cosgrave, give *de facto* recognition before talks could commence, were granted. This meeting was held on 6 October, the SDLP presenting their own socio-economic plan 'aimed at increasing the overall standard of living . . . sustaining full employment, and securing . . . planned growth'[8] as a basis for discussion. Agreement was reached in principle to form an Executive and the SDLP's plan became, with minor changes, the Executive's socio-economic programme.

With this initial basis of agreement talks commenced on 21 November on how the seats within the Executive would be apportioned. The Unionists demanded a majority of the seats commensurate with their role as representatives of the Protestant community. On the other hand, the SDLP argued that as they had the same number of members as Faulkner's party, 19,[9] they should have parity. At one stage Paddy Devlin even argued that as the Unionists were disunited, the SDLP should have a majority and nominate the Chief Executive. The problem was compounded by Section 8(1) of the Northern Ireland Constitution Act, which stated that the 'Executive shall consist of the Chief Executive member and not more than ten other members.'[10] The deadlock was resolved by the expedient of creating a two-tier administration. The first tier, the Executive, had 11 members and the second tier, the Administration, included the Executive plus four extra members. Within the Executive the SDLP had four seats, the Unionists six and Alliance one; the extra four seats in the Administration were apportioned to the SDLP, with two, and the Unionists and Alliance one each. Thus the overall ratio of six-seven-two preserved the Unionist majority at the expense of Alliance, who lost one seat.

The SDLP ministers were the Deputy Chief Executive (Gerry Fitt), the Ministers of Commerce (John Hume), Health and Social Services (Paddy Devlin), Housing (Austin Currie); and outside the Executive, Community Relations (Ivan Cooper) and Planning and Co-ordination (Edward McGrady). In spite of Roy Bradford seeking to portray himself through the media as a figure commanding more confidence among Protestants, Faulkner became Chief Executive. The formation of the Executive Designate was a compromise for both sides: the Unionists were unwilling to enter into negotiations concerning such issues as a Council of Ireland until they had formed an administration; the SDLP were reluctant to commit themselves until they were sure the Unionists accepted the Council concept.

Agreement opened the way for the next stage, tripartite talks between Westminster, Dublin and Ulster representatives, held at Sunningdale, Berkshire, between 6 and 9 December 1973. Originally it had been intended to exclude the loyalists from the conference by simply not inviting them, their views being conveyed to the conference by Whitelaw. The new Secretary of State, Francis Pym, evidently changed his mind, although the manner in which the invitation was delivered – while Paisley was speaking at the dispatch box – ensured a refusal. Paisley saw it as 'another studied insult to the Protestants of Northern Ireland.'[11]

On convocation, the conference almost immediately broke into five sub-committees to discuss in detail the main topics: the finance of the Executive; the functions of the Council of Ireland; policing; law enforcement; and the status of Northern Ireland. These sub-committees thrashed out the details of the agreement throughout the four days of the conference. In his book, *The Fall of the Northern Ireland Executive*, Paddy Devlin was in no doubt about the tenor of the SDLP approach. This was:

> To get all-Ireland institutions established which, with adequate safeguards, would produce the dynamic that could lead ultimately to an agreed single state for Ireland. . . . SDLP representatives would concentrate their entire efforts on building up a set of tangible executive powers for the Council which in the fullness of time would create and sustain an evolutionary process. All other issues were governed by that approach . . .[12]

The final outcome of the conference, a long and detailed communique, appeared to substantiate the efforts of the SDLP negotiators.[13] The most important points of the document from the point of view of the SDLP and Unionist participants were that a Council of Ireland would be created with executive functions, in return for which the Republic would recognise the constitutional position of Northern Ireland and take action against fugitive offenders.

The Council of Ireland was to have two tiers. The Council of Ministers, charged with 'executive and harmonising functions', would be composed of seven ministers each from the Irish government and the Northern Ireland Executive. The second tier, the Consultative Assembly, would consist of thirty members each from Dáil Eireann and the Northern Ireland Assembly and have as its role 'advisory and review functions'. To co-ordinate the activities of the Council, a secretariat composed of full-time officials would be formed. Eight separate areas were listed under which the council would have power of executive action, including agriculture, electricity, tourism and transport. These areas of common concern could only be broadly defined because of the 'constitutional anomaly of the council . . . linking on terms of equality a sovereign state and a subordinate jurisdiction of another sovereign state.'[14]

As an inducement to the Unionists to accept this substantive structure, the Republic 'solemnly declared that there could be no change in the status of Northern Ireland until a majority of the people of Northern Ireland desired a change in that status.' The British government correspondingly

affirmed its intentions to guarantee the present status of the province, but
that if a majority were to 'indicate a wish to become part of a united
Ireland, the British government would support that wish.' On the
contentious question of fugitive offenders, it was agreed to 'jointly set up a
commission to . . . recommend as a matter of extreme urgency the most
effective means of dealing with those who commit these crimes.' The
findings of the commission would be implemented by both governments.

The scope and detail of the Sunningdale Agreement were such that both
Unionists and SDLP could return to their supporters and justifiably claim
that they had achieved a compromise especially favourable to their own
side. The SDLP could claim that they had achieved a strong Council of
Ireland and rather than devalue the ideal of reunification they had helped
to create the institution that could bring it about. The Unionists could
similarly maintain that the Council was merely a body fostering mutual
aid and in return for accepting this, they had extracted from the Republic
a *de jure* recognition of the province's constitutional status plus action to
bring fugitive offenders to justice. Ultimately, 'the success of the Agreement depended on neither side listening to what their allies were saying
about it.'[15]

The fact that the two sides could make such divergent interpretations
reflected the Executive's fundamental problem, which was that the basis
for agreement did not exist between the prospective partners. The two
major issues of concern to the SDLP, internment and the police, were left
unresolved, apart from giving a vague hint that policing might at some
time become the responsibility of the Council of Ireland and that
internment would be brought to an end 'as soon as the security situation
permits'. Essentially, the Sunningdale Agreement helped to refract and
obscure the arguments to the point where each protagonist could draw
conclusions supporting a particular political point. While this facilitated
the reconciliation of the Executive parties, it did them a disservice in so far
as the process worked both ways: the loyalists were now able to intensify
their opposition to the new system and convince the Protestant majority of
the justification of their cause.

THE WORK OF THE EXECUTIVE AND ADMINISTRATION

Despite its short, five-month life, it is instructive to examine the general
outlines of Executive policy, with reference to the SDLP role. Two
questions are paramount. Firstly, to what extent were the departmental
and Executive plans original or merely developments of previous Stormont
and Northern Ireland Office policies? Secondly, how far was the overall
social and economic policy based on constructive agreement between the
coalition partners rather than just the highest common denominator?

The Executive's aims were published on 21 January 1974 in a policy document entitled *Steps Towards a Better Tomorrow*. Rather than setting out a comprehensive policy outline, the document consisted merely of a brief collection of general aims, largely set out by Hume and Devlin with minimal amendments from Faulkner. For the Executive to formally adopt a document so patently the product of one party indicates how little socio-economic thinking had been undertaken by the other two parties prior to the Executive's formation. To examine the plans to implement these aims, it is useful to briefly analyse the work of some of the government departments with SDLP heads; and of interest in this context is John Hume's work at the Department of Commerce, Austin Currie's at Housing, Local Government and Planning, Paddy Devlin's at Health and Social Services, and Ivan Cooper's at Community Relations.

Responsibility for the economy was divided between Hume, at Commerce, Herbert Kirk at Finance, and to a lesser extent Roy Bradford at Environment. At Commerce John Hume had to make the difficult decision of whether to pursue the well-established policies of his department or inaugurate new measures to encourage economic expansion in the province. Since the war successive Unionist governments had accepted that the problems of unemployment and regional depression could not be solved by the free play of market capitalism. It was acknowledged that limited state intervention in the economy was essential to attract new industries into areas of high unemployment. This policy was continued by Whitelaw and his ministers during the period of Conservative direct rule. *Steps Towards a Better Tomorrow* had committed Hume to maintaining these 'wide, generous and flexible industrial incentives,'[16] and the assumption underlying the document was that profitability would become a secondary consideration in the efforts to reduce unemployment.

Hume, however, made it clear that he regarded profitability and employment as synonymous and asserted that all concerns applying for aid would be judged on their commercial viability.[17] The two main bodies channelling aid to business and industry were the Local Enterprise Development Unit and the Northern Ireland Finance Corporation. The Local Enterprise Development Unit was designed primarily for dealing with the small local concerns needing small injections of capital. In 1972 and 1973, for example, it sponsored 95 projects, creating an estimated 1200 jobs.[18] The Northern Ireland Finance Corporation was geared to providing funds for larger concerns. The central decision was whether to sustain this policy of making 100 per cent grants available to industry, either to save them from liquidation or for development, or to implement the socialist extension to this, the initiation of entirely new state-owned industries created in advance of a suitable market. Hume chose the first path of aiding only existing concerns that had demonstrated their commercial potential. It is difficult to envisage how this policy would have attracted employment to the depressed areas west of the River Bann, for which Hume had so often declared he held a brief.

In the field of social services, the two departments were both headed by SDLP members, Austin Currie at the Department of Housing, Local Government and Planning, and Paddy Devlin at the Department of Health and Social Services (DHSS). Currie was entrusted with the more difficult area, housing. In 1971 Ulster's overall need had been estimated at between 130,000 and 230,000 new houses, and although a five-year plan had been adopted in 1970, aiming at 75,000 new houses – a target 'surpassing anything on a proportionate basis yet achieved in Great Britain'[19] – the construction industry and the new Housing Executive were not equal to the challenge. In 1972 to 1973, only 7061 new houses had been completed, indicating that the five-year total would be less than half the target. The housing shortage and concomitant social deprivation was compounded by the problem of intimidation, coupled with civil disobedience and the Housing Executive's large financial deficit.

In tackling these problems, Currie saw his priorities as fivefold. First, to resolve the widespread squatting problem; second, to reduce the housing waiting list; third, to move speedily in repairing and maintaining houses; fourth, to rehabilitate derelict houses; and fifth, 'to ensure that the rent strike is brought to an end.'[20] *Steps Towards a Better Tomorrow* had envisaged an annual house-building target of 20,000 and to help the construction industry reorganise its resources to cope with this, Currie proposed the formation of a consultative Construction Industry Council. To deal with the areas of special need, he promised to consider the concept of designated housing action areas and to examine the role of local housing associations and co-operatives, private landlords and home ownership.

If Currie's approach to the problems of housing was circumscribed by past policy, this was even more true of Paddy Devlin at the DHSS, an area determined by the doctrine of parity with British social legislation. In trying to impose local priorities on his department, Devlin's approach emphasised three points. Firstly, to introduce a comprehensive five-year plan for the health and social services in order to ensure that the various fields 'move ahead in an integrated way [and] that each element inter-relates with, and complements the others.'[21] Secondly, to initiate an extensive research programme to identify specific areas of social need which could be dealt with by drafting new legislation. Thirdly, he hoped to inculcate a whole new philosophy into the DHSS, one allowing 'people attending at the counters . . . [to] be treated at first class citizens . . . and made aware of all the benefits they are entitled to.'[22]

In general, then, the plans of the two SDLP ministers responsible for the social services did not deviate greatly from their British – or more distantly, Unionist – predecessors. Both possessed particular ideas about developing the social role of their departments, but available resources and the overall conservative economic philosophy of the Executive, determined by the other two coalition partners, the Faulkner Unionists and the Alliance Party, limited the scope of their plans. It is, for example, by no means certain that Currie would have found sufficient funds for introducing designated housing action areas or Devlin for sponsoring the research he proposed. The whole question of finance underlines the fact that the Executive was wholly dependent on Westminster, with the Treasury having an ultimate say in the allocation of funds. Local taxation was one idea floated to by-pass this problem, but implementing any such proposal would have been subject to the approval of Westminster.

At Community Relations, Ivan Cooper had the most unpredictable appointment, as head of a department that had seen four ministers of differing political persuasions in as many years. His department was charged with 'formulating policies likely to improve community relations . . . [and] to assist in the administration of the public services so as to improve community relations.'[23] In addition, it was empowered through the Social Needs (Grants) Act of 1970 to respond 'quickly and flexibly to . . . requests for help . . .'[24] A third major responsibility was for legislation relating to the Community Relations Commission (CRC) and the Commissioner for Complaints. Cooper saw his role as 'involving the entire community by participation and involvement in social reconstruction . . . [in] government at every level,'[25] and to this end various advisory bodies dealing with sport and recreation were formed as well as schemes to improve the physical appearance of areas hit by violence.

Perhaps Cooper's most contentious decision was to wind up the CRC. *Steps Towards a Better Tomorrow* had committed him to making a reappraisal of the 'existing institutional arrangements in the community relations field.'[26] The semi-autonomous nature of the CRC had often brought it into conflict with the Community Relations Department and the resignation of two directors in three months swiftly cast doubt upon the CRC's future. Official antagonism was fostered by informal and close contacts maintained by field workers with local associations and community groups, causing both central and local government to feel that their role was being undermined. In the event, Cooper bowed to the arguments of his civil servants and announced that because 'the format and range of activities of the Commission are no longer the most appropriate'[27] the CRC would be wound up. The CRC's consultative functions would thereafter be transferred to a new advisory council and the executive functions to a variety of already operating government agencies. The decision provoked considerable dissension and more than one backbencher asserted that, if the CRC was dismantled, another body outside the orbit of state control would have to be formed to continue its work.

Another main area of community services, education, was also of concern to the SDLP, although the department was not headed by an SDLP minister. Among other educational aims, *Steps Towards a Better Tomorrow* had set the target 'the development of pilot experiments, after consultation with interested parties, in integrated education.'[28] The

Minister of Education, Basil McIvor, proposed to tackle the problem through changes in the management of schools, with an alteration in the law 'to facilitate . . . the shared school . . . in which the two groups of churches would be equally involved in management.'[29] The Roman Catholic hierarchy was generally hostile to the plan, and indeed the Catholic bishop in Belfast had consistently refused to confirm into the Church children who had attended state schools. The situation contained the seeds of a confrontation between Church and state and hence the attitude of the SDLP was crucial. As it turned out, the emergent dispute was halted by the Executive's collapse. Although Fitt later stated that the Executive was united on the issue,[30] the SDLP has been less than enthusiastic about integrated education, and it is thus an open question whether the SDLP ministers would have supported Executive policy in the event of a major conflict with the Catholic hierarchy.

The remaining departments included in the Executive and Administration were largely makeweights incorporated to facilitate the apportionment of a sufficient number of posts to satisfy the three coalition partners. This was very obviously the case with the Department of Information, headed by John Baxter who spoke only four times during the life of the Assembly, and the Department of Planning and Co-ordination, headed by Edward McGrady. The Department of Manpower Services, headed by Robert Cooper, possessed a more instrumental role in that it performed the functions originally carried out by the Ministry of Labour and latterly the DHSS. The immediate concern of Oliver Napier's Office of Law Reform was with modernising the framework of law in the province.

Any overall assessment of the Executive's approach to government must invariably take into account its short existence. By May most departments had only managed to publish the financial estimates for the coming year and ministers make general statements of policy. Three main factors limited the formulation of Executive policy. Firstly, financial responsibility for the province, as mentioned above, rested with the Treasury in London. Secondly, the long-established tradition of parity with the social services in the rest of Britain and the previous policies pursued by the Stormont administration also militated against the introduction of radical or innovatory policies. Thirdly, in some departments there was the subtle pressure on ministers from civil service advisers to conform to their own policy priorities.

Bearing in mind these points, it is evident that the policy outline of the previous Stormont and direct rule eras were largely adhered to by the SDLP ministers. It would be speculative to conclude whether or not they would have formulated a less cautious and more distinctive approach to their departments in time; but if this had taken place, it is likely that the essentially conservative economic outlook of the Unionist members of the Executive would have proved a stubborn, and perhaps insuperable, obstacle.

The constructive work of the Executive was hampered by the obstructive and abstentionist tactics of the loyalist Assembly members. The loyalists evidently took a collective decision not to recognise the Executive by tabling formal questions and in any event, save for the Assembly's first four months, their participation in debates was low and those that they did participate in were invariably concerned with the constitutional question. By contrast some backbenchers from the Executive parties recorded exceptional interest. For example, Hugh Logue, an SDLP member, participated in 45 separate debates and asked 75 questions, a level surpassed only by Peter McLachlan, a Faulkner Unionist, who spoke in 82 separate debates and asked an incredible 222 questions.

Whatever attitudes the various political parties adopted towards the Assembly, what were the views of the population at large? An opinion poll conducted in March 1974 provided a unique opportunity to examine these political views on the eve of the Executive's collapse. The survey elicited respondents' views on the prevailing political and constitutional arrangements and on their perception of the ideal solution.[31] On the constitutional *status quo*, between one half and one third of Protestant respondents and an overwhelming majority of Catholic respondents expressed themselves content. Thus 52 per cent of Protestants said they thought Sunningdale a good idea, compared with 72 per cent of Catholics. Similarly, power-sharing found approval among 65 per cent of Protestants and 94 per cent of Catholics. The results indicated a Protestant majority in favour of making the Assembly work, with the recalcitrant loyalists finding endorsement among only 22 per cent of Protestant opinion. Catholic opinion was also unanimously behind the Executive concept with only 2 per cent expressing disapproval.

While the figures seem to indicate widespread affirmation of the new system, the results are misleading, for among Protestants there was general disagreement over what system they saw as their *most preferred solution*. Although a majority of Catholics (58 per cent) chose power-sharing, only 18 per cent of Protestants took this as an ideal solution and the remaining majority divided itself almost equally between a return to Stormont and full integration with the United Kingdom. There thus existed on the Catholic side a large proportion in favour of the Executive, willing and anxious for it to function successfully, but among Protestants superficial approval was underlaid by a basic uncertainty as to the system's practicality. This feeling that the Executive was little more than a transitory experiment was one the loyalists were ably equipped to exploit, aided, as it turned out, by the problems of the Dublin government.

THE COLLAPSE OF THE EXECUTIVE

While the immediate cause of the Executive's collapse was the strike organised by the Ulster Workers' Council (UWC), relations between the Executive parties had been under stress since January. There were four explanations for this tension, the first two affecting the SDLP, the second two the Unionist and Alliance parties. The problems clouding the SDLP's relations were the uncertainty surrounding the future of the police and the continuance of internment.

The policing problem has been the most intractable throughout the post-1969 troubles and stems from the paramilitary origins of the Royal Ulster Constabulary. The RUC's central problem was simultaneous responsibility for the security of the state and for the maintenance of a normal civilian policing role. The operation of these two roles by a single body within a divided society consequently harmed the RUC's credibility with the Catholic minority, who were suspicious of its political overtones and viewed it merely as an armed extension to the Unionist government. The well-documented misdemeanours of the RUC in 1968 and 1969 cemented the process of total alienation.[32] To detach the security from the policing role, the Hunt Report recommended the abolition of the paramilitary 'B' Special Police, proposed the raising of another part-time local defence force under the control of the British army, and civilianised the RUC, making it independent of the regime by the appointment of an autonomous Police Authority.

But the escalation of the troubles forced the RUC to keep its armed role despite the implementation of the Hunt reforms, and even with a large turnover in personnel the force was unable to win a measure of local Catholic confidence. As the Central Citizens' Defence Committee's *Black Paper* illustrated,[33] Catholic fears of the RUC could be dispelled only by radical reform and the continuing law and order crisis made some restructuring of the force an essential prerequisite for a permanent solution. While in office, Whitelaw was aware of the problem but mindful of the harm that could be done to already depleted RUC morale. He conceded that 'you can only have an efficient and acceptable police service by building on the existing foundations of the RUC. But to refuse to contemplate any changes at all in a constantly changing world is to deny oneself the opportunity to take advantage of new developments and to make improvements based on experience throughout the United Kingdom.'[34]

The political parties were ranged on either side of this statement: the Unionists would not tolerate any suggestion of change, the SDLP saw the solution 'not in isolation but as part of an overall political settlement'.[35] At Sunningdale the SDLP had pressed hard for 'the police on both sides of the border ultimately to be the responsibility of the Council of Ireland',[36] but the resultant communiqué gave only a vague commitment that the Council of Ministers should be consulted on appointments to the Northern Ireland Police Authority. The failure to ratify Sunningdale and in-augurate the Council of Ireland meant that the party refused to publicly support the police or urge Catholics to join it. This was certainly an anomalous position for a party contributing to the government and could be countenanced only so long as the security powers remained vested at Westminster. Even so, the situation imposed a severe strain on the Executive partners and put pressure on the Unionists and Alliance for swift ratification.

As with the policing question, the resolution of the SDLP's second problem, internment and civil disobedience, was also seen in the context of an overall political settlement. Throughout the negotiations on the formation of the Executive, the party refused to condemn the rent and rates strike or seek its end while detention persisted; conversely, after the *de facto* end of abstention in March 1972 they did nothing to intensify it. The existence of detention was obviously a bloc to progress and, recognising this, Whitelaw apparently agreed in October 1973 that it would be phased out, 'starting on the date on which the power-sharing Executive took up the reins of office.'[37] The party interpreted this as a binding agreement and on 28 December, three days before the Executive's installation, called on all those on strike to commence payment:

> In view . . . of the major advances made in recent times in establishing institutions which can remove the injustices under which the society has laboured for so long, we call on the people to give their full support to these institutions and as a positive indication of that support to withdraw from the rent and rates strike . . .[38]

The appeal, however, met with only a modest response, and the drop between December 1973 and June 1974 in the number of households participating in the rent strike was only slightly greater than what might have been expected from the overall downward trend.[39]

The dispute surrounding the collection of unpaid rent and rates was a much more emotive issue. Whitelaw had warned that 'unpleasant measures' were imminent for defaulters, but it was left to Austin Currie, Minister of Local Government, Housing and Planning, and ironically one of the instigators of the strike, to finalise these measures. On 3 April Currie announced the introduction of a 25 pence a week collection charge on unpaid rent and rates, to commence from 30 May. He repeated that 'payment in full will be required. There cannot be any amnesty. Arrears must be paid. Any other decision would be unfair to the great majority of tenants who have paid their rents.'[40] In the absence of a clear policy of phasing out internment, the decision caused consternation within the party. The SDLP ministers themselves were not averse to the principle of collection charges, but believed that it should be deferred until 22 July, the date fixed for a major increase in social security benefits and therefore an event that might obscure the introduction of the collection charge. Some SDLP ministers also thought that by July Sunningdale would have been ratified and internment wound up. In fact the earlier date was arrived at by pressure from two Unionist ministers, Herbert Kirk and Roy Bradford.

Paddy Devlin objected to the earlier date; and on 17 May, at a meeting between the Executive and Merlyn Rees at which the final decision on the charges was approved, resigned. The letter of resignation, passed to Rees during the meeting, stated that he 'would not remain on the Northern Ireland Executive in charge of the department which would be used as an instrument to impose penalties on rent and rates strikers unless there was hard evidence that internment and detention was being seriously phased out.'[41] The resignation was to take effect on 20 May, but in the event he was persuaded to freeze it until after the outcome of the UWC strike became known.

Also symptomatic of internal party friction caused by the persistence of internment was the formation of the 'Motion Number One' committee in January 1974, the title being a reference to the first anti-internment motion at the SDLP's annual conference the previous December. With the support of a small number of backbenchers and some middle-rank activists, the committee pressed the case for more action on detention with the party leadership. Although reflective of grass-roots concern, the committee's activities arguably assisted the presentation of the party case at Westminster, in that the leadership could claim that internment threatened party unity.

By contrast to the dissension caused within the SDLP by the internment and policing issues, the Executive's other problems directly affected the Unionist and Alliance members. One problem involved the Republic's inability to fulfil its obligations under the Sunningdale Agreement – recognition of Ulster's constitutional position and extradition – and the other the decisive loyalist victory in the February 1974 Westminster election. The Republic's two concessions of recognition and extradition were the Unionists' *quid pro quo* for their acceptance of a Council of Ireland embodying executive powers. The Republic's failure to honour these commitments in Unionist eyes logically cast into doubt the Council of Ireland and thus, also, SDLP participation in the Executive.

At Sunningdale the Republic agreed to recognise the North's position within the United Kingdom, but Article 2 of the Republic's 1937 Constitution states that 'the national territory consists of the whole island of Ireland . . .', although Article 3 concedes that 'pending re-integration' the legal jurisdiction of the state is limited to the twenty-six counties. A swift referendum to amend this irredentist claim would have removed the contradiction, but a delay enabled the leader of Aontacht Eireann, Kevin Boland, to question the legality of the Republic's declaration in the courts. The government won the case, but this proved to be of no comfort as their defence rested on the assertion that the declaration 'did not acknowledge that a portion of Ireland, therein described as "Northern Ireland", is part of the United Kingdom . . .'[42] Moreover, in dismissing Boland's action the Supreme Court found that the Sunningdale declarations 'were clearly distinct and in no sense an agreement on fact or principle.'[43]

The well-publicised legal proceedings were greeted with dismay by the Assembly Unionists, whose main plank in selling the concept of the Council of Ireland to their supporters had been the Republic's recognition of the province's constitutional status. An attempt by Cosgrave to give *de facto* recogntion by accepting that 'the factual position of Northern Ireland is that it is within the United Kingdom . . .'[44] failed to restore confidence, since he appeared to put one interpretation on the declaration when addressing Unionists and another when faced with litigation. To try and preserve party cohesion, Faulkner made it clear that he would need

> A solemn and binding declaration of the status of Northern Ireland if any of the other developments envisaged at Sunningdale are to continue, and if this portion of the Sunningdale Agreement were to be struck down, . . . it would be for the Dublin government to consider how any constitutional impediments should be overcome.[45]

The SDLP viewed the machinations of the Cosgrave administration and the Assembly Unionists with some disquiet since the Council of Ireland was central to their plans: without it their participation would be in doubt and the whole Sunningdale edifice would collapse. Under pressure from their Executive colleagues to accept a delay in signing the Agreement so as to allow the Council to meet initially at ministerial level only, the SDLP reiterated that Sunningdale must stand or fall only as a package.

Dublin's inability to deal with extradition and the whole question of making fugitive offenders amenable to the law was a further reason for down-grading Dublin's agreement and harming Executive credibility. The Irish Constitution contains no provision for extradition if the offence is deemed political. Sunningdale stated that 'persons committing crimes of violence, however motivated, in any part of Ireland should be brought to trial irrespective of the part of Ireland in which they are located.' To find the best possible legal means to this end, in an area fraught with legal pitfalls, a Law Enforcement Commission was set up, with the membership composed equally from North and South. The crucial requirement of the Commission was a speedy and practical report. But the legal intricacies dragged out the proceedings and eventually, after some acrimony, the Commission rejected the use of all-Ireland courts or a more simple amendment to the Republic's constitution, opting finally for the use of existing courts to exercise extra-territorial jurisdiction.

The inability to produce a decisive report, coupled with doubts expressed by Northern members of the Commission about the practicality of the course arrived at, further harmed the Republic's credibility. Once again the SDLP became a passive spectator while the other Executive parties voiced their misgivings about the whole Sunningdale pact. As Oliver Napier stated unambiguously in an Assembly debate, 'if effective means are not found to deal with fugitive offenders I shall not sign the Sunningdale Agreement.'[46]

The fourth and final factor undermining the Executive position and contributing to its fall was the February 1974 Westminster general election. The election came at a disastrous moment for the Assembly Unionists, as the guiding body of the party, the Ulster Unionist Council, had carried a motion rejecting the Council of Ireland by 457 to 374 votes just a month before. In response Faulkner resigned as leader and was in the process of drawing together his remaining supporters when the February election was announced. The loyalists – the anti-White Paper Unionists (with the departure of Faulkner now the official Unionist Party), the Vanguard and Democratic Unionists – had by now formed themselves into a united front, the United Ulster Unionist Council (UUUC), and fought the election as a single party. This contrasted with the Executive parties, which rejected any suggestion of electoral co-operation. With a single loyalist candidate in each constitutency possessing a strikingly simple policy and an efficient organisation, the disunited Executive parties were easily routed.

The result of the election was a decisive victory for the loyalists. The UUUC gained 11 of the 12 Ulster seats at Westminster and 51.1 per cent of the valid vote, compared to a combined vote of 38.6 per cent for the Executive parties. The SDLP maintained the strength of its Assembly vote, but with a split Catholic vote in two marginal constitutencies only managed to retain West Belfast with Gerry Fitt. The psychological blow to Sunningdale was undoubted, for the loyalists had captured a majority of the seats and a majority of the vote. As Craig's interpretation of the election outcome suggested, the loyalists had been given a mandate to oppose the Sunningdale Agreement: 'we must not prop up the undemocratic form of administration that now exists in Northern Ireland . . . there is not the necessary consent for the present constitutional formula.'[47] The loyalists realised that under Section 2 of the 1973 Northern Ireland Constitution Act, which stated that an Executive could only be formed if it 'is likely to be widely accepted throughout the community . . ,'[48] they could argue that the necessary support did not exist. By the end of April they had arrived at a set of common demands that included the abolition of the 'wholly undemocratic Executive', the repeal of the Northern Ireland Constitution Act and an immediate provincial election.[49]

The election defeat forced the Assembly Unionists to take cognisance of Protestant fears and Faulkner publicly accepted that the result 'reflected widespread concern in the Unionist community about the implications of the Sunningdale Agreement, and the proposed Council of Ireland in particular.'[50] As the Unionist and Alliance members began to bide their time, the SDLP became more adamant that the complete package would have to be speedily ratified. The dilemma was that early implementation would almost certainly destroy the Assembly Unionists, while delay would undermine the SDLP. Either way, the outcome would be, *inter alia*, the collapse of Sunningdale.

It was against this political background that on 14 May a hitherto obscure loyalist grouping, the Ulster Workers' Council, announced the commencement of a general strike to coincide with the rejection in the Assembly, by 44 votes to 28, of a motion requesting 'renegotiation of the constitutional arrangements'.[51] The aims of the UWC fluctuated throughout the course of the ensuing 14-day stoppage, but one common demand was for fresh Assembly elections which would, the loyalists believed, recreate the anti-Sunningdale majority they had polled in the February 1974 Westminster election. It is unnecessary to chronicle the course of the strike or its ramifications, a task already undertaken by Robert Fisk in his authoritative account, *The Point of No Return*.[52] What is relevant here is the SDLP's role in the episode and the immediate political consequences for the party.

During the strike, perhaps the fundamental mistake made by Westminster, and to a lesser degree by the SDLP, was to see the wide support given to the strike as emanating solely from paramilitary intimidation. While this was undoubtedly a factor, widespread Protestant support existed because of genuine uncertainties surrounding the Sunningdale Agreement. Significantly, the strikers gained the passive sympathy of a large section of the commercial and professional Protestant middle class, which the Executive (and notably Faulkner) had assumed would side with the *status quo*. As support for the strike increased, the SDLP's logical attitude was to suspect the veracity of the security forces in claiming that they were powerless to act. Of the Executive ministers, only Roy Bradford held any sympathy for the strikers' case and he consistently advocated negotiation, arguing in the two months following the February election that the Council of Ireland would have to be held in abeyance. The SDLP, in this instance personified by Paddy Devlin, suspected that Bradford was on the verge of betraying the Executive and Bradford did indeed later claim to have tendered his resignation on two separate occasions 'but the offer was not accepted.'[53]

As the disruption became daily more serious and Westminster emerged unwilling to underwrite the Executive's authority by military action, on 22 May Faulkner announced an Executive compromise on the Council of Ireland. There would be two separate phases. The first phase would consist of a Council of Ministers composed of seven members nominated by each government and providing a 'forum for consultation, co-operation and co-ordination of action . . .'[54] The second phase, the implementation of the Council's full powers, would only commence 'after a test of the opinion of the Northern Ireland electorate . . . this test would be the next general election to the Northern Ireland Assembly . . . due . . . in 1977−78.'[55] The response of the SDLP backbenchers was to press their ministerial colleagues to turn down the compromise and on a straight vote eleven backbenchers voted against the plan. The resultant 11 to 8 rejection provoked Stanley Orme, Minister of State at the Northern Ireland Office, to address the Assembly party in an effort to persuade them to change their minds. His dire warnings of civil war induced five previously opposed backbenchers into accepting the plan; and on a second vote the compromise was duly accepted – a prior agreement having been made that a majority verdict would be collectively binding.

On the following day, 23 May, John Hume presented a plan for a government takeover of the oil storage and distribution facilities as an initial step towards disarming the UWC's fuel monopoly. The Executive agreed that if the British refused to activate the plan, they would resign *en bloc*. On hearing of the impending mass resignations, Harold Wilson invited the three party leaders – Faulkner, Napier and Fitt – to meet him at Chequers on 24 May. During the course of a long talk, Wilson led them to believe that action by the British against the strikers would at last be forthcoming. He announced that he would speak to the nation on Saturday, 25 May; but, in the hours before the broadcast, arguments were put to him that the army should not, or could not, break the strike. When it came, Wilson's broadcast did not announce any new measures to re-establish the Executive's authority but rather appeared to exploit British national impatience with the Irish. The infamous reference to 'spongers' – people 'purporting to act as though they were an elected government . . . who spend their lives sponging on Westminster and British democracy'[56] – merely fuelled Protestant resentment and mobilised hitherto unaligned or passive sections of the Protestant community behind the UWC. The speech sealed the fate of the Executive.

The day after the broadcast, a new SDLP ultimatum threatened the resignation of the six SDLP ministers unless the oil plan was implemented within 24 hours. By this time, Paddy Devlin was already on the point of resignation. The ultimatum had the desired effect and the army moved into 21 petrol filling stations and storage depots. The UWC, who had been maintaining a limited power supply to ensure that sewage and water pumping stations and other essential services were maintained, announced that because of the army's intervention, all services would be withdrawn. At Stormont Faulkner was appraised of the consequences that would follow a complete breakdown of the electricity grid system. On 28 May he met his backbenchers, who informed him that he could no longer count on their support. At a meeting of the full Executive shortly after, Faulkner counselled negotiation with the UWC, a suggestion that was supported by Oliver Napier but which the SDLP still refused to consider. The decision was conveyed to Rees, who could obviously not deviate from his stated position of no talks with the UWC, and thus Faulkner and his fellow-Unionist ministers handed in their resignations. The SDLP and Alliance ministers refused to resign, though this was an empty gesture because the departing Unionists had taken with them the Executive's statutory basis.

Since the constitutional arrangements were essentially contrived in order to allow for coalition, the collapse of the Executive automatically meant the collapse of the constitution: there was, for example, no suggestion of another Executive being formed.

What were the immediate consequences of the fall of the Executive for the SDLP? Most prevalent was a feeling of disillusionment, but also considerable anger amongst middle-rank activists against the six SDLP ministers. This anger dated from 17 May, when the party executive had met in secret session at Cushendun, Co. Antrim. It was decided that, if pressed, SDLP ministers should agree to a phasing of the hitherto sacrosanct Council of Ireland only if full implementation was to be not later than December 1974.[57] The meeting concluded by submitting this plan to the Assembly party with the proviso that, if any changes were proposed, then the whole plan would be referred back to the party executive for a final decision. Thus when Faulkner announced the elaborate plan for a phased (and in SDLP eyes emasculated) Council, the party executive sensed betrayal by the SDLP ministers, especially since an inter-party sub-committee that included Hume and Devlin had been working on the modifications since 7 May.

In pioneering the concept of power-sharing at cabinet level in Northern Ireland the short and relatively undramatic life of the Executive was brought to an unfitting end by the Protestant veto. In his resignation statement Faulkner was forced to admit that 'from the extent of support for the present stoppage . . . the degree of consent needed to sustain the Executive does not at present exist.'[58] The necessity of winning loyalist consent for any future form of provincial government almost automatically precluded its acceptability to Westminster, or to the SDLP.

CONCLUSION

In a long-term perspective the power-sharing experiment in Northern Ireland failed for many reasons, of which the UWC strike was but one. In the first place, the basis for agreement between the coalition partners was insufficient to promote political cohesion. That the Executive was formed at all was the result of relegating the contentious powers, such as security, policing and the administration of justice, to Westminster. Even so, the Executive's published socio-economic policy was vague, ill-defined and little more than the highest common denominator between the three parties. Secondly, the participation of the SDLP in the Executive was contingent on the ratification of Sunningdale and responsibility for that rested with the Dublin government, a body outside the control of either Stormont or Westminster. Dublin's inability to resolve the dual problems or recognition and extradition was more a function of the constraints imposed by an antiquated constitution than lack of genuine commitment.

But whatever the cause, it further undermined the foundation for the Executive by discouraging Protestant support, enabling the loyalists to mobilise opposition against the power-sharing concept and the Council of Ireland.

The SDLP themselves did little until mid-1973 to promote the image of a legitimate governmental partner. The simple aim of participation in a regional administration was not enough to demonstrate their good intent in Protestant eyes in view of past actions. In this context, Paddy Devlin's view that 'a sustained run in office . . . could syphon off the sectarian poison from the atmosphere'[59] was naive in the extreme. The Executive's fate was finally sealed whenever the loyalists were able to convince a large number of Protestants as to the validity of their interpretation and the spectre of Irish unity that was raised was something their rhetoric was best equipped to exploit. The ultimate expression of this opposition, the UWC strike, was similar in aim but different in form to the Protestant veto originally used to prevent the application of the third Home Rule Bill to Ulster in 1912.

The reasons for the failure of the Executive also pinpoint the conditions necessary to sustain any future power-sharing experiment in Ulster. On the one hand, there would need to be a much wider field of common agreement between the coalition partners; and on the other, the natural opposition to the new regime would have to accept the aims of the partners as legitimate and confine their opposition to constructive constitutional forms. In a political system that feeds on extremism and has shown a remarkable degree of electoral stability in the nature and type of groups it produces, the prospects for finding a power-sharing formula that could command the necessary consent must seem remote, to say the least.

11 Impasse
(June 1974–March 1976)

For the Catholic community in Northern Ireland the various attempts to articulate their political demands have proved notably unsuccessful. The attempts to abolish partition through political channels and hence end their permanent minority status have achieved little, as has the reform of the province's electoral system. Attempts to shift the dimension of the conflict from religion has made only marginally better gains. On the other hand, the possibility of a change in the rules determining the formation of the government so that government by a numerical majority is replaced by government of the two communities has proved to be far-reaching. But the success of such a change in the political system is contingent on the acquiescence of the majority community, for, in other words, the expressions of opposition towards the new system must fall within the definable framework of constitutional practice.

The power-sharing system of government fell in 1974 because Protestant consent was not forthcoming, and because loyalist political opposition towards it transcended the constitutional framework and became an opposition of principle. Any hopes the Catholic community harboured that loyalism would welcome, or at least accept, institutionalised power-sharing were therefore dashed. By 1975 both sides, each equally united and cohesive, had again reached an impasse. In 1972 the impasse in the Stormont parliament had been broken by the British who tried to operate an alternative to majority rule. With the 1975 Convention the British again took the initiative, but for the tactical reason of not wishing to become embroiled in imposing a system of government on the province, left the onus for finding an alternative with local political forces.

THE AFTERMATH OF THE EXECUTIVE'S COLLAPSE

The disintegration of the Executive, and with it the whole system of government so carefully planned and expedited by the British, brought confusion in its wake. No immediate alternative policy existed, other than a reversion to direct rule which all the parties agreed was no solution: there was a need for a permanent, locally elected administration. The political repercussions were most severe on the Northern Ireland Office (NIO) and the SDLP, the former because they were forced to temporarily fill the governmental vacuum and concomitantly formulate an alternative policy, and the latter because they had built their political *raison d'être* around the maintenance of a Catholic presence in government, a demand now unambiguously rejected by the Protestant community.

Having initially dismissed the success of the strike as the result of intimidation, in a more considered atmosphere the NIO were forced to recognise the popular repudiation of the Executive. Excluding the temporary expedient of direct rule, only two options for seeking a new basis of political agreement in the province presented themselves. Firstly, all the powers of decision could be reserved to Westminster, or secondly, the Ulster politicians could themselves be asked to draft a constitution. Given the intractable nature of the problem, the NIO not unnaturally took the latter path. The Secretary of State, Merlyn Rees, was himself forced to recognise the rise of 'a new form of Protestant nationalism . . . which . . . has brought together many strands of what has hitherto been regarded as unionist opinion.'[1] The device of a constitutional Convention enabled Rees to sidestep this new element.

In July 1974 a White Paper, *The Northern Ireland Constitution*, was published which set out the details of the proposed constitutional Convention. Rees concluded after discussions with the parties that 'many people in Northern Ireland would welcome the chance of trying themselves to find a way of solving their own political and economic problems . . . the time has come to give representatives of all the people of Northern Ireland the opportunity to meet together to discuss the future.'[2] To this end the Convention was empowered 'to consider what provisions for the government of Northern Ireland would be likely to command the most widespread acceptance throughout the community . . .'[3] The method of election was identical to that of the Assembly. The Convention was to remain in existence until 'the date of laying its final report, or six months from the date of its first meeting, whichever is the earlier' and provision existed for a recall up to six months after dissolution. Powers were also enacted to allow 'the holding of a referendum or referenda on questions arising out of the work of the Convention.' The chairman was to be independent and not a member of the Convention; this person of 'high standing and impartiality from Northern Ireland' subsequently emerged as Sir Robert Lowry, the Lord Chief Justice.

In attempting to create a stable environment for the functioning of the Convention, the activities of the NIO apparently transcended that of the purely academic, and they arranged a ceasefire with the Provisional IRA.[4] Since 1972 and the revelation of Whitelaw's meeting with IRA leaders, the government had been unable to risk the opprobrium of renewing direct contacts with the organisation. On this occasion the initiative was taken by a group of Ulster Protestant clergymen who met the Provisional leaders at

Feakle, Co. Clare, on 10 December 1974 with at least the tacit approval of the NIO. The outcome was a ceasefire lasting initially from 22 December 1974 to 16 January 1975 and after an intervening breakdown, caused more by lack of communication than fundamental disagreement, renewed indefinitely from 9 February. The ceasefire was greeted with some alarm by the SDLP since it appeared to devalue their role as elected spokesmen for the Catholic community. The introduction of Sinn Féin 'incident centres' to 'act as a point of contact in either direction'[5] was another sinister aspect in SDLP eyes, since the function of these centres appeared less communication than an attempt by Sinn Féin to gain political credibility in Catholic areas by instituting advice centres.

Some suggestions were also made that IRA tactics were guided more by a secretive NIO admission that withdrawal from Northern Ireland – the principal IRA demand – would commence if and when the Convention failed. This view was propounded by one of the clergymen instrumental in arranging the Feakle talks, the Rev. William Arlow, who stated in May that he believed that 'the British government have given a firm commitment to the Provisional IRA that they will withdraw the army from Northern Ireland. This would be under circumstances such as if the present constitutional Convention fails to produce an agreed structure of government for the province.'[6] The statement was widely condemned and, whether or not true, negated any possible advantages gained by the halt in the IRA campaign by arousing loyalist (and even SDLP) fears that the British were undermining the role of the Convention. That the gains the IRA made from the ceasefire were modest gives credence to Arlow's contention. In the Commons, Rees admitted that 'the actions of the security forces . . . would be related to the level of any activity which might occur', adding, perhaps by way of a hint, that if a 'genuine and sustained cessation of violence' continued, then 'the room for response is considerable.'[7]

The SDLP's position was also difficult. Since 1973 the party's strategy had been built around the twin aims of power-sharing and an in-stitutionalised Irish dimension, but the loyalists had now emphatically rejected both. Moreover, the SDLP had risked losing support by participating in the ill-fated Executive before internment had been phased out, not to mention Austin Currie's introduction of collection charges on rent and rates arrears. The Executive's collapse did not produce the anticipated party split for two reasons. Firstly, the organisational structure helped to absorb the shock of the collapse and not least rank-and-file discontent with the Assembly party for their acquiescence in a phased Council of Ireland. Secondly, and more bluntly, Catholic politicians had no feasible alternative. The SDLP had become the major electoral choice of the Catholic community and from that fact enjoyed the peculiar political advantages that stemmed from having a single, organised party speaking for one community. A split would result in no single group having the ability to authoritatively articulate Catholic political demands. Thus, while a split was averted, much public dissension and acrimony emerged inside the party and also with the Dublin and Westminster governments who had begun to reassess and re-evaluate their respective roles in the light of the new situation.

Within the party a number of clashes occurred. In the course of one, Edward McGrady, who had called for a British declaration of intent to withdraw from the province, was publicly rebuked by Ivan Cooper. In a more serious disagreement, the differing views of Paddy Devlin and the then party treasurer, Paddy Duffy, came into sharp relief. Duffy had asserted that in order to 'create the common ground for a solution' he was prepared to accept the various facets of Protestantism and to recognise the constitutional position of Northern Ireland. In addition, he attacked his colleagues for 'failing to lead the Catholic community' in their efforts to be non-sectarian. Devlin issued a public rebuttal and declared that the main facets of Protestantism were malevolent and reaffirmed the party commitment to unity by consent. In criticising the view that the party's role was to 'lead the Catholic community', Devlin provided the interesting interpretation that the SDLP represented constituencies where 'the voters' by accident, happen to be Catholics.'[8] Although these and other disputes at times displayed a degree of bitterness rare to public intra-party disagreements, they were symptomatic not so much of irreconcilable dissension but rather of confusion as to how post-Executive party policy was to be defined and articulated.

The disputes with the Dublin government were perhaps more serious in so far as they had a bearing on the formulation of party policy. After the replacement of the traditionally nationalistic Fianna Fáil by a Fine Gael/Irish Labour coalition in 1973, Dublin had seen itself less and less as a latent guarantor of the Ulster Catholic minority. After the UWC strike government policy became, in the words of a confidential policy document prepared by Conor Cruise O'Brien, 'to avert the emergence of a loyalist majority in the Convention elections.'[9] To this end the government adopted a 'low profile', avoiding any reference to the Irish dimension that might 'reduce the chances of power-sharing, and increase loyalist strength.' In line with this policy, Cosgrave said in June that the people of the Republic did not desire 'unity or close association with a people so deeply imbued with violence and its effects.'[10] O'Brien himself remarked that the most practical aim could not be Irish unity, but to 'reconstruct power-sharing and. . . . make whatever sacrifices are required to that end.'[11] SDLP politicians saw themselves being abandoned to their fate.

Accompanying these fears was the suspicion that the British might also renege on their basic commitments. Despite explicit assurances in the White Paper, *The Northern Ireland Constitution*, that there would have to be 'some form of power-sharing and partnership' and that 'any political arrangements must recognise and provide for . . . an Irish dimension', it was a measure of the party's lack of confidence that they sought political undertakings directly from the Prime Minister, Harold Wilson. While assurances were quickly forthcoming on power-sharing, the delegation that met Wilson was less than happy about the British commitment to the Irish dimension.

The impact of these changes on the SDLP was not a fundamental reassessment of party policy – in any event no alternative existed – but rather a reiteration of the cardinal, non-bargainable points. A solution could only be found in the context of 'partnership between both sections of the Northern community and between both parts of this island based on agreement.'[12] In addition, a stronger British stand against the loyalists was demanded. If the loyalists refused to consent to the framework defined by the British and Dublin policies, the SDLP demanded 'a radical reappraisal of their position by both sovereign governments' involving a re-examination of 'the fundamental basis of British policy towards Northern Ireland since 1920.'[13] Ultimately it was hoped such a confrontation would lead to a British declaration that the province could remain in the United Kingdom 'only until such times as agreed institutions of government are established which allow the people of Ireland, North and South, to live together in harmony, peace and independence.'[14]

Tactically, the outcome of this policy was to shift the onus for defining the framework of the new situation on to the loyalists. The initiative did not rest with the SDLP, but with 'those who have rejected the existing institutions to make clear publicly whether or not they are prepared to work with us.'[15] Moreover, the issue on which the SDLP sought to confront the loyalists was power-sharing, not the Irish dimension, for the simple reason that a breakdown on power-sharing would mean that they could count on the moral support of the moderate Unionists, and of the Westminster and Dublin governments, support which would not be as readily forthcoming if the contentious issue was the Irish dimension. The approach of placing the responsibility for justifying their policy on to the loyalists, and explaining their own position only when it was specifically sought, remained the basic SDLP stance throughout the period of the Convention.

THE FIRST PHASE OF THE CONVENTION

The results of the Convention election gave the loyalists a resounding victory, with candidates endorsed by the UUUC securing 46 of the 78 Convention seats and another seat falling to an unaligned loyalist. The SDLP lost two seats from their Assembly total, with 17 successful candidatures. A large turnover of personnel occurred within the loyalist grouping. The expulsion of the pro-Faulkner Unionists from the official Unionist Party paved the way for an influx of mainstream (and in parliamentary terms inexperienced) Unionists into elective politics. Fighting the election as a component of a coalition further weakened the official Unionists and, with 19 seats, they emerged as an overall minority within the UUUC Convention party. The reduced influence of the official Unionists, further exacerbated by the indecisiveness of their leader, Harry West, meant that effective control of the coalition (and hence the Convention) fell to the more politically skilled and immensely energetic leader of the smallest component within the UUUC, the Rev. Ian Paisley.

The election campaign was fought by the SDLP on the basic principles of their philosophy, power-sharing and the Irish dimension. The only apparent compromise was that the institutions which would give the principles expression were vague and therefore negotiable. In its implications, the loyalist campaign sounded ominous to SDLP ears. The UUUC manifesto demanded a 'democratically elected parliament with a system of government broadly in line with the provisions to be made for constitutional devolution in the United Kingdom as a whole.' It rejected as 'inherently undemocratic any artificial device for giving any political party or interest a larger share of representation, influence or power than that to which its electoral support entitles it.'[16] In order to avoid the possibility of any ambiguity, a pledge was initiated which, signed by all prospective UUUC candidates, committed them unequivocally to the manifesto.[17]

After the Convention's initial meeting on 8 May 1975, a Standing Orders Committee, composed of seven loyalists, three SDLP members and one each from UPNI and the Alliance Party, was established to draw up the draft rules of procedure. Dissension developed within the committee at an early stage, initially over how the Convention should arrange its business, but later on how it should deliver its final report to Westminster. The SDLP's first premonition of how the loyalists would dominate the proceedings came in the form of Draft Rule 10 of the Standing Orders, which set up a 12-strong Business Committee to 'arrange the business of the Convention'.[18] Both SDLP and Alliance sought a greater role for the Chairman in that they had more faith in him to allow minority views representation than the loyalist-dominated committee. An amendment tabled by Alliance to instruct the committee only to 'advise and assist the Chairman'[19] was defeated by 44 votes to 29, and the UUUC Rule 10 was adopted on 4 June.

The second dispute involved the submission of the Convention's final report to Westminster. Under Draft Rule 15 the UUUC contended that only a single draft report need be submitted, provided that it had the support of a majority of the members. In the context of a failure to find agreement, this would mean that the loyalist report would become the formal submission of the whole Convention. The SDLP response to this was to consider seeking a High Court decision, arguing that Draft Rule 15 was *ultra vires* according to the terms of the Northern Ireland Constitution Act. Hume argued that not only the majority proposals needed to be included in the final report but also 'the proposals of any sizeable minority of the Convention.'[20] In the event, litigation was not pursued because of the time involved and instead, as 'both the speediest and most satisfactory method of dealing with the problem'[21], a ruling was sought from the Chairman. Somewhat to the surprise of the SDLP, after a lengthy and fully considered statement from the chair, Lowry found 'the proposed rule quite in order.'[22]

The animosities engendered by these initial disagreements were temporarily (but only temporarily) dispelled during the initial debates, which took place in a mood of almost universal harmony. Hume's approach was perhaps the most conciliatory and well-argued. In the course of an eloquent speech delivered during a debate on an all-party motion, he stated:

> One of the greatest weaknesses and causes of failure in this community has been that the ideals which different sections of it have held have been misrepresented by other sections. . . . Not only have both traditions on this island got to rethink their position but we have got to re-examine the fundamentals of our traditions, including the basic political commandments that have been handed down to us.[23]

But this conciliatory mood fostered a false repose, in that debating general, all-party motions did not deal with the basic contentious questions. Whatever the talk of compromise, neither side was, in the last analysis, retreating on its principles: the UUUC had pledged themselves never to have Catholics in government, but offered a committee system to give the minority a share in power; the SDLP would not give up the aim of securing representation at the highest levels of government, but were willing to compromise on the form of that presence.

The divisive questions were not discussed until the inter-party talks held between the UUUC and the three main groups, the SDLP, UPNI and Alliance, during the summer recess. The UUUC-SDLP talks, the most crucial, began on 8 August, with the UUUC negotiators consisting of William Craig, William Beattie and Austin Ardill. John Hume, Paddy Devlin and Austin Currie represented the SDLP. Paisley himself was not directly concerned in these talks and limited himself to acting as a negotiator in the UUUC-Alliance talks.

The critical meeting, which had been arranged directly between the parties and hence had no formal chairman and of which no formal record was kept, took place on 26 August when the UUUC presented a document outlining their main policy objectives. The SDLP expressed interest in paragraph 8 of the document which explicated the eventualities in which coalition government could come about. There were three possible situations:

1. By agreement between the parties before an election and obtaining approval from the electorate;

2. Where the largest party in parliament does not have an overall majority and needs to obtain it by agreement with another party. At best this can only be a short-term government;

3. Where an emergency or crisis situation exists and parties, by agreement, come together in the national interest for the duration of the crisis.[24]

At a further meeting the next day, the two sides unanimously agreed to seek outside advice on the question of voluntary coalition, as allowed for in paragraph 8(3) of the UUUC document. Lowry was approached and his office drafted a paper entitled 'The Voluntary Coalition Solution' which set out a possible agenda and was based on the twin assumptions that the SDLP would accept the principles of British parliamentary practice and that the UUUC would consider voluntary coalition.

At this stage the news leaked out that the two goups were exploring an area of possible compromise and grass-roots pressure came to bear on the UUUC leaders not to weaken their stand on power-sharing. In this connection, Paisley, who was not directly involved in the negotiations with the SDLP, made an irrational and dramatic statement, possibly to divert attention from the inter-party talks. Speaking after one of the province's periodic cycles of violence, and more significantly without reference to his coalition partners, he warned that loyalists would be 'forced to consider entire withdrawal from the Convention until such times as law and order are re-established.'[25] This outburst was quickly followed by a meeting on 8 September, while the UUUC-SDLP talks were in temporary suspension, at which the UUUC Convention group voted 37 to 1 to reject any possibility of power-sharing. The one dissident was William Craig, with his Vanguard colleague, David Trimble, and an official Unionist, William Morgan, abstaining. A further motion allowing the discussions with the SDLP to continue attracted only six votes in support.

Although confusion still surrounds the motives for the breaking off of the inter-party talks, it appears that it was precipitated by Paisley, who wished to halt any further exploration of the voluntary coalition idea. It is likely that he feared a compromise would split either his party or his church (or both) and in addition, a solution reached by the efforts of Craig would make him the obvious choice to lead such an administration. This interpretation is backed up by the Alliance negotiators who subsequently claimed that Paisley advocated the temporary coalition solution with some alacrity in their inter-party talks.[26]

The SDLP also supported this interpretation, pointing out that the UUUC policy document released to the press omitted a vital section. This dealt with law and order and stated that in times of grave emergency 'a special committee would exist . . . in respect of the declaration and acts of government . . . The chairmanship of such a committee would be for an opposition member.'[27] The SDLP underlined, with some justification, the illogicality of allowing them representation on such a crucial committee, but barring them access to the normal organs of government.

The repercussions of the failure of the inter-party talks were considerable. After the UUUC decision against power-sharing the SDLP viewed further talks as impractical. The events, Hume said,

> Have indicated to us that agreement is not possible. In these circumstances the responsible thing to do is . . . [to] take the necessary steps to complete our task as soon as possible and submit a report to Westminster . . . [it is] utterly pointless to engage in discussion on subjects proposed as solutions when parties to the discussions have already made up their minds.[28]

The repercussions were just as severe on the loyalists: Craig resigned as leader of the Vanguard Convention Party on 9 September, after failing to rally a sizeable proportion of his supporters behind him, the majority of whom left to form the United Ulster Unionist Movement, led by Craig's erstwhile deputy, Ernest Baird. The UUUC, hailed only months before as the catalyst for a new, all-inclusive loyalist political party, appeared on the verge of fragmentation.

By any standards the UUUC created a tremendous tactical blunder. If the inter-party talks had followed their intended path, the onus would have been placed on the SDLP to elucidate their position on the voluntary coalition concept. This would have presented two problems for the SDLP. Firstly, the concept did not allow for an institutionalised Irish dimension and while the SDLP might have absorbed this, the second problem, that no guarantees existed as to the SDLP's participation after 'the emergency' had ended, was fundamental. As Ivan Cooper declared, much to the annoyance of his colleagues, they would not 'accept less than full-blooded partnership throughout the community – in cabinet, on statutory boards and on councils.'[29] However the coalition proposals would not require such power-sharing, as they did not deviate from British parliamentary practice.

In the event of the coalition idea being put to the SDLP, a refusal would have left the UUUC in a far stronger position *vis-à-vis* Westminster, who would find it difficult to resist loyalist demands for a revived Stormont. As it turned out, internal loyalist dissension prevented this denouement coming about and the UUUC were cast as the obstructionists, a role which seemed to justify the SDLP's 'low profile' during the Convention and their reticence in commenting on voluntary coalition on the grounds that the loyalists had prematurely dismissed it.

The end of the inter-party talks marked the practical collapse of any possibility of agreement in the Convention. All that was left to do was to pass a report and submit it to Westminster. As the SDLP had feared at the beginning, the UUUC domination of the Business Committee meant that the majority loyalist report would be the formal Convention submission. Hume made it clear that they 'would have much preferred the final report of this Convention to have been drafted by impartial persons . . . after having had submitted to them the proposals of all the parties. In that way we could have had a report which generally reflected the views of all sections of the population.'[30] In view of this the party decided not to participate in further debate on the UUUC report, which could only add 'respectability to the views of a sectional majority.'[31] Despite a last-minute Alliance bid to have the report referred back, on 7 November it was resolved by 42 votes to 31 that the UUUC report be the formal Convention submission, exactly six months after the first Convention sitting.

Although the formal Convention submission, the finally published UUUC report also incorporated the detailed plans of the other major parties. This embarrassed the SDLP on two counts. Firstly, from a tactical point of view it appeared to contradict the SDLP interpretation of the Convention as an exercise in loyalist dominance, with the viewpoints of minority parties being consistently and consciously suppressed. Secondly, in terms of policies it brought the SDLP plans into public view for the first time, in contravention to the general party strategy of defining their plans only when specifically called upon to do so.

The report was discussed at Westminster on 12 January 1976. The Secretary of State, Merlyn Rees, concluded that although there was much agreement between the Convention parties, 'the report does not, in the view of the government, command sufficiently widespread acceptance throughout the community to provide stable and effective government.'[32] In a letter to Lowry, published on 16 January,[33] the Convention was ordered to reconvene on 3 February. The most intriguing aspect of the first phase of the Convention was the apparent volte-face by Craig on the issue of power-sharing. Craig's consent to SDLP participation in government was in fact the outcome of a gradual change initiated in 1974. His first Convention speech was notably conciliatory and after the formal rift with his UUUC colleagues he became a forceful proponent of the merits of coalition government. But like Faulkner, and more distantly Terence O'Neill, Craig fell victim to right-wing loyalism, in that as he moved towards a moderate or conciliatory position *vis-à-vis* the Catholic minority, he was immediately separated from the mainstream movement.

The problem for loyalist politicians was to state as unambiguously as possible to the electorate that they would not tolerate Catholics in government, although they employed the pejorative and emotive term 'republicans' in order to avoid appearing too overtly sectarian. Thus Faulkner had vacillated on the question, leading his electorate to believe that he rejected power-sharing. Craig had done the same by stating that there would be no deviation from British parliamentary practice. To most Protestants this meant a return to Stormont and the permanent exclusion of Catholics, but when Craig reinterpretated it as meaning that *in certain circumstances* it was admissible to tolerate a Catholic presence, he was ostracised, like Faulkner, not for having broken the word of his election commitment, but for breaking the spirit.

THE SECOND PHASE OF THE CONVENTION

After the dramatic events of the summer and the confusion wrought in loyalist ranks by Craig's conversion to voluntary coalition, the second phase of the Convention was an anticlimax. In order to reassert loyalist unity before the commencement of the new session the three UUUC groups met in Enniskillen in January 1976. In a remarkable display, all 40 – except one official Unionist, James Kilfedder – signed a written affirmation that there would be no deviation from the already submitted majority loyalist report. This attempt to patch up loyalist unity was aimed not just at cementing the coalition after the ejection of the four Vanguard members, but to prevent the gradual defection of some elements of the official Unionists known to favour voluntary coalition.[34]

Any hopes Westminster harboured that Craig might be a catalyst towards compromise were destroyed not just by the Enniskillen meeting but by the renewal of the SDLP policy on the RUC. At the December 1975 annual conference the leadership's non-recognition policy towards the police was overwhelmingly endorsed, despite a threat from one prominent member, Tom Donnelly, that he would resign if the policy was not rescinded (a threat subsequently carried out). The decision was attacked from all sides and interpreted as undermining Vanguard's coalition demands. Craig expressed regret that the party could not have given support so as to 'reassure the majority of their sincerity in seeking an agreement on the lines indicated during the inter-party talks.'[35]

The SDLP themselves felt their position was being misrepresented. On the one hand, it was claimed, they supported the police in the performance of their normal day-to-day duties; on the other, they would not give overall endorsement or partcipate in police liaison exercises in the absence of a general political settlement. They would support the police as 'agents of the responsible authority in impartially seeking out any criminal . . . [but] what we cannot do is to give unequivocal and blanket support to security forces for which we have no responsibility.'[36] To most Protestants the qualifications appeared to give credence to the accusations that the party was indulging in semantics. To some degree this was accurate, for the problem was that they recognised the immense post-1969 changes in the structure and membership of the RUC and were inclined to give their support, yet the tremendous animosity the RUC still created in Catholic areas dictated that they make support conditional, not absolute. Qualifying the policing issue by linking it to political change was advantageous in sustaining Catholic support, but highly detrimental to their image among Protestants. Aware of this, the party inserted a full-page advertisement in the main Protestant daily paper, the *Belfast News Letter*, in February, outlining their positions both on the police and the status of Northern Ireland.[37]

The Convention reconvened on 3 February and almost immediately a new series of inter-party talks commenced, this time arranged by the Chairman, chaired by him and officially recorded. After a number of meetings had been held between various groupings in a carefully planned series of fourteen, the first direct encounter between the UUUC and the SDLP took place on 12 February. As so often in Northern Ireland, the security situation had a direct influence on the day's events. The news broke that morning of the death of IRA hunger striker Frank Stagg. West Belfast and other Catholic areas experienced considerable violence and rumours circulated in the Convention that SDLP members who lived in these areas would be physically prevented from leaving their homes. The SDLP once again saw Catholic support slipping away from them towards the republican movement. Not only was the atmosphere therefore unconducive to compromise, but there must have been at least a shadow of doubt in the minds of the SDLP leaders as to whether a calmly worked out political solution with the loyalists, even if it were feasible, would not put them farther out of touch with grass-roots Catholic opinion.

At the UUUC-SDLP meeting no less than ten UUUC negotiators (including the three leaders) faced a four-man SDLP delegation, led by Gerry Fitt. After putting a series of questions to the UUUC, Fitt asked for an adjournment. When the SDLP delegation returned, Fitt restated the SDLP position and while Paisley was in the process of making a reply, the SDLP delegation walked out, saying that they were 'only prepared to engage in discussions which are seriously attempting to meet the partnership conditions – in our view, the UUUC are neither sincere nor serious about obtaining agreement with the SDLP.'[38]

While there was little hope that the second phase would produce agreement, the break-up of the talks marked the end of even a semblance of an attempt to find a solution. Only two minor attempts were made to try and resuscitate the Convention. Craig, who was still vigorously extolling the merits of voluntary coalition, took up a hint from Rees that the government would consider holding a referendum on the idea to try and undercut the UUUC. He moved a Convention motion to this effect recommending 'that the guidance of the Northern Ireland electorate should be sought through a referendum on the acceptability of any agreement founded on the commitment to a broadly based coalition government for a temporary period.'[39] The motion foundered on the opposition of the UUUC and the apathy of the SDLP. Hume stated that the SDLP would only welcome a referendum 'after full agreement, where everything is explicitly agreed.'[40] In the event the motion found support only from the Alliance Party.

The second attempt to revive the possibility of agreement came in the form of an Alliance plan for a three-tier government, incorporating a cabinet, a privy council and a series of committees. The cabinet would consist of five members drawn from the majority grouping in the legislature and would allocate resources between ten departmental chairmen selected or elected on a proportionate basis. A council of state would form the third component, composed of eight members proportionally elected and exercising advisory and executive powers in the security and human rights field.[41] Although the ingenuity of the proposals required study, it was a measure of the disillusionment that had crept into the SDLP that they dismissed the plan outright. The UUUC expressed some interest, but were motivated more by tactical concerns than genuine curiosity.

The Convention ended in direct contrast to how it had begun: in acrimony and dissension. It was formally dissolved from 5 March after the loyalists had again submitted their majority report. Speaking in the House of Commons, Rees wrote the epitaph of the Convention when he admitted that there was 'now no prospect of agreement between the parties there . . . it is clearly not possible at this time to make progress towards a devolved system of government for Northern Ireland . . . the government . . . does not contemplate any major new initiative for some time to come.'[42]

CONCLUSION

In a long-term perspective, the Convention was intended to act as a buffer between the UWC strike and indefinite direct rule. A means had to be found to dissipate loyalist euphoria which was being swiftly translated into uncompromising demands for a return to the Stormont system of government. To deny this to loyalists at such a time would have been to risk violence: thus the Convention was used to divert their energies. As a distraction it was successful and even left the loyalists in some disarray. Moreover, Paisley and some of the official Unionists were not opposed to direct rule, for they realised that the electorate themselves were also, apparently, not dissatisfied with it. In a poll conducted in early March, 74 per cent of the respondents (with the two religious groups in almost equal proportions) found direct rule an acceptable political alternative.[43]

The prospect of a long period of direct rule if the Convention report were rejected produced much negative thinking on the loyalist side even before the Convention met, so the prospect of agreement was always remote. But the structure of the Convention itself was not conducive to compromise, because, as a body based on established parliamentary practice, it encouraged 'built-in tendencies and pressures towards prepared attitudes,

set public speeches, confrontation, disagreement and majority voting.'[44]
For the SDLP the repercussions of failure were the possibility of their losing
electoral ascendancy over the Catholic community, for in six years they
appeared to have made little tangible gains. Militant loyalism had refused
to accept them as a legitimate opposition and militant republicanism still
waited to capitalise on their failures.

The one apparent hope of compromise, voluntary coalition, was
potentially disastrous for the SDLP. If the idea had been pursued, they
would have been forced to choose between the *aspiration* towards Irish
unity and the *fact* of accepting the permanence of the Ulster state. The
stark alternatives it left them were either to refuse voluntary coalition and
hence lose any credibility among Protestants and the British government,
or accept and thus participate in an Ulster administration without an
institutionalised link with the Irish Republic. Before they were formally
confronted with this invidious choice, the loyalists fortuitously divided on
the issue. Thus the SDLP were not only freed from having to choose,
something they had assiduously declined to do, but given an able publicist
in the form of Craig, who ignored no opportunity in saying that the SDLP
were a responsible and legitimate party with the interests of Northern
Ireland at heart.

A further consequence for the SDLP was a move away from the policies
inaugurated by the 1973 White Paper by the Westminster political parties.
Thus the SDLP were forced to revert to a pre-White Paper position and
seek explicit commitments from the Westminster parties about their
positions on power-sharing and the Irish dimension – still the cornerstones
of SDLP and, theoretically, British government, policy. This was illustrated by the exchange of letters between Denis Haughey, the SDLP
chairman, and Airey Neave, the Conservative party spokesman on
Northern Ireland, in October 1976. Haughey demanded explicit assurances that Conservative policy on Ulster was still guided by the 1973 White
Paper. Neave refused to give this, and would only say that he was
committed to 'a system of government that can command widespread
support throughout the community, including the minority', an answer
Haughey found 'quite unsatisfactory'.[45] The equivocal attitude of the
Conservatives to post-1973 British policy in Ulster was largely a more
public reflection of the Labour Party's attitude. By 1976 the SDLP's
demands for constitutional change in Northern Ireland, beginning in
1970, had in many ways turned full circle.

Conclusion

Moderate political conflict is an important prerequisite for the successful functioning of any democratic society. It depends upon the existence of individuals open to conversion on specific issues and willing to be recruited into political parties and groups. The supportive influence of conflict increases where individuals are subject to cross-pressures through over-lapping memberships and where a variety of cleavages cross-cut one another. Rather than resulting in disintegration, the diversity of political conflict tends to promote cohesion, since an individual may be a member of a majority on one issue and a member of a minority on another.[1] In a comparative context a bi-polar conflict, that is one which sustains two distinct and self-perpetuating communities ranged around a single all-pervasive cleavage, is rare. Extremism is likely to flourish because of the system's inability to resolve negotiable political issues and be encouraged by the tendency of the two groups to isolate their respective followers from conflicting stimuli, a process achieved by further intensifying the saliency of the dominant cleavage.[2]

The Northern Ireland political system is probably the best example of a bi-polar conflict. Since its formation in 1920 the system has sustained two uncompromising opponents, existing in a condition of virtual political atrophy. The problem has been further compounded by the fact that as the two communities are expressed in a majority and a minority within a democratic system, without substantive political (or societal) change, the conflict holds the prospect of preservation in perpetuity. The permanency of their respective positions, faithfully reproduced by successive elections, means that the system can be variously termed 'a majority dictatorship'[3] or 'a predominant-party system'[4] with one community continually repre-sented in power, the other in opposition. As the minority community is excluded from political power *sine die*, it possesses no motivation to participate in the conventional political process or to repudiate the elements within it who respond to political frustration by propagating extremist solutions.

As Rose suggests, any meaningful discussion of Ulster politics must be prefaced by the assumption that in theory the problem has no solution.[5] The two communities are so deeply polarised that there is a zero-sum equation: the gains of one community will always be inversely pro-portional to the losses of the other. Whatever means the two sides adopt to channel their political demands will have a direct and substantial impact on the system as a whole. To return, therefore, to the conceptual problem initially raised in the Introduction: how does a community that constitutes one-third of the population of the state articulate its political demands? The SDLP has provided one such method of articulation, but what have been its major successes and innovations in endeavouring to mitigate this minority status?

The response of the Catholic community in Ulster to permanent political opposition, expressed up to 1969 through the medium of the Nationalist Party, was to seek to widen the boundaries of the state. Such an exogenous change would increase the size of the Catholic electorate and hence alter the *weight* of their community within the political system by creating an all-Ireland Catholic majority. The SDLP's answer has been to demand endogenous change and not to attempt to alter the weights, but *the institutions within which the weights are applied*. The goal is thus a change in the rules governing the organisation and procedure of the political system. Two aims have been paramount: a change in the electoral system, and more importantly, a change in the rules governing the formation of the executive government, so as to require the inclusion of the political representatives of the Catholic community. To date, only the change in the electoral system has been accepted as legitimate by the loyalists, and then only tenuously.

In electoral terms, between 1929 and 1969 the plurality system favoured the two major groups, the Nationalists and the Unionists. The pre-1929 electoral system, proportional representation, had favoured smaller parties by lowering the threshold of representation. Between 1929 and 1969 under the plurality system the Nationalists gained an average of 13.3 per cent of the valid vote and 16.2 per cent of the seats, an over-representation that was due to the high level of uncontested seats. In the Assembly and Convention elections, conducted under PR, the SDLP won 22.9 per cent of the vote and 23.1 per cent of the seats, a highly proportional result. In fact the benefits to the Catholic community of PR have rested not so much on the proportionality of the outcome, but in the incentive given by the large multi-member constituencies to nominate candidates over the whole province and particularly in areas containing small minorities of Catholics hitherto untouched by anti-partitionist politics.

But by far the more important strategy adopted by the SDLP is the demand for participation, as of right, in the executive level of government. As the normal rules of governmental formation exclude a minority, unless in coalition with another group with whom it constitutes a majority, a change in the rules to accommodate minority participation stimulates the main aim of most political parties: the desire for political office. It further provides an incentive for a minority to engage in electoral competition, since, although it has no prospect of attaining a majority, electoral strength provides an indicator of what level of representation the minority should gain within the executive. The articulation of this power-sharing demand has led to four important innovations that mark the SDLP out as a new element in Ulster politics and have important repercussions in the post-1970 political debate.

Firstly, the prerequisite to power-sharing is constructive participation in the state. While favouring eventual Irish reunification, the SDLP constitution states that it seeks unity only 'by the consent of a majority of the people in Northern Ireland'. As this consent is not forthcoming, unity is consigned to a secondary position, and participation within the prevailing constitutional framework is justified. There remains, however, some equivocation on unity, for despite the commitment to the *status quo*, unity has been positively sought on a number of occasions without regard to its practicality. Thus, for example, when the condominium plan was drawn up, Irish unity rather than participation in the present framework was given priority, as also was the case in party pronouncements with regard to the proposed Council of Ireland in early 1974. But it is worthy of note that whenever the SDLP has been under pressure, as during the period of the 1975 constitutional Convention, in practical negotiations the demand for an institutionalised link (though not the psychological bond) with the Irish Republic has been relegated in favour of the demand for a community administration that would include themselves.

Secondly, the power-sharing demand has transferred a majority within the Catholic community that previously withheld consent from the regime but complied with its basic political laws into a majority conceding both consent and compliance. Thus those Catholics previously refusing to recognise the Stormont regime have been willing to at least temporarily forgo the main alternative, Irish unity, by supporting a provincial regime containing representatives of both communities. That the SDLP has been able to both mould and reflect Catholic opinion on this issue demonstrates that it is, in Neumann's phrase, 'a party of representation'[6] in so far as it is electorally oriented. This is emphasised by the attempt to legitimise the system by creating greater consensus, even though its support is contingent on the declared willingness of the majority to initiate qualitative political change on the party's own terms.

Thirdly, as a 'party of representation', organisation is essential for electoral strength and maximising the weight of the power-sharing argument. The prospect of political power inherent in the argument creates the rationale for a mass party organisation, as such a body cannot be maintained without the prospect of attaining a practical, meaningful, goal. The adoption of a socialist pattern of organisation, incorporating a mass membership and based around the branch, makes the SDLP structurally similar to most socialist and social democratic political parties in Western Europe. The utilisation of mass party organisation has been an innovation within the Ulster party system as almost all the parties (including those in the Irish Republic) are based on the cadre, a form of organisation that depends on 'the grouping of notabilities'.[7]

While novel in Irish terms, the structure conforms to the pattern of the distribution of power within socialist parties. As Michels was the first to conclude, a small element within the organisational framework takes decisions and controls the direction of the party, not the mass itself.[8] Within the SDLP this oligarchic control is exercised not by the executive committee, a group of activists who have risen from the ranks of the membership, but by the elected representatives. The exercise of this power by an elected group (theoretically sub-ordinate to the executive committee which itself expresses the wishes of the mass) is consonant with Catholic social structure and political attitudes. In Ireland as a whole political relationships tend to be familial, personalistic and encompass a strong link between the broker (the politician) and client (the voter). The pattern of attitudes that these clientelist relationships engender fosters a deference to authority, in this case personified by the local politician, that negates the ability of any group of ordinary party members to have their wishes implemented.

The inclusion of socialist organisation and symbols as part of the SDLP appeal emphasises class and socio-economic concerns, a cleavage that cross-cuts the dominant religious divide. Although an attempt to organise within one community, the non-sectarian socialist structure with open membership leaves open the possibility of recruiting limited numbers of socially conscious Protestants whose aims are not catered for within any of the loyalist political parties. Downs concluded that parties seek to maximise their support by offering material inducements to the widest number of electors,[9] while Riker has modified this by contending that although parties will seek to maximise their support, they will do so only to the point of creating 'coalitions just as large as they believe will ensure winning and no larger.'[10] The determinant of the degree to which the coalition exceeds the minimum necessary size is information, for in a perfect situation groups will know exactly how much is needed to create a minimum winning coalition, but with imprecise information, larger coalitions have to be aimed at.

The size principle has important implications for SDLP strategy in Northern Ireland. As a minority, the party has only two possible directions to go to change its size: either to become a smaller minority or to gain a majority. Since cleavage lines in Northern Ireland are so clear-cut and the electorates that correspond to each political tendency so stable, almost perfect information is available, hence facilitating the deployment of a definitive coalition strategy. Thus the party's open structure allows for Protestant membership and opens the possibility of a future minimum majority. This strategy has not contradicted the aim of power-sharing, the object of which is to change the context in which the weights are applied, but in many ways it has been a parallel tactic. In any event, few positive attempts have been made to gain support from the Protestant majority, for to do so would be, in the present context of Northern Ireland, to risk defections from among the party's own Catholic supporters.

A further point in relation to organisation is its ability to ensure a continuity of allegiance among the membership that stretches beyond the dominance or charisma of individual personalities. This helps the party to preserve its values and objectives intact and to protect its members from potentially divisive forces within the political environment. Initially the SDLP appeared to represent a mere aggregation formed to articulate a variety of rudimentary political demands. However, since 1973 the development of the power-sharing concept and the growth of the organisation have enabled it to absorb certain values from the political context with which it has become identified. This process has been facilitated by the party leadership's ability to clearly define the SDLP's role in the political system and shape the structure towards that role, and by maintaining a set of values, aside from power-sharing, which have helped to preserve the organisation's character.[11]

A shared understanding has thus been diffused among the SDLP membership, through the medium of organisation, about the organisation's ultimate objectives. A widespread commitment to these objectives has become the key criterion for adapting action to the changing political environment. While this has had the consequence of preserving internal party stability, it has also meant that in crucial negotiations various objectives have not been capable of compromise because of their centrality to the organisation's survival. Thus power-sharing is a non-negotiable demand, even though in many ways it can only deliver symbolic and not real power. Other areas of government that have the potential to deliver real power have been correspondingly ignored, because they fall outside the organisation's schema of political objectives.

The fourth and final consequence of the SDLP's articulation of power-sharing has been the high level of electoral unanimity it has achieved, a level unprecedented for any single Catholic political group in Ulster. While this unanimity within the Catholic community was not demonstrated until the 1973 Assembly elections, since 1970 the party had been projected as the main elected representative of the minority and consistently fulfilled that role. Thus it formed a political counterpoint to the recrudescence of physical force republicanism, embodied in the Provisional IRA. The IRA's ability to disrupt the life of the province created the necessity for political negotiation to find a solution and brought in the British government to act as an arbiter between the conflicting aspirations of the two communities. Political change stemmed not so much from IRA violence itself as from the disinclination of the British government to tolerate that violence; after their intervention, the British assumed the role of seeking to identify and extend the possible areas of agreement and accommodation.

In the evolving conflict, the need for a political group to negotiate on behalf of the Catholic community was thus a further implication of this electoral unanimity and a role that the SDLP was well-equipped to fulfil. Prior to 1970 a significant element absent in the political situation was a single body enjoying Catholic confidence to act as a negotiator. The British government's attempt to reconstruct a power-sharing system in 1973 depended crucially on the existence of such a Catholic group whose political dominance was unchallenged and who possessed the authority to convince their supporters of the efficacy of such a solution. In turn, while emotionally and politically opposed to violence, the SDLP's negotiating role enabled them to capitalise on the potential for political reform introduced by the IRA campaign.

Ultimately, the construction of the power-sharing administration in January 1974 was made possible not only by Catholic political unity, but by Protestant disunity; in other words, a reverse of the pre-1970 situation, when Catholic fragmentation and Protestant unity had disproportionately harmed Catholics. As the experience of another divided society, the Netherlands, has illustrated, where bargaining on substantive political issues takes place, the internal political cohesion of the community, and specifically the ability of the political group to retain the allegiance of its supporters, is a vital condition.[12] With the reformation of Protestant unity in 1974 the system collapsed for the simple reason that the Protestant leaders within the administration did not hold the allegiance of their community. An impasse had again been reached and the zero-sum nature of the conflict clearly exposed.

Despite the ability of the wholly political and constitutional SDLP to win strong electoral support, the tenuous relationship of the Catholic community to physical force still exists. The symbiotic relationship between violent and constitutional political activity within both communities obviously transcends party labels and is a problem of history rather than of political science. But the ambiguity towards violence that remains, which the SDLP has strenuously sought to eradicate, must rank as the party's major failure. Thus, while the SDLP attains strong *political* endorsement, the republican movement gains widespread *latent* support as the last guarantor of the community's safety in the event of a disaster. The Catholic community may thus be said to have a dual personality, in so far as the SDLP (as the constitutional leaders) accept the system's legitimacy while parts of the grass-roots remain isolated, disaffected and willing to acquiesce in the use of republican violence. In Western countries where it has been prevalent, this duality has usually been transitional, but this is not the case in Ulster where each community expresses its fear of the other by the maintenance of an armed faction.

But whatever criticisms are made of the SDLP do not detract from the very real and significant achievements the party has made since 1970. These achievements have been made within an environment that has been at the very least hazardous, and at worst, all too frequently fatal. The party has provided a non-violent alternative to physical force, and its absence would undoubtedly have led to a greater political role for the IRA and the probable consignment of Catholics to permanent political opposition. Both of these consequences would clearly have led to a greater intensity of conflict than has so far befallen Northern Ireland.

Appendix:
The Constitution
of the Social Democratic
and Labour Party

Clause One: Name
The Association shall be called the Social Democratic and Labour Party.

Clause Two: Principles and Objects
The objects of the Party shall be as follows:
1. To organise and maintain in Northern Ireland a Socialist Party;
2. To promote the policies decided by the Party Conference;
3. To co-operate with the Irish Congress of Trade Unions in joint political or other action;
4. To promote the cause of Irish unity based on the consent of the majority of people in Northern Ireland;
5. To co-operate with other Labour Parties through the Council of Labour and to co-operate with other Social Democratic Parties at an international level;
6. To contest elections in Northern Ireland with a view to forming a Government which will implement the following principles:
(*a*) The abolition of all forms of religious, political, class or sex discrimination; the promotion of culture and the arts with a special responsibility to cherish and develop all aspects of our native culture.
(*b*) The public ownership and democratic control of such essential industries and services as the common good requires.
(*c*) The utilisation of its powers by the state, when and where necessary, to provide employment, by the establishment of publicly owned industries.

Clause Three: Membership
1. There shall be two classes of members, namely,
(*a*) Individual members;
(*b*) Corporate members.
2. Any person who subscribes to the Principles and Objects of the Party

and is not a member of any other political party may be accepted as an individual member of the Party.

3. An individual member must be accepted into membership by a Branch of the Party in the Northern Ireland Assembly Constituency where he resides or for which he is registered as an elector.

4. Where there is no Branch of the Party in the area in which he resides, a member shall be entitled to join the Branch nearest him provided that no member shall be a member of more than one Branch.

5. The Executive Committee may expel from the Party any member whose activities they consider injurious to the Party or inconsistent with its Principles and Objects.

6. A Branch of the Party may refuse into membership any person or may expel an existing member, but such persons may appeal to the Executive Committee who may confirm or reverse the decision.

7. Corporate members shall consist of Trade Unions affiliated to the Irish Congress of Trade Unions, Co-operative Societies, Socialist Societies, Professional Associations and Cultural Organisations.

8. A corporate member must accept the Principles and Objects of the Party and agree to conform to its Constitution.

9. The Executive Committee may refuse the application of any organisation for corporate membership and may expel any existing corporate member if they consider its membership would be injurious to or inconsistent with the Principles and Objects of the Party, but such an organisation may appeal against the decision of the Executive Committee to the Party Conference whose decision shall be final.

10. The Executive Committee shall report to the Party Conference all expulsions of individual or corporate members and all rejections of appeals against expulsion from Branches.

11. Each Branch shall pay to Headquarters a minimum annual subscription of £1 in respect of each of its members.

12. Each corporate member shall pay to the Executive Committee before 30th September each year an annual subscription of 25p. for each member who wishes to affiliate.

13. Annual subscriptions shall become due on the first day of January in each year and shall relate to that calendar year.

Clause Four: Branch, District and Constituency Organisation

1. A Branch of the Party shall be formed in any district with the approval of the Executive Committee which shall, if necessary, define the functional area of the Branch.

2. Each Branch shall forward, before 30th September each year, an affiliation fee of £1 for each member of the Branch together with the name and address of each paid-up member.

3. Each Branch shall hold an Annual General Meeting before March 31st at which it shall elect the following Branch Officers: Chairman, Vice-

Chairman, Secretary and Treasurer, and a Committee at which it shall transact any other relevant business. It shall, in addition, hold at least six business meetings during the year.

4. Each Branch shall promote the policies of the Party, maintain an effective organisation within its functional area and support Party candidates in local and parliamentary elections.

5. Each Branch shall draw up a set of Branch rules and deposit a copy with the Executive Committee, which shall have the power to declare all or part of the Branch's rules repugnant to the Constitution. Any amendment of or addition to a Branch's rules shall be notified to the Executive Committee.

6. Each Branch shall forward to the Treasurer before 30th September each year, a statement of the financial position of the Branch.

7. The functional area of any Branch shall not cross the boundaries of a Northern Ireland Assembly constituency.

8. A Constituency Council shall be formed in each Northern Ireland Assembly Constituency. It shall consist of representatives from each Branch of the Party in the constituency appointed according to the following scale:

Membership	Number of Representatives
10—30	2
31—60	3

and additional representatives in these proportions. Branch representation, at any time, shall be determined by the membership registered at Party H.Q. on the previous registration date. The registration dates shall be March 31st, June 30th, September 30th and December 31st each year.

9. Each Constituency Council shall hold an Annual Meeting at which it will elect the following officers: Chairman, Vice-Chairman, Secretary and Treasurer, and transact any other relevant business. It shall, in addition, hold a minimum of three business meetings during the year.

10. The following shall be members of the Constituency Council ex-officio:

(a) The members of the Legislative Assembly for the constituency and the members of the United Kingdom Parliament who are members of the Party;

(b) The Party's prospective candidates for the constituency;

(c) Those members of the Executive Committee who reside in the constituency;

(d) The members of the District Councils who reside in the constituency.

11. The functions of the Constituency Council shall be as follows:

(a) To promote, through publicity and other means, the policies of the Party in the constituency;

(*b*) To co-ordinate the work of the Branches in the constituency;

(*c*) To organise, with the approval of the Executive Committee, new Branches of the Party in the constituency where it is deemed necessary;

(*d*) To create and maintain in the constituency an effective electoral organisation.

12. Where there is only one Branch of the Party in a constituency the Branch shall perform the functions of the Constituency Council.

13. A District Executive of the Party shall be formed in each District Council area. It shall be constituted as follows:

(*a*) Representatives from each Branch in the District Council area according to the following scale:

Membership	Number of Representatives
10–30	2
31–60	3

and additional representatives in these proportions. Branch representation, at any time, shall be determined by the membership registered at Party H.Q. on the previous registration date. The registration dates shall be March 31st, June 30th, September 30th and December 31st each year;

(*b*) Members of the Legislative Assembly, members of the United Kingdom Parliament who sit for constituencies whose boundaries encompass all or part of the District Council area;

(*c*) Members of the District Council who are members of the Party;

(*d*) Members of the Party Executive resident in the District Council area.

(*e*) Members of the Area Boards, Housing Executive, District Committees or other Statutory Bodies resident in the District Council Area, who are members of the Party.

14. Each District Executive shall hold an Annual General Meeting before March 31st at which it shall elect the following officers: Chairman, Vice-Chairman, Secretary and Treasurer, and transact any other relevant business. It shall, in addition, hold a minimum of three business meetings during the year.

15. The functions of a District Executive shall be as follows:

(*a*) To co-ordinate the work of the Party's Councillors on the District Council;

(*b*) To provide a means of communication between the Party's Councillors and the Branches;

(*c*) To organise, in accordance with Clause Seven, Section 11, meetings to select the Party's candidates in each District Electoral area of the District Council areas;

(*d*) To organise and direct the Party's campaign in local government elections.

Clause Five: The Party Conference

1. The Party Conference shall be the supreme governing authority in the Party. It shall be the duty of each individual member and section of the Party to promote the policies decided by the Conference.

2. The Conference shall normally be held in the period 15th October to 30th November each year on a date to be determined by the Executive Committee.

3. A special Conference may be held if the Executive Committee so decides or if more than one third of the Branches so request the Executive Committee.

4. The Conference shall be constituted as follows:

(*a*) Delegates appointed by each Branch in accordance with the following scale:

Membership	Number of Representatives
10—20	2
21—30	3
31—40	4
41—50	5

and additional delegates in these proportions.

(*b*) Delegates appointed by corporate members in accordance with the following scale:

Membership	Number of Delegates
10—200	1
201—400	2
401—600	3

and additional delegates in these proportions up to a maximum of 50 delegates.

(*c*) Members of the Legislative Assembly and members of the United Kingdom Parliament who are members of the Party;

(*d*) Members of the Executive Committee;

(*e*) Elected Local Government Representatives who are members of the Party.

5. Every delegate attending the Conference must be a fully paid-up individual member of the Party.

6. Each person attending the Conference by virtue of Section 4 of this clause shall have one vote.

7. Only Branches and corporate members who have paid the appropriate affiliation fees to the Executive Committee before 30th September shall be entitled to send delegates to the Conference.

8. Motions for the Conference and amendments to motions may be submitted by the Executive Committee, the Assembly Party, Branches and corporate members.

9. Motions shall be received by the Executive Committee not less than seven weeks before the Conference. The preliminary agenda shall be circulated to Branches and corporate members not less than six weeks before the Conference. Amendments to motions and the names and addresses of the delegates appointed by the various Branches and corporate members shall be received by the Executive Committee not less than four weeks before the Conference. The Conference agenda, credentials and other documents shall be circulated to those entitled to attend Conference not less than one one week before Conference. Emergency motions may be submitted with the consent of the Conference.

10. The Executive Committee shall submit to the Conference a report of its work since the previous Conference.

11. The Assembly Party shall submit to the Conference a report of its work since the previous Conference.

12. The following Party Officers shall be elected at the Conference: Chairman, two Vice-Chairmen, Treasurer and Assistant Treasurer. The elections shall be by secret ballot using the Single Transferable Vote.

13. The Conference shall elect fifteen individual members to serve on the Executive Committee. The election shall be by secret ballot using the Single Transferable Vote.

14. Candidates for Party Office and for the Executive Committee shall be nominated by Branches or by corporate members. The Executive Committee shall be informed in writing of such nominations and receive the written consent of the candidates at least seven weeks before the date of the Conference. The names of the candidates shall be circulated along with the preliminary agenda.

Clause Six: The Executive Committee and the Central Council

1. The Executive Committee shall consist of the Party Officers elected at the Party Conference, fifteen individual members elected at the Party Conference, the Leader and Deputy Leader of the Assembly Party in the Northern Ireland Assembly and one other member elected by and from the Assembly Party. A Chairman who does not seek re-election shall be a member of the following year's Executive Committee ex-officio.

2. All members of the Executive Committee must be individual members of the Party.

3. Casual vacancies shall be filled by co-option.

4. The day-to-day control of the organisation and the administrative affairs of the Party shall be in the hands of the Executive Committee. It shall interpret the Constitution and make provision for any matter not contained therein. The Executive Committee shall be responsible for implementing Conference decisions and developing policy between Conferences.

5. The Executive Committee shall meet at least twelve times each year.

6. The Executive Committee shall have the power to engage such

fulltime administrative and research staff as it deems necessary and shall have the power to determine the renumeration, conditions and tenure of office of such persons.

7. A bank account shall be opened in the name of the Executive Committee. The funds of the central organ of the Party shall be lodged in that account and withdrawals shall require the signature of the Treasurer and one other Officer. Money may be borrowed on that account for the general purposes of the Party with the approval of the Executive as expressed by a resolution to that effect.

8. Trustees shall be appointed by the Executive to hold on behalf of the Party such premises as the Executive may from time to time decide to acquire, and the said Trustees shall be empowered by resolution of the Executive to borrow money on the security of any such premises.

9. There shall be a Central Council of the Party which shall be constituted as follows:

(*a*) Members of the Executive Committee;

(*b*) Members of the Legislative Assembly and members of the United Kingdom Parliament who are members of the Party;

(*c*) District Councillors;

(*d*) Representatives of each Branch of the Party appointed according to the following scale:

Membership	Number of Representatives
10—50	2
51—100	3
101—150	4

and additional representatives in these proportions. Branch representation, at any time, shall be determined by the membership registered at Party H.Q. on the previous registration date. The registration dates shall be March 31st, June 30th, September 30th and December 31st each year.

(*e*) Two representatives from each Constituency Council and two representatives from each District Executive.

10. The function of the Central Council shall be to provide a means of communication between the membership and the central organs of the. Party.

11. The Central Council shall meet at least three times each year and shall hear reports from the Executive Committee, the Assembly Party and the Party organisation in the various constituencies.

Clause Seven: Selection of Candidates

1. The Party's candidates in any Assembly or United Kingdom constituency shall be selected by a Selection Convention called for that purpose.

2. The Selection Convention shall be organised by the Executive

Committee which shall have power to determine the procedure to be followed by the Convention.

3. The Selection Convention shall consist of delegates appointed by the Branches affiliated to the Constituency Council according to the following scale:

Membership	Number of Delegates
10—20	4
21—30	6
31—40	8
41—50	10

and additional delegates in these proportions. Branch representation, at any time, shall be determined by the membership registered at Party H.Q. on the previous registration date. The registration dates shall be March 31st, June 30th, September 30th and December 31st each year.

4. A prospective candidate must be an individual member of the Party. He must be proposed and seconded in writing by individual members of the Party and this nomination document must be forwarded to the Executive Committee.

5. The Executive Committee shall forward to each Branch affiliated to the Council the names of the prospective candidates at least one week before the meeting of the Convention.

6. The candidate shall be elected by secret ballot.

7. Only delegates shall have the right to vote and each delegate shall have one vote.

8. The Executive Committee shall appoint the Chairman of the Convention who shall forward its decisions to the Executive Committee.

9. The decision to contest the election shall be made by the Executive Committee who shall also have the power to ratify or to refuse to ratify the choice of candidates.

10. If there is only one Branch in the constituency the candidate shall be elected at a full meeting of the Branch called for that purpose by the Executive Committee which shall appoint the Chairman of the meeting.

11. Candidates for District Council elections in each District Electoral area shall be selected at a General Meeting of the Party members residing in the District Electoral area called for that purpose. Such selection meetings shall be organised by the appropriate District Executive.

Clause Eight: Amendment
Any addition to or amendment of the above Constitution shall only be made at the Party Conference provided that at least two thirds of those voting support the proposition. Such additions or amendments shall come into force immediately upon the ending of the Conference at which they have been approved.

Notes

INTRODUCTION

1. The terms 'Northern Ireland' and 'Ulster' are used interchangeably in the interests of euphony. For their precise definition see M. W. Heslinga, *The Irish Border as a Cultural Divide* (Assen: Van Gorcum, 1962) ch. 3. The terms 'Catholic' and 'Protestant' are used solely to identify a community.

2. W. J. M. Mackenzie, *Free Elections* (London: Allen & Unwin, 1967).

3. Extracted from Dankwart D. Rustow, *A World of Nations* (Washington: Brookings, 1967) Table 1. Figures relate to the situation in 1966 and the other six countries are Afghanistan, Congo Brazzaville, Ceylon, Czechoslovakia, New Guinea and Pakistan.

4. Extracted from Thomas T. Mackie and Richard Rose, *The International Almanac of Electoral History* (London: Macmillan, 1974). The other two countries are South Africa (between 1953 and 1970) and Japan (1958 to 1972).

5. See D. von Eschen *et al.*, 'The Conditions of Direct Action in a Democratic Society', *Western Political Quarterly* 22:2 (1969) pp. 309–25.

6. For an elaboration of the different types of political violence, see Peter K. Eisinger, 'The Conditions of Protest in American Cities', *American Political Science Review* 68:1 (1973) pp. 11–26, and H. L. Nieburg, 'The Threat of Violence and Social Change', *American Political Science Review* 56:4 (1962) pp. 865–73. For the background to political violence in Ulster, see Paul F. Power, 'Violence, Consent, and the Northern Ireland Problem' *Journal of Commonwealth and Comparative Politics* 14:2 (1976) pp. 119–40.

7. F. S. L. Lyons, 'Charles Stewart Parnell' in Brian Farrell (ed.), *The Irish Parliamentary Tradition* (Dublin: Gill & Macmillan, 1973) p. 193.

8. Quoted in Joseph Lee, *The Modernisation of Irish Society 1848–1918* (Dublin: Gill & Macmillan, 1973) p. 163.

9. Giuseppe di Palma, 'Disaffection and Participation in Western Democracies: the Role of Political Oppositions', *Journal of Politics* 31:4 (1969) p. 986.

10. See Richard Rose, 'On the Priorities of Citizenship in the Deep South and Northern Ireland', *Journal of Politics* 38:2 (1976) pp. 247–91, and W. Don Carroll, 'The Search for Justice in Northern Ireland' *New York University Journal of International Law and Politics* 6:1 (1973) pp. 28–56.

11. See E. E. Schattschneider, *The Semi-Sovereign People* (New York: Holt, Rinehart & Winston, 1960) ch. 3; and more generally, Gabriel A. Almond, 'Approaches to Developmental Causation', in Gabriel A. Almond *et al.*, *Crisis, Choice and Change* (Boston: Little Brown, 1973).

CHAPTER 1

1. Karl W. Deutsch, 'Social Mobilisation and Political Development',

American Political Science Review 55:3 (1961) p. 493. The main themes of this chapter are also examined in Ian McAllister, 'Political Parties and Social Change in Northern Ireland: the Case of the SDLP', *Social Studies* 5:1 (1976) pp. 75–89.

2. W. G. Runciman, *Relative Deprivation and Social Justice* (Harmondsworth: Penguin, 1966) p. 11.

3. For succinct collations of evidence, see Campaign for Social Justice, *The Plain Truth* (Dungannon: Campaign for Social Justice, 1969); Ambrose MacAuley, 'Catholics in the North, 1870–1970' *Newman Review* 2:1 (1970) pp. 21–32; Frank Gallagher, *The Indivisible Island* (London: Gollancz, 1957) ch. 15. For more objective disseminations of the evidence, see Richard Rose, *Governing Without Consensus* (London: Faber, 1971) and Gerard Francis Rutan, 'Northern Ireland Under Ulster Unionist Home Rule: the Anti-Movement Political System, 1920–63' (Carolina: unpublished University of North Carolina PhD dissertation, 1964) chs. 5–11. For an analysis of how Protestants reacted to Catholic allegations of discrimination, see Sarah Nelson, 'Protestant "Ideology" Considered: the Case of "Discrimination"' in Ivor Crewe (ed.), *British Political Sociology Yearbook* vol. 2 (London: Croom Helm, 1975).

4. Runciman, op. cit., p. 43.

5. Cited in Claude Mertens, 'Report on Civil and Social Rights in Northern Ireland', *Human Rights Journal* 2:3 (1969) p. 514.

6. *Disturbances in Northern Ireland* [the Cameron Report] (Belfast: HMSO, Cmd. 532, 1969) para. 134.

7. Cited in Martin Wallace, *Northern Ireland: Fifty Years of Self-Government* (Newton Abbot: David & Charles, 1971) p. 117.

8. *Second Report of the Northern Ireland Commissioner for Complaints* (Belfast: HMSO, HC 2048, 1970) paras. 52–3.

9. Denis P. Barritt and Charles F. Carter, *The Northern Ireland Problem* (Oxford: Oxford University Press, 1972) p. 96.

10. *Disturbances in Northern Ireland*, para. 138.

11. Rose, op. cit., p. 298.

12. Ibid., pp. 292–6.

13. *Disturbances in Northern Ireland*, paras. 139–41.

14. Cited in Derek Birrell, 'Relative Deprivation as a Factor in Conflict in Northern Ireland', *Sociological Review* 20:3 (new series) (1972) pp. 317–43.

15. Rose, op. cit., p. 301 (original italics).

16. *Disturbances in Northern Ireland*, para. 11.

17. Russell Stetler, *The Battle of the Bogside* (London: Sheed & Ward, 1970) p. 32.

18. R. J. Lawrence, *The Government of Northern Ireland* (Oxford: Oxford University Press, 1965) p. 122.

19. Unless otherwise stated, all the statistics in this chapter are calculated from *The Ulster Year Book* (Belfast: HMSO, various dates).

20. Barritt and Carter, op. cit., p. 76.

21. *Irish Times*, 28 November 1961.

22. F. S. L. Lyons, *Ireland Since the Famine* (London: Collins/Fontana, 1973) p. 689.

23. See Cornelius O'Leary, 'The Catholic in Politics', *Christus Rex* 17:4 (1963) p. 289 *et seq.*

24. P. A. Fahy, 'Some Political Behaviour Patterns and Attitudes of Roman

Catholic Priests in a Rural Part of Northern Ireland', *Economic and Social Review* 3:1 (1971) p. 22.

25. G. B. Newe, 'The Catholic in the Northern Ireland Community', *Christus Rex* 18:1 (1964) pp. 26–7. See also Newe's introduction to John Biggs-Davidson, *Catholics and the Union* (Belfast: Unionist Party, 1972).

26. David Kennedy, 'Whither Northern Nationalism', *Christus Rex* 13:4 (1959) p. 275.

27. Daniel Lerner, *The Passing of Traditional Society* (New York: Free Press, 1958) p. 43. For another application of the modernising thesis to Ulster, see Roger Scott, 'Ulster in Perspective: the Relevance of Non-European Experience', *Australian Outlook* 23:3 (1969) pp. 246–57.

28. P. A. Compton and F. W. Boal, 'Aspects of the Inter-Community Population Balance in Northern Ireland', *Economic and Social Review* 1:4 (1970) Table 2.

29. William Peterson, 'A General Typology of Migration', *American Sociological Review* 23:3 (1958) p. 263.

30. Samuel P. Huntington, *Political Order in Changing Societies* (New Haven: Yale University Press, 1968) p. 461.

CHAPTER 2

1. F. S. L. Lyons, 'Dillon, Redmond, and the Irish Home Rulers', in F. X. Martin (ed.), *Leaders and Men of the Easter Rising* (London: Meuthen, 1967) p. 39.

2. James O'Reilly quoted in *Irish News*, 1 November 1966.

3. Rose, *Governing Without Consensus*, p. 228.

4. Eddie McAteer quoted in *Irish News*, 13 December 1965.

5. John Duffy in *Irish Press*, 16 November 1964.

6. J. L. McCracken, 'The Political Scene in Northern Ireland, 1926–37' in Francis McManus (ed.), *The Years of the Great Test, 1926–39* (Cork: Mercier, 1967) p. 154.

7. Quoted in Nicholas Mansergh, *The Government of Northern Ireland* (London: Allen & Unwin, 1936) p. 248.

8. Tim Pat Coogan, *Ireland Since the Rising* (London: Pall Mall, 1966) p. 309.

9. Eddie McAteer quoted in *Irish News*, 13 December 1965.

10. Ibid., 16 October 1959.

11. Cf. McAteer's reasons for participating in the 5 October 1968 march given in W. H. Van Voris, *Violence in Ulster* (Amherst: University of Massachusetts Press, 1975) p. 73.

12. Quoted in J. Bowyer Bell, *The Secret Army* (London: Sphere, 1972) pp. 394–5.

13. See Gerard F. Rutan, 'The Labour Party in Ulster: Opposition by Cartel', *Review of Politics* 29:4 (1967) pp. 526–35.

14. Richard Rose, 'Discord in Ulster', *New Community* 1:2 (1971) p. 124.

15. John F. Harbinson, *The Ulster Unionist Party, 1882–1973* (Belfast: Blackstaff, 1973) p. 154.

16. See Ian McAllister, 'Political Opposition in Northern Ireland: the National Democratic Party, 1965–1970', *Economic and Social Review* 6:3 (1975) pp. 353–66.

17. John F. Harbinson, 'A History of the Northern Ireland Labour Party,

1891—1949' (Belfast: unpublished Queen's University MSc thesis, 1966) p. 233.

18. *Nusight*, 27 November 1967.

19. Cornelius O'Leary, 'Belfast West' in D. E. Butler and Anthony King, *The British General Election of 1966* (London: Macmillan, 1967) p. 255.

20. See M. Lipskey, 'Protest as a Political Resource', *American Political Science Review* 62:4 (1968) pp. 1144—58.

21. James Thompson, 'The Northern Ireland Civil Rights Movement' (Belfast: unpublished Queen's University MA thesis, 1973) p. 52. For other accounts of the movement, see John J. Kane, 'Civil Rights in Northern Ireland', *Review of Politics* 33:1 (1971) pp. 54—77; Donald E. Leon, 'The Politics of Civil Rights in Northern Ireland: Some Views and Observations', *Cithara* 10:1 (1970) pp. 3—17; Paul F. Power, 'Civil Protest in Northern Ireland', *Journal of Peace Research* 9:3 (1972) pp. 223—36; Vincent E. Feeney, 'The Civil Rights Movement in Northern Ireland', *Eire-Ireland* 9:2 (1974) pp. 30—40.

22. *Irish News*, 9 July 1965.

23. Ibid., 24 June 1968.

24. Ibid.

25. Rose, 'Discord', p. 124.

26. Cited in Richard Rose, 'The Dynamics of a Divided Regime', *Government and Opposition* 5:2 (1970) p. 183.

27. *Irish Times*, 7 February 1969.

28. See Paul Arthur, *The People's Democracy, 1968—73* (Belfast: Blackstaff, 1974) p. 45.

29. *Irish Times*, 13 February 1969.

30. Ibid., 7 February 1969.

31. Owen Dudley Edwards, *The Sins of Our Fathers* (Dublin: Gill & Macmillan, 1970) p. 269. For an analysis of the election, see Cornelius O'Leary, 'The Northern Ireland General Election (1969)' in F. A. Hermens (ed.), *Verfassung und Verfassungswirklichkeit* (Verlag: Köln und Opladen, 1969).

CHAPTER 3

1. *Irish Times*, 26 February 1969.

2. HC Deb (NI) 71, c218 (22 January 1969).

3. Ibid., 72, c680 (20 March 1969).

4. See *Irish Times*, 4 December 1969. The spokesmen were: Austin Currie and John Hume, Development; Michael Keogh and Paddy O'Hanlon, Commerce; Ivan Cooper, Education; Tom Gormley, Finance; Paddy Kennedy, Attorney-General; John Carron and Ivan Cooper, Community Relations; Paddy Devlin and James O'Reilly, Health and Social Services.

5. *Strategy of the Seventies Conference: Agenda* (Belfast: mimeo, 31 January 1970).

6. *Irish Times*, 27 May 1970. For general accounts of the election, see Roger Scott, 'The British General Election in Northern Ireland', *The Dalhousie Review* 5:2 (1970) pp. 249—61 and by the same author, 'The 1970 British General Election in Ulster', *Parliamentary Affairs* 24:1 (1970) pp. 16—32.

7. See Barry White, 'The SDLP', *Fortnight*, 25 September 1970.

8. *Irish Times*, 17 August 1970.

9. Another Senator, Claude Wilton, formerly a Liberal, joined the SDLP on 10

November 1970. Patrick Wilson was murdered on 26 June 1973.

10. *Irish Times,* 19 August 1970.

11. Ibid., 22 August 1970.

12. Ibid., 20 August 1970.

13. Ibid., 26 August 1970.

14. Ibid., 22 August 1970.

15. *Minutes of National Democratic Party Special Conference* (Belfast: mimeo, 3 October 1970).

CHAPTER 4

1. SDLP, *Party Constitution* (Belfast: SDLP, 1976) p. 1. The full constitution is also reproduced in the Appendix.

2. Ulster figure from David Bleakley, 'The Northern Ireland Trade Union Movement', *Journal of the Social and Statistical Inquiry Society of Ireland* 19 (1953–54) p. 164. British figure from Robert McKenzie, *British Political Parties* (London: Heinemann, 1970) p. 484. Republic's figure from Basil Chubb, *The Government and Politics of Ireland* (Oxford: Oxford University Press, 1970) p. 90.

3. John Graham, 'The Consensus Forming Strategy of the Northern Ireland Labour Party, 1949–68' (Belfast: unpublished Queen's University MSSc thesis, 1972) p. 247.

4. Due to the problems of matching census and constituency boundaries and dealing with the large 'not stated' religion category in the 1971 census, Catholics are slightly under-represented in some constituencies.

5. *Irish Times,* 3 August 1974.

6. Michael McKeown, 'SDLP: All Kinds of People', *Hibernia,* 24 January 1975.

7. *Belfast Telegraph,* 15 August 1975.

8. *Irish Times,* 7 September 1972.

9. Ibid., 7 November 1972.

10. Leon D. Epstein, *Political Parties in Western Democracies* (New York: Praeger, 1967) p. 293.

11. For an authoritative study of pre-1973 elections in Northern Ireland, see Sydney Elliott, 'The Electoral System in Northern Ireland Since 1920' (Belfast: unpublished Queen's University PhD thesis, 1971) 2 vols.

12. For example, Denis Haughey from Co. Tyrone, the party chairman since 1973, was nominated for North Antrim in the Convention. The SDLP seat in the constituency went to a relatively unknown, but local (and Protestant) candidate, John Turnly.

13. Correlations between the proportion of Catholics in a constituency and the proportion of postal votes gives an r value of 0.19 for the Assembly election and 0.73 for the Convention election.

14. Michael Laver, 'On Introducing STV and Interpreting the Results: the Case of Northern Ireland, 1973–75', *Parliamentary Affairs* 29:2 (1976) p. 218.

15. Calculated from R. J. Lawrence *et al., The Northern Ireland General Elections of 1973* (London:HMSO, Cmnd. 5851, 1975)Table 36, and Ian McAllister, *The 1975 Northern Ireland Convention Election* (Glasgow: Survey Research Centre Occasional Paper No. 14, 1975) Table III. 7.

16. Ian McAllister, 'Social Influences on Voters and Non-Voters: a Note on Two Northern Ireland Elections', *Political Studies* 24:4 (1976) pp. 462–8.

17. See Carrick James Market Research, *Northern Ireland: Reaction to the White Paper and Other Subjects* (London: mimeo, 1973) Table 18.

18. Brian Wilson, 'The Alliance Party of Northern Ireland: a Study of a Bi-Confessional Party' (Glasgow: unpublished University of Strathclyde MSc dissertation, 1976) Table 1. In December 1972 the membership stood at 8670, but thereafter central figures were no longer recorded.

CHAPTER 5

1. Saul Rose, 'Policy Decision in Opposition', *Political Studies* 4:2 (1956) p. 128.

2. *Irish Times*, 22 August 1970.

3. Alliance Party, *Constitution and Rules* (Belfast: Alliance Party, 1974) p. 20 (original italics).

4. SDLP, *Towards a New Ireland* (Belfast: SDLP, 1972).

5. Donal Barrington, 'The Council of Ireland in a Constitutional Context', *Administration* 20:4 (1972) p. 36.

6. See *Irish Times*, 12 February 1972. See also Charles F. Carter, 'Permutations of Government', *Administration* 20:4 (1972) pp. 50–7.

7. *Irish Times*, 16 October 1972.

8. SDLP, *A New North, A New Ireland* (Belfast: SDLP, 1973).

9. SDLP, *Speak With Strength* (Belfast: SDLP, 1975).

10. See, for example, Paddy Devlin in *Irish Times*, 3 December 1976.

11. SDLP, *Sixth Annual Conference: Agenda, Annual Reports and Other Conference Papers* (Belfast: SDLP, 1976) p. 31.

12. Ben Caraher in *Social Democrat*, 1 March 1976.

13. E. Rumpf and A. C. Hepburn, *Nationalism and Socialism in Twentieth Century Ireland* (Liverpool: Liverpool University Press, 1977) p. 222.

14. See SDLP, *Women in Society* (Belfast: SDLP, 1975); SDLP, *Alcoholism: a Forgotten Problem* (Belfast: SDLP, 1975); SDLP, *Community Relations in the New North* (Belfast: SDLP, 1975).

15. SDLP, *Economic Analysis and Strategy* (Belfast: SDLP, 1976). Cf. *Economic and Industrial Strategy for Northern Ireland* [the Quigley Report] (Belfast: HMSO, 1976).

16. SDLP, *Housing: the Way Ahead* (Belfast: SDLP, 1976).

17. SDLP, *Education: the Need for Reform* (Belfast: SDLP, 1975).

18. See Rose, *Governing Without Consensus*, p. 336. Significantly, the SDLP's relatively mild policy on integrated education has attracted strong private condemnation from the Catholic hierarchy in Belfast.

19. SDLP, *Policing: Realities and Responsibilities* (Belfast: SDLP, 1975) p. 1.

20. Brian Farrell, 'Labour and the Irish Political Party System: a Suggested Approach to Analysis', *Economic and Social Review* 1:4 (1970) p. 486.

21. Quoted in Basil Chubb (ed.), *A Source Book of Irish Government* (Dublin: Institute of Public Administration, 1964) p. 227.

22. *Irish Times*, 4 June 1969.

23. Ibid., 8 February 1973.

24. *Times*, 9 February 1974.

25. Samuel H. Beer, *Modern British Politics* (London: Faber, 1971) p. 127.

26. Rose, *Governing Without Consensus*, Table V. 3.

27. 1974 figure extracted from data cards; 1976 figure cited in *Belfast Telegraph*, 19 March 1976.

CHAPTER 6

1. For separate studies, see Patrick McGill, 'The Senate in Northern Ireland, 1921–62' (Belfast: unpublished Queen's University PhD thesis, 1965) and Richard Rose, *Northern Ireland: a Time of Choice* (London: Macmillan, 1976) pp. 111–16.

2. David Butler and Donald Stokes, *Political Change in Britain* (Harmondsworth: Penguin, 1971) p. 327.

3. Brian Farrell, 'Dáil Deputies: "the 1969 Generation"', *Economic and Social Review* 2:3 (1971) p. 315.

4. Richard Rose, *Class and Party Divisions: Britain as a Test Case* (Glasgow: Survey Research Centre Occasional Paper No. 1, 1969) Table 12.

5. Farrell, op. cit., p. 314.

6. Edmund A. Aunger, 'Religion and Occupational Class in Northern Ireland', *Economic and Social Review* 7:1 (1975) p. 6.

7. See, for example, Mart Bax, 'Patronage Irish Style: Irish Politicians as Brokers', *Sociologische Gids* 17:3 (1970) pp. 179–91.

8. Robert E. Agger, 'Lawyers in Politics: the Starting Point for a New Research Program', *Temple Law Quarterly* 29:3 (1956) p. 436.

9. Calculated from *The Times Guide to the House of Commons, 1974* (London: Times, 1974) p. 265.

10. See, for example, Basil Chubb, 'Going About Persecuting Civil Servants: the Role of the Irish Parliamentary Representative', *Political Studies* 11:3 (1963) pp. 272–86, and Paul Sacks, 'Bailiwicks, Locality and Religion: Three Elements in a Dáil Constituency Election', *Economic and Social Review* 1:4 (1970) pp. 531–54.

11. Quoted in Thomas N. Brown, 'Nationalism and the Irish Peasant, 1800–48', *Review of Politics* 15:4 (1953) p. 403.

12. See Mart Bax, *Harpstrings and Confessions: an Anthropological Study of Politics in Rural Ireland* (Amsterdam: University of Amsterdam, 1973) p. 261.

13. William H. Riker, *The Theory of Political Coalitions* (New Haven: Yale University Press, 1962) pp. 32–3.

14. Samuel J. Eldersveld, *Political Parties* (Chicago: Rand McNally, 1964) p. 71.

15. Rose, *Governing Without Consensus*, Table III. 2.

16. Herbert Jacob, 'Initial Recruitment of Elected Officials in the United States: a Model', *Journal of Politics* 24:4 (1962) p. 711.

17. Al Cohan, *The Irish Political Elite* (Dublin: Gill & Macmillan, 1972) p. 40.

18. John Whyte, *Dáil Deputies* (Dublin: Tuairim pamphlet no. 15, 1966) p. 36.

19. W. J. M. Mackenzie, 'Local Government in Parliament' *Public Administration* 32:4 (1954) pp. 409–24.

20. Farrell, op. cit., p. 320.

21. The Association for Legal Justice, the Derry Citizens' Action Committee and the Minority Rights Group are all considered synonymous with the NICRA.

CHAPTER 7

1. Giuseppe di Palma, *Apathy and Participation* (New York: Free Press, 1970) p. 90.
2. Robert A. Dahl, *Political Oppositions in Western Democracies* (New Haven: Yale University Press, 1966) p. 345.
3. *Commentary by the Government of Northern Ireland to Accompany the Cameron Report* (Belfast: HMSO, Cmd. 534, 1969) p. 4.
4. Quoted in Richard Deutsch and Vivien Magowan, *Northern Ireland: a Chronology of Events, 1968–74* Vol. 1 (1968–71) (Belfast: Blackstaff, 1973) p. 152.
5. Kevin Boyle *et al.*, *Law and State* (London: Martin Robertson, 1975) p. 24–5.
6. See *Commentary Upon the White Paper (Cmd. 558)* (Belfast: Irish News, 1971).
7. *Report of the Advisory Committee on Police in Northern Ireland* [the Hunt Report] (Belfast: HMSO, Cmd. 535, 1969) para. 183.
8. HC Deb (NI) 78, c15 (3 February 1971).
9. Maurice Hayes, 'The Role of the Community Relations Commission in Northern Ireland', *Administration* 20:4 (1972) p. 90.
10. The only legislation the Stormont opposition managed to initiate and pass in 51 years was the Wild Birds Act of 1931.
11. *Irish Times*, 26 November 1970.
12. Cf. Sean MacStiofain, *Memoirs of a Revolutionary* (London: Gordon Cremonesi, 1975) pp. 133–8.
13. Conor Cruise O'Brien, *States of Ireland* (London: Hutchinson, 1972) p. 205.
14. See Provisional IRA, *Freedom Struggle* (Dublin: Provisional IRA, 1973).
15. *Irish Times*, 6 March 1971.
16. Ibid., 8 December 1970.
17. Quoted in Deutsch and Magowan, op. cit., p. 153.
18. HC Deb (NI) 78, c2057 (24 February 1971).
19. Ibid., 82, c21–3 (22 June 1971).
20. Ibid., c23–5.
21. Ibid., c40.
22. Ibid., 82, c96 (23 June 1971).
23. Ibid., 82, c179–82 (24 June 1971).
24. Ibid., c269.
25. Ibid., c246.
26. Ibid., c329.
27. Phelim O'Neill had previously been expelled from the Order for attending a Catholic church service. He joined the Alliance Party on 18 February 1972. For a succinct summary of these events, see Henry Kelly, *How Stormont Fell* (Dublin: Gill & Macmillan, 1972).
28. HC Deb (NI) 82, c187 (24 June 1971).
29. *Violence and Civil Disturbances in Northern Ireland in 1969* [the Scarman Report] (Belfast: HMSO, Cmd. 566, 1972) ch. 29.
30. HC Deb (NI) 81, c468 (25 May 1971).
31. Quoted in Kelly, op. cit., p. 25.
32. *Irish Times*, 10 July 1971.
33. Ibid.
34. Ibid., 9 July 1971.

35. Ibid., 12 July 1971.
36. Ibid.
37. 821 HC Deb, 5s, c31 (12 July 1971).
38. *Irish Times*, 14 July 1971.
39. Ibid.
40. Ibid., 15 July 1971.
41. Ibid., 12 July 1971.
42. Ibid., 16 July 1971.
43. Ibid., 17 July 1971.
44. Ibid., 16 July 1971.

CHAPTER 8

1. *Irish Times*, 1 April 1971.
2. See MacStiofain, op. cit., pp. 183–4.
3. John McGuffin, *Internment* (Tralee: Anvil, 1973) p. 86.
4. Figures supplied by the RUC Press Office. For the contrary view on internment, see Unionist Party, *The Case for Internment* (Belfast: Unionist Party, 1972).
5. *Irish Times*, 10 August 1971.
6. Ibid., 23 August 1971.
7. Ibid., 20 August 1971.
8. Ibid., 7 September 1971.
9. Quoted in Gary MacEoin, *Northern Ireland: Captive of History* (New York: Holt, Rinehart & Winston, 1974) p. 256.
10. *Irish Times*, 17 August 1971.
11. *Fortnight*, 1 October 1971.
12. HC Deb (NI) 82, c919 (6 October 1971).
13. *Irish Times*, 12 November 1971.
14. Ibid., 9 December 1971.
15. Joe Boyle *et al.*, 'Respondents' Perceptions of the Causes of the Northern Ireland Conflict' (Belfast: Attitudes in Ireland Report No. 4, mimeo, 1976) Tables 2 and 3.
16. Joe Boyle *et al.*, 'Summary Tables of Attitudes in Northern Ireland' (Belfast: Attitudes in Ireland Report No. 1, mimeo, 1976) Table 81.
17. Terence Carroll, 'Political Activists in Disaffected Communities: Dissidence, Disobedience and Rebellion in Northern Ireland' (Ottowa: unpublished University of Carleton PhD thesis, 1974) p. 338.
18. Ibid., p. 344.
19. *Irish Times*, 6 October 1971.
20. Ibid.
21. Ibid.
22. Ibid., 27 October 1971.
23. Ibid., 6 December 1971.
24. Ibid., 12 August 1971.
25. Ibid., 16 August 1971.
26. Ibid., 9 November 1971.
27. Ibid., 1 September 1971.

28. J. C. Beckett, *The Making of Modern Ireland, 1603–1923* (London: Faber, 1973) pp. 446–7.

29. Robert Taber, *The War of the Flea* (St Albans: Paladin, 1972) p. 130.

30. *Irish Times*, 6 November 1971.

31. *Future Development of the Parliament and Government of Northern Ireland* (Belfast: HMSO, Cmd. 560, 1971) p. 9.

32. *Irish Times*, 28 October 1971.

33. Ibid., 21 December 1971.

34. *Fortnight*, 3 September 1971.

35. John Whyte, *The Reform of Stormont* (Belfast: New Ulster Movement, 1971).

36. *Irish Times*, 6 November 1971.

37. 823 HC Deb, 5s, c16 (22 September 1971).

38. *Irish Times*, 16 December 1971.

39. 826 HC Deb, 5s, c1588 (25 November 1971).

40. *Irish Times*, 1 February 1972.

41. Ibid., 1 February 1972.

42. This seemingly trivial distinction was necessitated by a clause in the Republic's Offences Against the State Act which prohibits civil disobedience for political purposes.

43. *Irish Times*, 22 February 1972.

44. 833 HC Deb, 5s, c1860 (24 March 1972).

45. *Irish Times*, 25 March 1972.

46. 833 HC Deb, 5s, c1860–61 (24 March 1972).

47. Quoted in *Irish Times*, 20 March 1972.

48. Ibid., 25 March 1972.

49. Ibid., 3 April 1972.

50. Ibid., 27 March 1972.

51. Conor Cruise O'Brien, *States of Ireland* (London: Hutchinson, 1972) p. 276.

52. Peter Pyne, 'The Third Sinn Féin Party, 1923–26: Part 2, Factors Contributing to Collapse', *Economic and Social Review* 1:2 (1970) p. 230.

CHAPTER 9

1. Rose, *Governing Without Consensus*, Tables V. 3 and V. 5.

2. 833 HC Deb, 5s, c1861 (24 March 1972).

3. *Fortnight*, 1 July 1972.

4. *Irish Times*, 27 May 1972.

5. Ibid.

6. *Irish Times*, 30 May 1972.

7. Ibid., 15 June 1972.

8. Ibid., 23 June 1972.

9. 839 HC Deb, 5s, c722 (22 June 1972).

10. Cf. Pablo Pistoi, 'Conflict in Northern Ireland: Operation Motorman in Ballymurphy' (Colchester: unpublished University of Essex MA dissertation, 1972).

11. *Irish Times*, 2 August 1972.

12. Ibid., 11 August 1972.

13. 841 HC Deb, 5s, c1329 (24 July 1972).

14. *Irish Times*, 15 August 1972.

15. Ibid., 22 September 1972.

16. SDLP, *Towards a New Ireland* (Belfast: SDLP, 1972). For a more detailed discussion of the plan, see pp. 56–8.

17. T. E. Utley, *Lessons of Ulster* (London: Dent, 1975) p. 97.

18. 457 HC Deb, 5s, c239 (28 October 1948).

19. Northern Ireland Office, *The Future of Northern Ireland* (London: HMSO, 1972) para. 40.

20. Ibid., para. 75.

21. Ibid., para. 78.

22. Ibid., para. 79 (f).

23. *Irish Times*, 20 February 1973.

24. Ibid., 27 November 1972.

25. Ibid.

26. See *Belfast News-Letter*, 4 March 1973.

27. 833 HC Deb, 5s, c1859 (24 March 1972).

28. *Irish Times*, 24 January 1973.

29. Ibid., 25 January 1973.

30. 849 HC Deb, 5s, c402 (23 January 1973).

31. 840 HC Deb, 5s, c722 (6 July 1972). For an exhaustive analysis of the poll, see R. J. Lawrence and S. Elliott, *The Northern Ireland Border Poll, 1973* (London: HMSO, Cmnd. 5875, 1975).

32. *Northern Ireland Constitutional Proposals* (London: HMSO, Cmnd. 5259, 1973).

33. *Irish Times*, 23 March 1973.

34. *Fortnight*, 21 May 1973.

35. *Irish Times*, 7 May 1973.

CHAPTER 10

1. Otto Kirchheimer, 'The Waning of Opposition in Parliamentary Regimes' in Mattei Dogan and Richard Rose (eds), *European Politics* (London: Macmillan, 1971) p. 285. For a development of some of the themes in this chapter, see Ian McAllister, 'The Legitimacy of Opposition: the Collapse of the 1974 Northern Ireland Executive', *Eire-Ireland* (forthcoming). See also Michael James, 'The Failure of Britain's Irish Policy', *Australian Quarterly* 47:1 (1975) pp. 51–64, and Donal Barrington, 'After Sunningdale', *Administration* 24:2 (1976) pp. 235–61.

2. Quoted in David Bleakley, *Faulkner: Conflict and Consent in Irish Politics* (London: Mowbray, 1974) p. 126.

3. *Irish Times*, 4 June 1973.

4. See *Belfast News-Letter*, 14 June 1973.

5. Michael Laver, *The Theory and Practice of Party Competition: Ulster, 1973–75* (London: Sage Contemporary Political Sociology Series 06–014, 1976) p. 30.

6. *Irish Times*, 31 July 1973.

7. Ibid., 2 April 1973.

8. Paddy Devlin, *The Fall of the Northern Ireland Executive* (Belfast: published for the author, 1975) p. 45.

9. Faulkner's original 23 members had been whittled down by one death, two defections and the appointment of one menber as Speaker.

10. *Halsbury's Statutes of England*, Vol. 43 (1973) (London: Butterworth, 1974) p. 1188.

11. Ass Deb (NI) 1, c1447 (5 December 1973).

12. Devlin, op. cit., p. 32.

13. The document is reproduced in Richard Deutsch and Vivien Magowan, *Northern Ireland: a Chronology of Events, 1968–74* Vol. 2 (1972–73) (Belfast: Blackstaff, 1974) Appendix 7.

14. Keith Kyle, 'Sunningdale and After: Britain, Ireland and Ulster', *The World Today* 31:11 (1975) p. 442.

15. Michael Farrell, *Northern Ireland: the Orange State* (London: Pluto, 1976) p. 311.

16. *Irish Times*, 22 January 1974.

17. See ibid., 29 January 1974.

18. *Fortnight*, 2 November 1973.

19. Quoted in A. Murie *et al.*, 'Developments in Housing Policy and Administration in Northern Ireland Since 1945', *Social and Economic Administration* 6:1 (1972) p. 49.

20. Ass Deb (NI) 2, c762 (12 February 1974).

21. Ibid., 3, c1123 (22 May 1974).

22. *Irish Times*, 3 January 1974.

23. Ass Deb (NI) 3, c64 (3 April 1974).

24. Ibid.

25. Ibid., 2, c506 (5 February 1974).

26. Ibid., 2, c1975 (21 March 1974).

27. Ibid., 3, c75 (3 April 1974).

28. *Irish Times*, 22 January 1974.

29. Ass Deb (NI) 3, c299 (30 April 1974).

30. See 876 HC Deb, 5s, c1259 (9 July 1974).

31. The survey was conducted by National Opinion Polls. The figures used here have been extracted from data cards.

32. See *Disturbances in Northern Ireland*, paras. 168–84 and *Violence and Civil Disturbances in Northern Ireland in 1969, passim.*

33. See Central Citizens' Defence Committee, *The Black Paper: the Story of the Police* (Belfast: Central Citizens' Defence Committee, 1973).

34. *Irish Times*, 5 September 1973.

35. SDLP, *Policing: Realities and Responsibilities* (Belfast: SDLP, 1975) p. 1.

36. Devlin, op. cit., p. 35.

37. Ibid., p. 46.

38. *Irish Times*, 29 December 1973.

39. See Table 8.1.

40. Ass Deb (NI) 3, c51 (3 April 1974).

41. *Irish Times*, 30 May 1974.

42. Ibid., 15 March 1974.

43. Ibid., 5 March 1974.

44. Dail Deb 271, c8 (13 March 1974).

45. Ass Deb (NI) 2, c521 (5 February 1974).

46. Ibid., 2, c2067 (26 March 1974). On this general question, see C. R. Symmons, 'The Law Enforcement Commission Report and Article 29 of the Irish Constitution', *The Irish Jurist* (new series) 8:1 (1973) pp. 33–54.

47. 870 HC Deb, 5s, c737–8 (18 March 1974).
48. *Halsbury's Statutes of England* Vol. 43, pp. 1181–2.
49. *Irish Times*, 27 April 1974.
50. Ibid., 5 March 1974.
51. Ass Deb (NI) 3, c843 (14 May 1974).
52. Robert Fisk, *The Point of No Return* (London: André Deutsch, 1975).
53. *Belfast Telegraph*, 27 March 1975.
54. Ass Deb (NI) 3, c1155–56 (22 May 1974).
55. Ibid., c1157–58.
56. Quoted in Fisk, op. cit., p. 201.
57. *Irish Times*, 25 May 1974.
58. Ibid., 29 May 1974.
59. Devlin, op. cit., p. 33.

CHAPTER 11

1. 874 HC Deb, 5s, c882 (3 June 1974).
2. 876 HC Deb, 5s, c611 (4 July 1974).
3. *The Northern Ireland Constitution* (London: HMSO, Cmnd. 5675, 1974) para. 50.
4. The IRA termed the cessation of violence a *truce* in order to emphasise the bilateral aspect; the NIO always referred to it as a *ceasefire* to characterise it as a unilateral action.
5. 886 HC Deb, 5s, c208 (11 February 1975).
6. *Belfast Telegraph*, 26 May 1975.
7. 884 HC Deb, 5s, c201–2 (14 January 1975).
8. *Irish Times*, 13 September 1974.
9. Ibid., 25 September 1974.
10. Ibid., 14 June 1974.
11. Ibid., 1 July 1974.
12. Ibid., 19 June 1974.
13. SDLP, *Another Step Forward* (Belfast: SDLP, 1974).
14. Ibid.
15. *Irish Times*, 19 June 1974.
16. Ibid., 17 April 1975.
17. One official Unionist, James Kilfedder, refused to sign but retained UUUC endorsement.
18. Conv Deb, p. 123b (11 June 1975).
19. Ibid.
20. Ibid., p. 13b (27 May 1975).
21. Ibid., p. 13a.
22. Ibid., p. 45a (28 May 1975).
23. Ibid., pp. 283b–4b (19 June 1975).
24. *Irish News*, 12 September 1975.
25. *Belfast Telegraph*, 4 September 1975.
26. See *Alliance*, 1 October 1975.
27. *Irish News*, 12 September 1975.
28. Conv Deb, pp. 517b–8a (17 September 1975).

29. *Belfast Telegraph*, 9 September 1975.
30. Conv Deb, p. 763a (23 October 1975).
31. Ibid., p. 763b. For the UUUC view of the report, see UUUC, *A Guide to the Convention Report* (Belfast: UUUC, 1976).
32. 903 HC Deb, 5s, c54 (12 January 1976).
33. See *The Northern Ireland Convention: Text of a Letter from the Secretary of State for Northern Ireland to the Chairman of the Convention* (London: HMSO, Cmnd. 6387, 1976).
34. At least nine of the 19 official Unionists were thought to be not unreceptive to the coalition concept. See *Irish Times*, 14 October 1975.
35. *Irish Times*, 9 December 1975.
36. Ibid.
37. See *Belfast News-Letter*, 4 February 1976.
38. *Irish Times*, 13 February 1976. The exchange that precipitated the split was as follows:

> Mr Hume: Are we to understand Mr West as saying that there are no circumstances in which the UUUC would serve in cabinet with the SDLP?
> Mr West: That is right.

Northern Ireland Convention Inter-Party Talks (Belfast: mimeo, 1976) p. 204.
39. Conv Deb, p. 966a (2 March 1976).
40. Ibid., p. 977a.
41. See *Alliance*, 1 March 1976.
42. 906 HC Deb, 5s, c1716 (5 March 1976).
43. *Belfast Telegraph*, 19 March 1976.
44. John A. Oliver, 'The Ulster Convention', *Blackwoods Magazine* 320:1930 (1976) p. 130.
45. *Social Democrat*, 1 November 1976.

CONCLUSION

1. S. M. Lipset, *Political Man* (London: Heinemann, 1971) pp. 87–9.
2. Robert A. Dahl, *Regimes and Oppositions* (New Haven: Yale University Press, 1973) pp. 4–5.
3. Arend Lijphart, 'The Northern Ireland Problem: Cases, Theories and Solutions', *British Journal of Political Science* 5:1 (1975) p. 94.
4. Giovanni Sartori, *Parties and Party Systems* (Cambridge: Cambridge University Press, 1976) p. 196.
5. Richard Rose, *Northern Ireland: a Time of Choice* (London: Macmillan, 1976) p. 139.
6. Sigmund Neumann, *Modern Political Parties* (Chicago: University of Chicago Press, 1962) p. 403.
7. Maurice Duverger, *Political Parties* (London: Meuthen, 1967) p. 64.
8. Robert Michels, *Political Parties* (New York: Free Press, 1962).
9. Anthony Downs, *An Economic Theory of Democracy* (New York: Harper, 1957).
10. Riker, op. cit., pp. 32–3. See also Joseph A. Schlesinger, 'The Primary Goals of Political Parties: a Clarification of Positive Theory', *American Political*

Science Review 69:3 (1975) pp. 840–9.

11. For one case study of organisational maintenance, see Gianfranco Poggi, *Catholic Action in Italy* (Stanford: University of California Press, 1967).

12. Arend Lijphart, 'Consociational Democracy', *World Politics* 21:2 (1969) p. 221.

Bibliography

Arthur, Paul, *The People's Democracy, 1968–73* (Belfast: Blackstaff, 1974).

Aunger, Edmund A., 'Religion and Occupational Class in Northern Ireland' *Economic and Social Review* 7:1 (1975) pp. 1–18.

Barritt, Denis P. and Carter, Charles F., *The Northern Ireland Problem* (Oxford: Oxford University Press, 1972).

Bax, Mart, *Harpstrings and Confessions* (Amsterdam: University of Amsterdam, 1973).

Biggs – Davidson, John, *Catholics and the Union* (Belfast: Unionist Party, 1972).

Birrell, Derek, 'Relative Deprivation as a Factor in Conflict in Northern Ireland' *Sociological Review* 20:3 (new series) (1972) pp. 317–43.

Bleakley, David, 'The Northern Ireland Trade Union Movement' *Journal of the Social and Statistical Inquiry Society of Ireland* 19 (1953–54) pp. 159–69.

—*Faulkner: Conflict and Consent in Irish Politics* (London: Mowbray, 1974).

Boyd, Andrew, *The Rise of the Irish Trade Unions, 1729–1970* (Tralee: Anvil, 1972).

Bowyer – Bell, J., *The Secret Army* (London: Sphere, 1972).

—'The Escalation of Insurgency: the Provisional Irish Republican Army's Experience, 1969–71' *Review of Politics* 35:3 (1973) pp. 398–411.

Boyle, Kevin, *et al.*, *Law and State* (London: Martin Robertson, 1975).

Budge, Ian and O'Leary, Cornelius, *Belfast: Approach to Crisis* (London: Macmillan, 1973).

—'Permanent Supremacy and Perpetual Opposition: the Parliament of Northern Ireland, 1922–72' in A. Eldridge (ed.), *Legislatures in Plural Societies* (London: Sage, 1974).

Callaghan, James, *A House Divided* (London: Collins, 1973).

Carroll, Terence, 'Political Activists in Disaffected Communities: Dissidence, Disobedience and Rebellion in Northern Ireland' (Ottowa: unpublished University of Carleton PhD thesis, 1974).

Carroll, W. Don, 'The Search for Justice in Northern Ireland' *New York University Journal of International Law and Politics* 6:1 (1973) pp. 28–56.

Darby, John, 'Northern Ireland: the 1973 White Paper' *New Community* 2:2 (1973) pp. 202–5.

—*Conflict in Northern Ireland* (Dublin: Gill and Macmillan, 1976).

De Paor, Liam, *Divided Ulster* (Harmondsworth: Penguin, 1970).

Deutsch, Richard and Magowan, Vivien, *Northern Ireland: a Chronology of Events, 1968–74* (3 Vols.) (Belfast: Blackstaff, 1973, 1974 and 1975).

Devlin, Paddy, *The Fall of the Northern Ireland Executive* (Belfast: published for the author, 1975).

Edwards, Owen Dudley, *The Sins of Our Fathers* (Dublin: Gill and Macmillan, 1970).

Elliott, Sydney, *Northern Ireland Parliamentary Election Results, 1921–72* (Chichester: Political Reference Publications, 1973).

Farrell, Brian (ed.), *The Irish Parliamentary Tradition* (Dublin: Gill and Macmillan, 1973).

Farrell, Michael, *Northern Ireland: the Orange State* (London: Pluto, 1976).

Feeney, Vincent E., 'The Civil Rights Movement in Northern Ireland' *Eire-Ireland* 9:2 (1974) pp. 30–40.

Fisk, Robert, *The Point of No Return* (London: André Deutsch, 1975).

Graham, John, 'The Consensus-Forming Strategy of the Northern Ireland Labour Party, 1949–68' (Belfast: unpublished Queen's University MSSc thesis, 1972).

Harbinson, John F., *The Ulster Unionist Party, 1882–1973* (Belfast: Blackstaff, 1973).

Hastings, Max, *Ulster 1969* (London: Gollancz, 1970).

Heslinga, M.W., *The Irish Border as a Cultural Divide* (Assen: Van Gorcum, 1962).

James, Michael, 'The Failure of Britain's Ireland Policy' *Australian Outlook* 47:1 (1975) pp. 51–64.

Kane, John J., 'Civil Rights in Northern Ireland' *Review of Politics* 33:1 (1971) pp. 54–77.

Kelly, Henry, 'Northern Ireland: So Far' *Eire-Ireland* 6:4 (1971) pp. 6–14.

— *How Stormont Fell* (Dublin: Gill and Macmillan, 1972).

— 'Northern Ireland: Beginning or End?' *Eire-Ireland* 7:1 (1972) pp. 39–45.

Kennedy, David, 'Whither Northern Nationalism' *Christus Rex* 13:4 (1959) pp. 269–83.

Kyle, Keith, 'Sunningdale and After: Britain, Ireland and Ulster' *The World Today* 33:11 (1975) pp. 439–50.

Larkin, Emmet, 'Socialism and Catholicism in Ireland' *Church History* 33 (1964) pp. 462–83.

Laver, Michael, *The Theory and Practice of Party Competition: Ulster, 1973–75* (London: Sage Contemporary Political Sociology Series No. 06–014, 1976).

Lawrence, R. J., *The Government of Northern Ireland* (Oxford: Oxford University Press, 1965).

Lawrence, R.J., *et al.*, *The Northern Ireland General Elections of 1973* (London: HMSO, Cmnd. 5847, 1975).

Leon D., 'The Politics of Civil Rights in Northern Ireland: Some Views and Observations' *Cithara* 10:1 (1970) pp. 3–17.

Lijphart, Arend, 'The Northern Ireland Problem: Cases, Theories and Solutions' *British Journal of Political Science* 5:1 (1975) pp. 83–106.

McAllister, Ian, 'Political Opposition in Northern Ireland: the National Democratic Party, 1965–70' *Economic and Social Review* 6:3 (1975) pp. 353–66.

— *The 1975 Northern Ireland Convention Election* (Glasgow: Survey Research Centre Occasional Paper No. 14, 1975).

— 'Social Influences on Voters and Non-Voters: a Note on Two Northern Ireland Elections' *Political Studies* 24:4 (1976) pp. 462–8.

MacAuley, Ambrose, 'Catholics in the North, 1870–1970. *Newman Review* 2:1 (1970) pp. 21–32.

McCann, Eamonn, *War and an Irish Town* (Harmondsworth: Penguin, 1974).

McCarthy, Charles, 'Civil Strife and Trade Union Unity: the Case of Ireland' *Government and Opposition* 8:4 (1973) pp. 407–31.

MacEoin, Gary, *Northern Ireland: Captive of History* (New York: Holt, Rinehart and Winston, 1974).

McGuffin, John, *Internment* (Tralee: Anvil, 1973).

— *The Guinea-Pigs* (Harmondsworth: Penguin, 1974).

MacStiofain, Sean, *Memoirs of a Revolutionary* (London: Gordon Cremonesi, 1975).

Magee, John (ed.), *Northern Ireland: Crisis and Conflict* (London: Routledge and Kegan Paul, 1974).

Mansergh, Nicholas, *The Government of Northern Ireland* (London: Allen and Unwin, 1936).

Moody, T. W., *The Ulster Question, 1603–1973* (Cork: Mercier, 1974).

Nealon, Ted, *Ireland: a Parliamentary Directory, 1973–74* (Dublin: Institute of Public Administration, 1974).

Newe, G. B., 'The Catholic in the Northern Ireland Community' *Christus Rex* 18:1 (1964) pp. 22–36.

O'Brien, Conor Cruise, *States of Ireland* (London: Hutchinson, 1972).

O'Leary, Cornelius, 'The Catholic in Politics' *Christus Rex* 17:4 (1963) pp. 285–97.

— 'Ireland: the North and South' in S. E. Finer (ed.), *Adversary Politics and Electoral Reform* (London: Anthony Wigram, 1975).

Oliver, John A., 'The Ulster Convention' *Blackwoods Magazine* 320:1930 (1976) pp. 123–32.

Palley, Claire, 'The Evolution, Disintegration, and Possible Reconstruction of the Northern Ireland Constitution' *Anglo-American Law Review* 1 (1972) pp. 368–476.

Power, Paul F., 'Civil Protest in Northern Ireland' *Journal of Peace Research* 9:3 (1972) pp. 223–36.

— 'Violence, Consent, and the Northern Ireland Problem' *Journal of Commonwealth and Comparative Politics* 14:2 (1976) pp. 119–40.

Provisional IRA, *Freedom Struggle* (Dublin: Provisional IRA, 1973).

Pyne, Peter, 'The Politics of Parliamentary Abstention: Ireland's Four Sinn Féin Parties, 1905–26' *Journal of Commonwealth and Comparative Politics* 12:2 (1974) pp. 206–27.

Rose, Richard, *Governing Without Consensus* (London: Faber, 1971).

—*Northern Ireland: a Time of Choice* (London: Macmillan, 1976).

—'On the Priorities of Citizenship in the Deep South and Northern Ireland' *Journal of Politics* 38:2 (1976) pp. 247–91.

Rumpf, E. and Hepburn, A. C., *Nationalism and Socialism in Twentieth Century Ireland* (Liverpool: Liverpool University Press, 1977).

Sacks, Paul, *The Donegal Mafia* (New Haven: Yale University Press, 1977).

Scott, R. D., 'Ulster in Perspective: the Relevance of Non-European Experience' *Australian Outlook* 23:3 (1969) pp. 246–57.

—'Northern Ireland: the Politics of Disintegration' *Australian Outlook* 27:1 (1973) pp. 40–9.

Sunday Times Insight, *Ulster* (Harmondsworth: Penguin, 1972).

Thompson, James, 'The Northern Ireland Civil Rights Movement' (Belfast: unpublished Queen's University MA thesis, 1973).

United States Congress, *Northern Ireland Hearings Before the Sub-Committee on Europe* (Washington: Government Printing Office, 1972).

Utley, T. E., *Lessons of Ulster* (London: Dent, 1975).

Van Voris, W. H., *Violence in Ulster* (Amherst: University of Massachusetts Press, 1975).

Wallace, Martin, *Drums and Guns* (London: Chapman, 1970).

—*Northern Ireland: Fifty Years of Self-Government* (Newton Abbot: David and Charles, 1971).

Whyte, John, *The Reform of Stormont* (Belfast: New Ulster Movement, 1971).

—*Church and State in Modern Ireland, 1923–70* (Dublin: Gill and Macmillan, 1973).

—'The Catholic Factor in the Politics of Democratic States' *American Behavioural Scientist* 17:6 (1974) pp. 798–812.

Wilson, Brian, 'The Alliance Party of Northern Ireland: a Study of a Bi-Confessional Party' (Glasgow: unpublished University of Strathclyde MSc dissertation, 1976).

Winchester, Simon, *In Holy Terror* (London: Faber, 1974).

Index